Table of Contents

Acknowledgments

In updating *Web-Based Training*, I relied on a number of colleagues, professional organization, and vendors. As I revised the chapters I was fortunate to have access to students and to IBM Mindspan customers who kept me focused on the real issues and concerns in the field. They provided insight into the important issues and they raised the technical, business, and educational questions that need to be answered. I am particularly indebted to those who shared their stories, best practices, and advice. The wisdom of practitioners such as Barbara Ash Linda Barrille, Ann Barron, Kay Bell, Pat Brogran, Tim Brown, Saul Carliner, Lance Dublin, Ryann Ellis, Ken McDonald, Mike Glass, Dave Grebow, Nancy Harkrider, Jennifer Hofmann, Becky Holden, Bill and Kit Horton, Tom Keating, David Metcalf, Alex Moulder, Tony O'Driscoll, Fred and Marilyn Pula, Catherine Rickelman, Art Shirk, Steven Teal, and Mike Zimmerman.

In a technical field, where it can be difficult to understand concepts such as synchronous, asynchronous, adaptive learning, learning objects, and communities of practice, I was blessed by the generosity of the vendor community. Without exception, vendors such as Centra, Colaborative Learning Network, EnglishTown, Gold Standard Media, IBM Mindspan, Interwise, Macromedia, Placeware, Ill Online, and UserActive generously supplied screen captures.

Margaret Driscoll
January 2002

MARGARET DRISCOLL

SECOND EDITION

Web-
BASED TRAINING

Creating e-Learning
Experiences

JOSSEY-BASS/PFEIFFER
A Wiley Company
www.pfeiffer.com

Published by

JOSSEY-BASS/PFEIFFER

A Wiley Company
989 Market Street
San Francisco, CA 94103-1741
415.433.1740; Fax 415.433.0499
800.274.4434; Fax 800.569.0443

www.pfeiffer.com

Jossey-Bass/Pfeiffer is a registered trademark of Jossey-Bass Inc., A Wiley Company.
ISBN: 0-7879-5619-8

Library of Congress Cataloging-in-Publication Data

Driscoll, Margaret
    Web-based training : creating e-learning experiences / Margaret Driscoll.—2nd ed.
       p. cm.
    Includes bibliographical references and index.
    Contents: Web-based training : tactical & strategic advantages—Best practices for WBT implementation—Principles of
adult ed. & instructional design—Tools of the trade—Analyzing needs and selecting delivery methods—Selecting
the most appropriate eLearning method—Designing asynchronous interactions—Designing synchronous interactions—
Developing blue prints—Implementing & evaluating WBT programs—Looking ahead.
    ISBN 0-7879-5619-8 (alk. paper)
    1. Employees—Training of—Computer network resources. 2. Employees—Training
of—Computer-assisted instruction. 3. World Wide Web. I. Title

HF5549.5.T7 D75 2002
658.3'124'02854678—dc21
                                                  2001006385

Acquiring Editor: Josh Blatter
Director of Development: Kathleen Dolan Davies
Editor: Rebecca Taff
Senior Production Editor: Dawn Kilgore
Manufacturing Supervisor: Becky Carreño
Cover Design: Blue Design
Printing 10 9 8 7 6 5 4 3 2 1

Introduction

The first edition of this book was called *Web-Based Training: Using Technology to Design Adult Learning Experiences.* It was written four years ago. At the time, Web-based training was in its infancy and most people developing programs were early adopters. I had the good fortune of interviewing these early adopters as part of the research for my dissertation at Columbia. The first edition was a compilation of best practices, stories of success and failure, and a recommended process for developing programs synthesized from real-world practitioners. One of the aha's that resulted from my research for the first edition was that there were four distinct kinds of Web-based training. Understanding the four kinds of WBT programs—Web/computer based training, Web/electronic performance support, Web/virtual asynchronous classrooms, and Web/virtual synchronous classroom programs—was important because each delivery mode had specific strengths and limitations. As a result of the characteristic differences among the delivery platforms, there was a need to design programs that could optimize the technology, and the first edition addressed this issue.

Over the past four years one of the changes in Web-based training is the name. The term Web-based training has been replaced with a broader term *e-learning.* E-learning is used to provide an umbrella term for referring to all the technologies involved in the process of designing, delivering, and managing instruction using computers. One can gain a sense of how this field is still evolving by trying to find a definition of e-learning on which everyone can agree. The change in terminology is much more than semantics. The breadth of the term has widened the scope for what is to be included in the training professionals' toolbox of instructional technologies and the scope of this book. In addition to four kinds of Web-based training, e-learning now includes technologies for tracking and managing training; applications that assist in authoring and managing content; and a host of new collaboration and knowledge management applications that I discuss in this edition.

The second change is the growth of a $23 billion dollar e-learning industry. People interviewed for the first edition were primarily designing their programs using homegrown programs that they programmed using simple HTML

1

authoring tools. Today, the software programs for creating e-learning abound. There are literally hundreds of software programs from which to choose.

A third change is the emergence of e-learning front and center in the business environment due to increased globalization and competition and the emergence of the Internet as a major force for commerce. E-learning is bringing training to the attention of upper management in a way that other learning technologies have never done. What had once been the domain of "those nice people in training" is now the place where organizations can reduce costs, reach customers, stimulate the supply chain, and speed up innovation. The change in status for training and development brings new decision makers and new criteria for what is to be regarded as training, education, and learning.

As a result of the growth of the e-learning industry there have been other significant developments. First, the people who are now responsible for developing e-learning do not need to have deep technical skills to produce programs. The availability of commercial software means that anyone who can afford the program and, in some cases, people who can simply connect to a website can author programs. This has lowered the barrier to entry and has enabled organizations to develop programs that would not have been possible in the past.

Another is the preponderance of commercial software applications. The significance and growth of commercial software applications for designing, developing, delivering, and managing online learning programs has gone unnoticed. Practitioners have paid little attention to the assumptions that underlie these programs as far as how people learn, how assessments are designed, how materials are created, and how roles of learners, facilitators, instructional designers, and managers are evolving. Most of the attention has been paid to financial aspects, such as stock prices, mergers and acquisitions, and the number of customers each vendor serves. The real story is the impact these programs are having on the design of adult learning experiences. Unlike much of the instructional technology that came before, e-learning technology dictates much of what designers can and can not do. These programs are not value-free, blank sheets of paper, but rather they are software applications built on assumptions regarding the roles of facilitators and learners and how skills and knowledge are transmitted, practiced, and tested. This second edition addresses these issues of roles and adult learning theory.

Four years is a long time. Web-based training is a child of the Internet, and like all Internet technology it thrives on Internet time. Four years in Internet time is said to be like twenty-four years of regular time. In the last four years, I have been an active participant in the e-learning conferences, have spent a great deal of time working with organizations that implement e-learning, and have taught graduate education courses. These experiences have shaped the book.

The purpose of this book is to provide an overview of the process for designing adult learning experiences to be delivered via e-learning. The book takes into consideration the complex decisions and tradeoffs among business, technical, and educational factors. There are three primary audiences for this book: business managers, training managers, and instructional designers/course developers. The three threads of business, technology, and education are woven together and are often messy—as the e-learning business often is.

Business managers may find few new ideas relative to the knowledge economy or return on investment of Web-based training, but they may find the steps required to build a WBT program and the descriptions of risks from skipping steps to be informative. This book does not pretend to provide a deep review of the instructional design process or of learning methods and development techniques. The business reader will find enough details to enable him or her to manage a group of Web-based training professionals, who have strong instructional design and andragogical skills, or to write a request for proposal for WBT and specify requirements for a project to be outsourced.

Training managers who have not managed an online learning project will find the steps in the ADDIE process simplistic but affirming. Yes, a great deal of the process for designing and developing e-learning materials remains the same as for traditional training, but of course there are some differences. New insights for training managers may be (1) a greater appreciation for the technical considerations and (2) a heightened awareness of the business issues that must inform their decisions. Because business, technology, and education are woven together in this book, critical decision points such as choosing a team, selecting a delivery mode, and anticipating the need to link to other back-end applications such as the HRIS system or the corporate ERP system are clear.

Instructional designers and course developers who have never created an e-learning program will find the ADDIE model easy to follow and the resources at the back of each chapter a good starting point for additional learning. Those who have created an e-learning program will find the ADDIE model a good framework in which to anchor the business and technology topics. Veteran instructional designers and course developers will find understanding the larger picture helpful as they move on to manage their own e-learning projects.

This book is a good starting point for business managers, training managers, and instructional designers/course developers, and each audience is expected to graduate to other materials that will strengthen this knowledge of business, technology and education. The second edition of this book has made changes to the organization of the chapters and the optional exercises have been strengthened. The initial chapters provide a foundation for the business considerations, the educational principles, and the technology that underlies e-learning. Based on this foundation, the reader is introduced to the ADDIE (analysis, design, development, implementation, evaluation) process. This simplistic framework provides an overview of the steps while also looking at the business and technical issues. The last chapter pushes the reader to make the connections between trends within the business environment and the evolving e-learning field.

This book uses tenets of adult learning—the value of experience and the role of reflection in learning. Readers who choose to complete the exercises will find ample opportunity to gain first-hand experience with four kinds of Web-based training, knowledge management applications, and software for authoring courses. The decision to modify these exercises was a difficult one. In the first edition, I choose to avoid using URLs because there was no guarantee they would remain viable. In this edition, I have recommended URLs because readers told me that having to find sites on their own was time-consuming and frustrating. So be patient if not all links work. Where possible, I have given hints as to how you might search for more sites like the suggested links. I want to extend my thanks to all those who contributed to my first edition by participating in interviews, testing the book, and suggesting changes. For this, the second edition, I would like to thank the customers who have shared their educational, technical, and business dilemmas. Working with these practitioners on the front lines of e-learning has been a reality check and a constant source reshaping this book. I would also like to thank my colleagues who provided practical insights on topics such as costs, team roles, and technology considerations. In particular I would like to thank my developmental editor, Maryanne Koschier, who has been a champion for the reader and has always been able to see the forest for the trees.

Chapter 1

Tactical and Strategic Advantages

The concept of Web-based training has attained something of cult status in the popular media. It is hard to pick up a training magazine or a professional newsletter or attend a conference without finding the lion's share of attention being given to Web-based training. Leaders in the field and studies suggest that Web-based training will be central to the design and delivery of workplace learning in the 21st Century. Recent industry reports, such as *Training* magazine's Annual Industry Report state that 13 percent of all courses are delivered by computer; and, according to International Data Corp (IDC), the online training market is estimated to reach $11.6 billion in 2003.

Web-based training is advocated as an enterprise-wide training solution because all members of an organization can access it and because it can fill almost any gap in skills and knowledge. Online learning is a mission-critical application that helps organizations compete in the new economy. It has also been heralded as reducing training costs, improving return-on-investment, and delivering just-in-time training. Although these are often overstated, it is still clear that WBT is indeed a powerful tool.

Before advocating that your organization invest in Web-based training, it will be helpful to understand the advantages in a business context.

Tactical and strategic issues related to WBT are important to human resource managers, and training managers must understand these business themes in order to build a case for implementing Web-based training. It is imperative to be able to describe the value of WBT to an organization in terms of cost and benefits when talking to senior level managers and decision makers.

What You Will Learn in This Chapter

After completing this chapter you will be able to

- Assess the tactical and strategic benefits of Web-based training; and

- Determine whether or not Web-based training is the appropriate method for your program.

When to Use WBT

Strategic Reasons

There is a great deal of marketing hype regarding the *strategic advantages* of Web-based training. The term *strategic* comes from the military. In the military, leaders have a vision as to the general direction of the war and regarding what to attack and what to defend. This broad vision is called a strategy, and the adjective "strategic" is applied to those things relating to the overall direction of the endeavor or enterprise.

Web-based training is strategic only when it is used in support of broad goals having long-term significance. *Strategic reasons* for implementing Web-based training include:

Developing a Global Workforce. Web-based training is an excellent tool for developing a global workforce. The Web delivers consistent, timely, and quality training to staff members around the world.

Responding to Shorter Product Development Cycles. Web-based training is a powerful tool when dealing with short development cycles. In the past a new product would be released every twelve or eighteen months. Today organizations release new products or point releases of software every six to eight months. This rapid pace of development demands a training solution that can keep pace. Web-based training can be used to provide the needed training without taking employees away from their jobs.

Managing Flat Organizations. The downsized and flatter organizations are part of a lean and competitive landscape. This trend has placed the responsibility of training on line managers, who already have too much to do. Web-based training can deliver foundation skills, such as desktop application training and product training. This frees up managers, allowing them to focus on mentoring and coaching or on more advanced skills and knowledge.

Adjusting to Needs of Employees. The recent labor shortages and changing trends in the workplace have led to telecommuting, virtual offices, and flex-time. These trends make it possible for organizations to recruit and retain workers more easily. These same workers benefit from a training delivery methodology that can adjust to their hours and work styles.

Enabling a Contingent Workforce. Contingent workers, such as temporary workers, self-employed workers, and consultants, increased by 57 percent between 1980 and 1994. Given organizations' growing reliance on a contingent workforce to deal with peak demands for labor, Web-based training can provide a way to quickly train these people.

Retaining Valued Workers. Education is a core benefit for employees who understand that training, retraining, job hopping, and even career hopping are part of the new economy. Web-based training programs that offer college degrees, technical certification, and skill-building courses are powerful benefits organizations can use to retain workers.

Increasing Productivity and Profitability. E-learning programs can increase skills and knowledge, making it possible for employees to sell more products, service a wider range of products, take on more complex assignments, and complete work faster and with few errors. All of these outcomes improve productivity and in turn increase profitability.

The strategic benefits of Web-based training are often overlooked for the more tactical benefits. Understanding your organization's strategic mission and the vision for moving the business forward is essential. Web-based training is expensive and requires the commitment of a cross-functional team. It is far easier to gain this commitment for a Web-based training program that is aligned with strategic goals.

A call center manager talks about initiating an e-learning program for tactical reasons and achieving strategic results

When we started, we knew what we wanted to accomplish, and we had a good business case for implementing Web-based training. The call center trained about one hundred new customer service representatives every quarter using an eleven-week face-to-face program. The Web-based training program reduced the new hire training time from eleven weeks to nine. The saving resulting from reducing class time and getting new hires on the phones sooner meant that the Web-based training system paid for itself the first year. As we forecast, Web-based training reduced our training costs.

What surprised us was the performance improvement. After completing the Web-based training program, new hires were able to sell 80 to 110 percent as well as customer service representatives who had been on the job a year.

Tactical Reasons

Tactical benefits are often easier to understand, and they tend to generate more enthusiasm because of the anticipated savings. These benefits meet important short-term needs, but they are less significant in achieving long-term goals.

Tactical reasons for implementing Web-based training include:

Reducing Travel and Related Costs.   One of the easiest ways to show cost savings is to calculate the savings related to airfare, hotels, meals, and other travel expenses over a two- or three-year period. Keep in mind, this is simply a cost-savings tactic.

Enabling Learning Any Time and Any Place.   Web-based training technically can make it possible for learners to complete programs at their desks, at home, or during slow periods.

Providing Just-in-Time Learning.   If training programs are available on the Web, the learners can take training just before they need the content rather than enrolling in a class weeks before they *might* need the training. It is also easy for learners to return to the program for a refresher course.

Leveraging Existing Infrastructure.   Organizations often seek to justify their investments in intranets, remote dial in access, new multimedia PCs, and other technology. Web-based training makes use of the existing equipment and staff, thus providing greater reason to adopt it as a training solution.

Enabling Delivery Independent of a Platform. Unlike older computer-based training technologies, Web-based training program can run on PCs, Macintoshes, and UNIX systems. Using Web-based training allows the training organization to create a program once and use that same program on all systems.

Providing Tools for Tracking and Record Keeping. Organizations that are required to keep records for government or insurance reasons are able to track student participation and completion. Some Web-based training programs offer powerful tools that use databases to keep accurate records and allow for succession planning and workforce development.

Making Updates Easy. Web-based training courses are easier to update than traditional computer-based training programs developed for delivery via CD-ROMs because changes do not require the pressing and shipping of new disks each time a module is updated. These reasons are summarized in Table 1.1.

A quick scan and analysis of the success stories featured in trade publications, such as *Training, Online Learning, InternetWorld,* and *e-Learning* magazine highlight two findings. First, most organizations initially justify Web-based training based on simple cost reductions or cost avoidance rationale. Analysts suggest that cost reduction may be the primary rationale because it is easy to demonstrate and defend. A second finding of equal interest is the fact that strategic benefits such

Table 1.1. Strategic and Tactical Advantages of WBT

Strategic	Tactical
Developing a global workforce	Reducing travel and related costs
Responding to shorter product development cycles	Enabling learning any time and any place
Managing flat organizations	Providing just-in-time learning
Adjusting to needs of employees	Leveraging existing infrastructure
Enabling a contingent workforce	Enabling delivery independent of a platform
Increasing productivity and profitability	Providing tools for tracking and record keeping
Retaining valued workers	Making updates easy

as improved productivity and increased profitability are often discovered after a Web-based training program has been conducted, rather than being the reason for running the program. In an Eduventures.com report, *Corporate E-Learning ROI Scoreboard*, Yegin Chin was unable to find any companies that were able to demonstrate measurable revenues directly related to an e-learning solution. In the best cases, organizations showed net benefits but not true ROI because they were not able to account for direct and indirect costs.

The Disadvantages of WBT

The business reasons for adopting Web-based training are easy to understand. It is also important to understand the disadvantages, as these may not be as obvious.

Substantial Technical Infrastructure

A clear disadvantage of Web-based training is the substantial technical infrastructure required to run programs. In addition to developing educationally effective training programs, designers must contend with computer system requirements, network capacity, and network access.

Generally, Web-based training programs can be used from a variety of platforms such as UNIX work stations, IBM personal computers and clones, and Macintosh computers. Of course, this may not be true if developers use highly complex tools. Even ubiquitous Web browsers such as Netscape Navigator® and Microsoft's Internet Explorer® present subtle differences in how they display a page of text or a graphic.

Other technical infrastructure issues are network capacity and access. Training programs compete with other applications such as e-mail. Unlike workbooks that stand on their own, Web-based programs require access to the organization's network.

Yet another issue is network access. Learners must be able to log in to an intranet or the Internet. Programs are limited by the kind of dial-in connections available. If learners are using a 28.8 modem, they may not have the capacity to download large files quickly. If learners are accessing the Internet from a corporate network, they may encounter security problems that prevent them from running Java code or downloading plug-ins.

New Learning Methods

Workbooks, videocassette programs, and job aids are familiar tools, but Web-based training is new for many learners. It requires learners to master using a browser, navigating nonlinear programs, and interacting with classmates using unfamiliar tools such as chat rooms and threaded discussions.

Required Range of Skills

Web-based training is labor-intensive, requiring broad-range skills. Because resources are frequently in short supply, trainers have become adept at playing multiple roles, but Web-based training should not be designed, developed, and delivered by a single person. The team should include graphic designers, network managers, server installers, end-user support personnel, and programmers. Managing a cross-functional team requires the coordination of schedules to accomplish project milestones in parallel. As the training group writes the program, the customer-support group may be talking with potential learners to determine whether they have sufficient RAM and a current version of the browser software.

Management of External Resources

Another disadvantage of Web-based training is that it relies on external resources such as other organizations' websites, adequate hardware, and reliable access to the network. One is at the mercy of others. An external website can be eliminated, leaving a hole in the program. Or a department may have no other use for sound cards, and so not have them installed. The trainer is also dependent on the information systems (IS) group to support end users and to keep the network running nights and weekends.

Figure 1.1 summarizes the disadvantages of Web-based training.

New Ways of Thinking

Organizations must learn to think about training as something that happens in places other than training centers and offsite programs. There is a tendency to think of Web-based training as something less than "real training." Managers feel that it is less than real training because workers are sitting at their desks and appear to be

Figure 1.1.   Disadvantages of Using WBT
✔ Requires substantial technical infrastructure
✔ Requires learners to adapt to new learning methods
✔ Requires a team to design, develop, and deploy
✔ Requires management of resources beyond the training organization
✔ Requires organization to embrace new ways of thinking
✔ Requires significant time and money

surfing or not doing anything. This attitude leads managers and peers to regard workers engaged in Web-based training as being interruptible with questions, phone calls, and casual conversations. This attitude can make WBT a difficult learning solution to implement unless organizations begin to think about WBT as real training and important enough to give workers time to focus on the course.

In organizations such as IBM, attitudes are being changed using a number of strategies. The first strategy is formal accountability. At IBM, a management development program called Basic Blue is a required program of all first-line managers. This program is 75 percent online learning and 25 percent traditional classroom learning. The learners and their managers are accountable for successfully completing the online portion of the course. This accountability is part of a formal process that includes communication and rules regarding who can attend the traditional classroom portion. If learners fail to complete the Web-based training program or have difficulty with segments of the program, their managers and training professionals provide mentoring and support. Permission to travel and participate in the face-to-face class is also determined by successful completion of the online course. A second tactic is to make it clear that e-learning is a valued training method for both exempt and nonexempt employees. One clear indicator of the value of e-learning at IBM is the fact that five thousand managers worldwide enroll and complete the program. These managers are not only setting an example for other employees but they are learning first-hand about the value of e-learning.

Significant Time and Money

Web-based training requires more time to design and develop than instructor-led courses or self-paced workbooks. The act of creating Web-based training is similar to the act of creating software. This means that training professionals are required to take extra steps to program and test their courses. These extra steps add to the cost and extend the development time.

Now that we've looked at both the potential advantages and disadvantages of incorporating Web-based training into your organization, let's look at where it can best fit into your training strategy, what skills it best teaches, and the potential challenges of this training medium.

When to Use WBT

Web-based training is not the solution for every training problem, but it is appropriate for teaching certain skills and imparting particular kinds of knowledge, such as software applications, management skills, or business writing. The medium can also be highly effective to teach learners the skills needed to close a sale, diagnose a problem, or evaluate the merits of competing solutions. Table 1.2 shows a matrix for determining when to use WBT.

Gap in Learners' Skills and Knowledge

Web-based training is a potential solution to a performance problem if the learners lack skills or knowledge. Like any training, it will not work if the performance problem is the result of factors other than lack of skill or knowledge.

Technically and theoretically, just about anything can be taught on the Web, but it can be impractical. Consider the following types of skills:

Cognitive Skills. Cognitive skills include solving problems, applying rules, and distinguishing among items. Tasks that require the manipulation of symbols and numbers are well-suited to being taught on the Web, such as completing an income tax form. Cognitive skills are traditionally taught using text, graphics, and symbols and such instructional strategies as reading, writing answers, solving computational problems, and completing exercises. All are well-suited to Web-based training.

Psychomotor Skills. Psychomotor skills require a complex combination of physical movement and thought, such as operating a crane or driving a golf ball. These skills are difficult to teach in a WBT program, as they require an environment with coaching and detailed feedback. Given adequate funding and time, however, it is possible to design such a program.

Table 1.2. When WBT Is Appropriate

Type of Learning	Well Suited for Pure e-Learning Solution	Best as Part of Blended Solution
Cognitive skills: Complete a tax form, balance a checkbook	X	
Psychomotor skills: Hit a golf ball, use a table saw		X
Attitudinal skills: Value diversity, choose to recycle		X

Attitudinal Skills.   Teaching learners to change their opinions and, in turn, to change their behavior is challenging in any medium, but it is particularly challenging in Web-based training. For example, if the objective is to teach learners to care about the environment and, therefore, to choose to recycle, there is no opportunity to use reinforcement strategies available in the traditional classroom. The tools that allow trainers to develop simulations, conduct discussions, and facilitate group learning can be expensive and usually require that learners have access to powerful computers.

It is possible to teach psychomotor and attitudinal skills on the Web, but such programs are difficult to design and develop. I will discuss these types of learnings/skills in more detail in Chapter 6, Selecting the Most Appropriate e-Learning Method.

Adequate Computer Skills

The learners must have computer, browser, and Internet skills. Even learners with these skills must be carefully assessed, and the program must be matched to their skill level. Learners with novice-level computer skills do best in programs that simply run in the browser. Offer more technically advanced learners complex WBT programs with video and audio that require the downloading and installation of plug-in software.

Organization Has Capacity to Deliver

Organizations must have adequate hardware, software, and staff to support learners. Determine whether your organization has the technical infrastructure to connect to the Internet or the organization's intranet. Be sure that computers have sufficient memory and RAM; provide support staff to assist local and remote offices with network problems, hardware failures, and browser installation.

Some Potential Problems and Recommendations

Three important problem areas that you should be aware of when planning programs are discussed below. Other ideas on how best to implement Web-based training programs are discussed in the next chapter.

Inadequate Resources

Avoid Web-based training for psychomotor or attitudinal skills unless you have adequate resources. Designing Web-based training for complex psychomotor skills is expensive. Teaching them requires more than instructing learners to execute steps in a process; it requires opportunities for practice that bring together the mental and physical knowledge and skills required to act. A successful WBT program requires high-quality simulations, two-way video for coaching, and a network that can handle a large volume of traffic. For example, it is technically possible to develop a WBT program to teach newly hired warehouse workers to drive a forklift, but it would require substantial programming, editing, network bandwidth, and computer resources. Before starting a project like this, develop a detailed cost estimate and compare it to alternative training options such as on-the-job training, one-on-one training sessions, or a mentoring program. Even if the program could be delivered on the Web, does it make sense? Even when teaching cognitive skills, not having the necessary resources can present difficulties.

Inadequate Materials

Avoid using existing materials for a Web-based training program without redesign. Although existing courses are a good starting point for material, they will require instructional, graphic, and technical redesign to take advantage of the Web. Existing materials such as student guides, computer-based training programs, and video-cassette programs were probably created with tools such as Microsoft's Word™ or PowerPoint™ and Macromedia's Director™ or Authorware™. If materials were created with these tools, it is relatively easy to convert them to a Web-ready format.

Lack of Variety

Avoid using the same software tool for every program. The four kinds of Web-based training methods will be covered in Chapter 6. Suffice it to say for now that it is not advisable to use a single software application or developmental tool to create all of your programs. Distinct software applications and tools are available for creating text-intensive learning, live instructional video, radio-like broadcast programs, and animation. Each of these offers wonderful training possibilities, but no single tool will be equally effective for solving all training problems. Use a combination.

Think of Web-based training within an overall training plan and as an additional method for delivering instruction, along with videotapes, CD-ROM, and workbooks.

Select the appropriate combination of media, one that is easy for learners to use and that delivers the learning objectives. In some cases it is appropriate to deliver the entire class via the Web. In others, it is more appropriate to use the Web to complement instructor-led classes, for example, as a prerequisite for videoconference training or as advanced training for those who have completed internships or apprenticeships. Learn the unique advantages of this medium, and then use it judiciously.

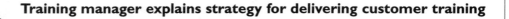

Training manager explains strategy for delivering customer training

Our customers are not big fans of e-learning; they want face-to-face classes where they can get to know the new product, talk to the guys who built it, and ask questions. These new release classes work great. The problem is keeping customers updated on changes in the product after the initial new release class. Sometimes we make changes to the product that require a half day of training to understand. We know that customers aren't going to travel all the way here for four hours, so we use e-learning for update training. The update training enables people to get what they need without the travel and to still be able to talk to the instructor and other students, and to ask questions.

Summary

Devoting the opening chapter of a book on Web-based training to business issues may seem odd, but it is essential that those responsible for corporate training start here. Web-based training is simply a delivery methodology and it is no better or worse than traditional classroom training, video-based training, or correspondence course training. Choosing to adopt online learning for a corporation is a business decision that rests on two factors: Is there a tactical and/or strategic benefit? and Can this delivery methodology do the job? The next chapter will move beyond the "go/no go" decision and look at best practices for implementing Web-based training.

Suggested Readings

Driscoll, M. (1997, April). Defining Internet-based and Web-based training. *Performance Improvement, 36*(4), 5–9.

Barron, T. (1999, September). Harnessing online learning. *Training & Development, 53*(9), 28–33.

Cross, J. (2001). *A fresh look at ROI.* Learning Circuits. [Online]. Available: www.learningcircuits.org/2001/jan2001/cross.html

Ganzel R. (2001). *Associated learning* [Online]. Available: www.onlinelearningmag.com/new/may01/printer/feat2prt.htm

Chen, Y. (2001, June). *Corporate e-learning ROI scoreboard: Early leaders emerge.* Boston, MA: Eduventures Consulting.

Horton, W. (2000). *Designing Web-based training.* New York: John Wiley & Sons.

Industry Report 2000. (2000, October). *Training,* pp. 45–95.

Watson, J.B., & Rossett, A. (1999, May/June). Guiding the independent learner in Web-based training. *Educational Technology, 39*(3), 27–36.

Wetzel, M. (2001, February). Stuck in the middle. *Online Learning Magazine,* pp. 30–32, 34.

Chapter 2

Best Practices for WBT Implementation

In the last chapter we explored the strategic and tactical advantages of instruction on the Web. We also explored some of the potential pitfalls when implementing WBT programs. This chapter continues to focus on the foundations of WBT. There are a number of best practices that have been identified by practitioners who have successfully implemented e-learning programs. Best practices are not simple formulas for how to implement Web-based training; they are insights that help you assess the options and craft your own plan. Use these considerations when educating decision makers, interacting with the information technology organization, and working with vendors.

What You Will Learn in This Chapter

After completing this chapter you will be able to explain best WBT implementation practice, with guidelines on how to

- Make WBT a business-driven activity;
- Match Web-based solutions to business needs;
- Prepare for an adequate budget and timeline;
- Form a successful cross-functional team;
- Set standards for development of WBT in your organization;

- Be successful in your first program implementation;
- Evaluate WBT based on productivity goals;
- Educate trainers that WBT is a form of software development;
- Plan for future WBT programs and maintain existing ones; and
- Educate management about the value and uses of WBT.

The Business of Education and Training

Training in profit and nonprofit organizations is an intervention that helps the organization achieve a goal. This seems like an obvious point, but it is easy to lose sight of this fact in the excitement created by new technology and the potential offered by Web-based training. Before diving into designing solutions, it is essential to check your assumptions and to have a solid grounding in the business issues associated with e-learning.

Ten Lessons from Those Who Have Implemented WBT
1. Make WBT a Business-Driven Activity
The first and most important lesson learned is the importance of linking e-learning to a business need. As discussed in Chapter 1, there are strategic and tactical reasons for adopting Web-based training. When possible link WBT to strategic business initiatives such as developing a global workforce to service new products more quickly, responding to shorter product development cycles by providing faster sales training, and supporting flat organizations by reducing the time managers spend teaching new hires the basics.

Linking WBT to a strategic business issue is essential. There must be a business unit manager who is accountable for achieving a strategic goal and who is accountable for championing Web-based training. For example, a business unit manager who has a major stake in launching new products more quickly and training a national salesforce faster should initiate the Web-based training program. On the other hand, the training manager, like the information systems manager, is a service provider with a specialized skill set related to training and development of human resources. It is not the job of the training manager or information systems manager to set the direction or define what should be accomplished. The role of both of these functions is to use their expertise to guide and support the business unit manager.

For example, the training manager should be able to explain in simple "technobabble"-free language what WBT can and cannot do. He or she should also be able to recommend solutions that the business unit manager may not be aware of. It is the partnered efforts of the business, training, and IS managers that ensures a successful project.

2. Match Web-Based Solution to Business Needs

The starting point for any WBT initiative is to determine first whether training is needed, and second, what kind of solution is appropriate. This may sound obvious, but there is a great deal of confusion when choosing among information, presentations, and training. These three distinct solutions can look very similar. All of these solutions service a different need and have different outcomes for the learners (see Table 2.1).

As you can see, information and presentation solutions are closely related but require different considerations. In fact, training may have components of pure information and pure presentation, but the purpose of these segments is subordinate to the greater training solution. At the end of this chapter there are resources for learning more about designing informational sites and online presentations.

The four distinct kinds of WBT solutions that we discuss later in this book are (1) Web/computer-based training, (2) Web/electronic performance support systems (W/EPSS), (3) Web/virtual asynchronous classroom (W/VAC), and (4) Web synchronous classroom (W/VSC).

3. Demand Adequate Budget and Time

One of the first questions you will have to answer is "How much does it cost?" The answer is, "How much do you have to spend?" Off-the-shelf programs cost as little as $7 for a monthly subscription to thousands of dollars for an executive MBA program delivered online. The cost of custom-developed programs can also vary. Simple linear, text-intensive "page turners" cost as little at $3,000 per hour of training. Complex programs using rich media, sophisticated video, and highly interactive exercises can cost from $50,000 to $70,000 per hour of seat time.

Organizations are often surprised that the hardware and software needed to create and deliver Web-based training is the smallest part of the budget. Web-based training costs are directly related to three variables:

- *Degree of Interactivity and Production Values.* The degree of interactivity refers to the number of possible paths or branches, the amount of remediation, and the richness of feedback. Production values are the invisible factors

Table 2.1. Comparing Training, Information, and Presentation Solutions

Solution Definition	Characteristics	Examples
Training is a deliberate process for bringing about a change in behavior, attitude, or cognitive structures.	Designed to create predicable and measurable outcomes Guides learner through the program Results in a change in behavior or skill Provides practice and feedback	SmartForce (www.smartforce.com) NETg (www.netg.com)
Information is composed of data that have been given meaning by a process of analysis and organization and that has been communicated in a meaningful and recognizable form, in time to affect some outcome.	Designed to organize data Navigated by learner who uses information as he or she sees fit No practice provided Not prescribe the outcomes No assessment or feedback	Yale Style Guide (http://info.med.yale.edu/caim/manual/contents.html) WebMD Health (http://my.Webmd.com/)
Presentations are structured one-way communications of facts, concepts, principles, and procedures using multiple media, designed either to provide information or persuade the reader.	Designed to share ideas or to persuade Structured flow of information No practice or feedback	Patient Education (www.surgery.mc.vanderbilt.edu/surgery/Trauma/Powerpoint/casemgmt/sld001.htm) ASTD Road Map for E-Learning (www.astd.org/virtual_community/Comm_elrng_rdmap/roadmapintro.html)

that make the difference between a polished finished project and an amateur project. Think about the difference between a car commercial produced by Ford for broadcast on ABC television and a commercial for a local used car lot on cable. Both advertisements attempt to sell cars but the Ford advertisement is of better quality and demonstrated high production values. Needless to say, quality and production value affect the price.

- *Type of Learning and Complexity of Content.* The nature of what is being taught will impact the budget. There are significant cost differences among teaching facts, concepts, principles, and procedures. Teaching a medical student simple facts related to identifying heart disease if going to be far less expensive than teaching a medical student to apply principles of internal medicine needed to diagnose heart disease.

  Some things don't change, as in the design of traditional classroom programs. Simple content is easiest and cheapest to develop; for example, it costs and takes less time to develop a communication skills program than an advanced JAVA scripting program. The more complicated the content, the longer it will take the designer to chunk and sequence it, as well as develop exercises.

- *Stability of Content.* Program costs can double or triple if the content changes frequently and dramatically during the design and development phase. Creating WBT is a form of software development. Changes in the program can send you back to start if they impact the navigation or perquisites or require massive rework of the interface. A change in the scope of the project will result in a change in the timeline and budget.

These variables are directly related to labor costs. When asking for a budget, be sure to define what you want to accomplish and determine, what you can do, and what you will need to hire outside help to accomplish.

There are a few nuances of the pricing model that are helpful to understand. First, the cost of a program is dependent on the point at which you need resources. Like all training programs, Web-based training requires analysis, design, development, implementation, and evaluation (ADDIE). The cost of the program will be higher if outside resources must be brought in to do all five phases. On the other hand, if an organization can complete the analysis, implementation, and evaluation with internal resources the cost should be less.

The second challenge in budgeting is to determine who owns other hidden expenses. Unlike traditional non-computer-based training programs, WBT has ongoing expenses. A few expenses to consider are

- *Helpdesk Support.* Web-based training programs, like other software programs, require that learners have access to technical support staff who can address questions regarding computer problems, network issues, difficulties with passwords, and system crashes. Rather than adding staff to the training department, it is common to give the headcount to the information systems group to allow them to increase their staff.

- *Infrastructure.* Depending on the solution, the organization may need to purchase additional hardware, such as modems, servers, or Internet service provider (ISP) accounts for learners working offsite or connecting from home. In some organizations, training may need to supplement the cost of new computers if WBT increases the system requirements. For example, an accounting department would not have to purchase sound cards or modems for their work. In this case the company must make provisions to supplement the hardware budget to ensure the computers would be able to accommodate WBT programs.

- *Connect Time.* If programs are designed for an international audience, telephone charges can be a major issue. Before rolling out the program, determine who pays for the connect time. This can be a major cost in the Asia Pacific region.

- *Localization and Translation.* Learners may technically be able to view Web-based training worldwide, but this does not mean they will comprehend it. Training is most effective when delivered in the learners' primary language. Consider how many languages the program will be translated into and determine whether your authoring tools support localization and translation. *Localization* is the process of adapting a product or service to a particular language or culture by creating the desired local "look and feel." This is an added expense and challenge because Web-based training programs can include text, graphics, and other media-rich elements that are expensive to revise. In addition, the authoring tools must be able to create an interface that can accommodate the translation of buttons with long German words and double byte Asian characters.

- *Maintenance.* One of the benefits of live instructor-lead training is that the materials do not have to be updated until the course is next taught. Web-based training programs are on display seven days a week, twenty-four hours a day, and obsolete content can create problems. As part of the initial project plan, there should be a plan to maintain and update the program until it is retired. Be sure to budget for ongoing maintenance. The formula below can be used to guestimate the costs.

> Cost of Original Program × Percentage of Change Per Year
> = Maintenance Per Year
> EXAMPLE:
> $100,000 × 15% change = $15,000 maintenance budget

Estimating the cost of Web-based training is complex. The best advice is to estimate carefully and to share your budget assumptions with a cross-functional team, including members of the information systems group, the client, and the business unit. If the estimate seems shockingly large, don't reduce it or assume it is a mistake. Review your numbers, and then ask for adequate budget.

One of the best tools for estimating time is to draw a Gantt chart or bar chart (or use Microsoft Project Manager) to create a drawing. The drawing will illustrate that most tasks are on the critical path and this makes timelines inflexible (see Figure 2.1).

In the 1990s Katherine Golas did research estimating development time for interactive courseware (ICW). Although the technology has changed, the metrics are worth considering because most of the costs in ICW and WBT are related to instructional design activities that have not changed. Like Brandon Hall's estimates, Golas' estimates span a wide range. Golas estimates that the hours needed to develop one hour of interactive courseware range from 50 to 200 for basic programs, 150 to 400 for medium simulations, and 200 to 600 for programs with a high degree of interactivity and extensive branching. (For more detail see her paper at www.coedu.usf.edu/inst_tech/resources/estimating.html.)

4. Form a Cross-Functional Team with a Powerful Champion

E-learning initiatives such as launching a Web-based training program, implementing a training management system, and creating an online certification program require a cross-functional team. The team may include the learners, as well as those involved in the development and delivery of the course. It is important to

Figure 2.1. Most WBT Tasks Are on the Critical Path

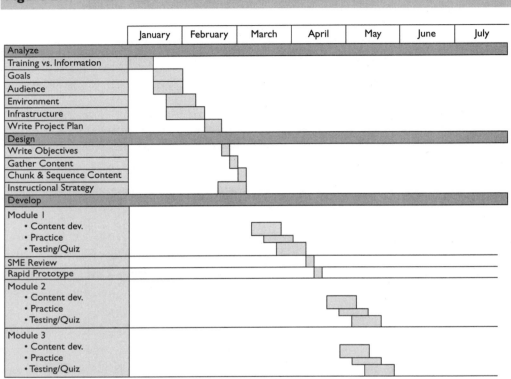

	January	February	March	April	May	June	July
Analyze							
Training vs. Information							
Goals							
Audience							
Environment							
Infrastructure							
Write Project Plan							
Design							
Write Objectives							
Gather Content							
Chunk & Sequence Content							
Instructional Strategy							
Develop							
Module 1							
• Content dev.							
• Practice							
• Testing/Quiz							
SME Review							
Rapid Prototype							
Module 2							
• Content dev.							
• Practice							
• Testing/Quiz							
Module 3							
• Content dev.							
• Practice							
• Testing/Quiz							

Training manager shares his experience with sticker shock

There was an e-learning conference last year for HR executives and senior managers. I didn't get to go, but the head of the HR department went. She came back really jazzed about what she saw, so we had a meeting. She wanted to talk about what we were doing with e-learning. We are a small department, so we outsource all our e-learning. She described the kind of program she had in mind for new hires, you know—high-dollar stuff with video, simulations, and personalization. I called our vendor and asked them to come in and to bring some examples of what they had done for other clients.

My guess is that no one had talked price at that conference. The head of HR was pretty surprised by the price tags on the programs she liked. . . . I'd say she got sticker shock. It was helpful to have the vendor show her what the difference was between the basic and the deluxe versions. Working with the vendor we got a good program in line with our budget.

identify the people who should be involved early in the process. Do not limit the team to instructional designers and subject-matter experts. Table 2.2 shows the members of the WBT development team and their involvement at each phase.

Developing Web-based training requires many team members with specialized skills. In some organizations people play more than one role, for example, the project manager may also be responsible for the instructional design and the system manager may act as the webmaster and network specialist. The following paragraphs describe the major responsibilities of each role.

- *Project Manager.* The project manager is responsible for leading the overall WBT effort, setting milestones, negotiating for resources, and communicating changes to the team. He or she has responsibilities at every phase of the project.

Table 2.2. Phases and Roles of Web-Based Training Team

Roles	Analysis		Design	Development	Delivery	Evaluation
	Instructional Goal	Select Most Appropriate WBT Methodology				
Project Manager	X	X	X	X	X	X
Instructional Designer(s)	X	X	X	X	X	X
System Managers		X		X	X	
Subject-Matter Expert(s)	X	X			X	X
Learners	X			X	X	X
Learners' Manager(s)	X				X	X
Legal Counsel			X	X	X	
Editor(s)				X	X	X
Programmer(s)		X	X	X	X	X
Graphics Artist(s)			X	X		
Webmaster		X			X	
Instructor(s)					X	X

- *Instructional Designer(s).* The instructional designer is responsible for conducting the needs assessment, choosing the most appropriate form of Web-based training, designing lessons, and developing blueprints. During the website-development phase, the instructional designer must be available to clarify directions in the blueprints and to negotiate changes in the design necessitated by technical limitations or changes in time or funding. The instructional designer leads the effort to evaluate the program.

- *System Manager(s).* The system manager provides technical guidance and support for the program. When the team is choosing the most appropriate form of Web-based training, the system manager provides insights into the organization's technical capabilities and limitations. As the instructional designer creates lessons and blueprints, the system manager reviews them to ensure that the network and software can support the design. During the site-development phase, the system manager provides the team with system resources, such as access to servers, passwords, and development accounts. During the evaluation phase, the system manager assists the pilot learners with network issues and installation of WBT software, plug-ins, and browsers.

- *Subject-Matter Expert(s).* The subject-matter expert contributes to the needs-assessment phase by helping to define program goals. When the blueprints are ready for review, the subject-matter expert reviews the documents for gross omissions and inaccuracies. During the program-evaluation phase, he or she continues to identify omissions and inaccuracies as well as recommend improvements to the program.

- *Learners' Manager(s).* The learners and their managers are involved at the beginning and again at the end. Both groups are expected to complete questionnaires and participate in interviews and observation sessions. When the program has been developed and is ready to pilot, the learners and their managers review the program and provide feedback.

- *Legal Counsel.* The role of legal counsel is to review the design documents and program blueprint to ensure that there are no problems regarding copyright, use of trademarks, or improper use of proprietary information. For example, if the Web-based training program is using sections of a multimedia program developed by a third party, legal counsel will help the developer secure the copyright for use of the program on the Web.

- *Editor(s).* Editors are responsible for the grammar, consistency, and clarity of the text used on website pages. Reviewing the blueprint before it goes to programmers and graphic artists reduces the amount of rework during the development of the website. Editors continue to make corrections and recommendations during the website development and during the evaluation phase of the program.

- *Programmer(s).* Programmers play an active role during the last three phases of development. As the blueprint is being developed, they review the design and make technical recommendations. For example, if the instructional designer wants to create an exercise that tracks learner responses and provides dynamic feedback, the programmer gives recommendations regarding how to accomplish this. During the development stage, programmers are responsible for developing HTML pages, creating Java applets, and developing interactions using tools such as mBED™ or Macromedia's ShockWave™. During the program evaluation phase, the programmers make the necessary iterative changes from the pilot.

- *Graphic Artist(s).* The responsibility of the graphic artist is to help translate the lesson designs and storyboards into Web pages. The graphic artists provide creative direction and style. The images, navigation, and layout of screens developed and agreed on during the blueprint phase are put into production during site development. The graphic artist works with programmers to create joint photographic experts group (JPEG) and GIF images to be included in HTML pages. They design the images programmers use to create maps for navigation. After the evaluation phase, the graphic artist makes changes to the Web pages as needed.

- *Webmaster.* The webmaster is responsible for maintaining the Web server and the site on a day-to-day basis. During the blueprint stage, he or she estimates the server capacity and hard drive space required to support the program. During the website development phase and the program evaluation phase, the webmaster puts pages on the server or grants access to the team as needed.

- *Instructor(s).* Instructors are responsible for delivering asynchronous and synchronous (real-time) programs. They are involved in the program evaluation phase to identify any delivery problems and may make recommendations for timing and sequencing in a synchronous class.

A cross-functional team is the only way to bring together the resources and experience needed to develop complex solutions. No one group has the technical expertise, subject-matter knowledge, process experience, or budget. Just as you need subject-matter experts, training professionals, and others in the development of classroom courses, in WBT you need varying expertise for your WBT team.

Technical writer talks about becoming a victim of her own success

Last year I became Ms. E-Learning! I'm a technical writer, and I created a small Web-based training lesson to go with a section of a users' manual I was writing. It was fun. I got to use Flash, Dreamweaver, and some other stuff that I learned on my own. When my boss showed my lesson to some other people, they thought it was great. They wanted me to make lessons to go with the whole manual. I was really glad they liked it, but there was no way I could develop all that e-learning by myself. A big project like making e-learning to accompany the users' manual takes a team. I had to explain how long it would take if I had to do the writing, artwork, programming, and testing all by myself for every lesson.

Finding a Champion

The key to bringing together a cross-functional team is to find a powerful champion. It takes more than identifying the business unit manager with a strategic need. It is important to find a business manager who can act as the project's champion. The qualities of a champion are

- *Can Secure Resources.* Champions must command the budget and authority to get resources such as headcount, hardware, office space, and, most importantly, cooperation from other organizations.

- *Has Mission-Critical Training Need.* Champions will be supportive if they perceive the success of training as a critical factor in accomplishing their missions.

- *Willing to Communicate Support.* Champions should be willing to communicate their support in visible and meaningful ways. In addition to attending kickoff meetings and sending the obligatory memos, they should be willing to provide incentives and rewards as well as punish those who will not cooperate.

- *Understands the Benefits/Limitations of WBT.* Champions do not see WBT as a silver bullet but rather they know what this technology can and cannot accomplish.

The champion should not be confused with the project leader. Table 2.3 provided a comparison of the roles. The champion is involved in the strategic decisions, while the project leader is responsible for the tactical day-to-day decisions and tasks.

5. Drive Simplicity and Standards

Standards used in WBT relate to (1) the operating guidelines of hardware and software, (2) the selection of software tools, and (3) the development process. Let's look at each one.

Organizations should consider standards at three levels. At the most detailed level, software and hardware products will list the standards to which they adhere. The most common training software standard is the AICC or Aviation Industry CBT Committee standard. The AICC develops guidelines for the aviation industry, which promotes the interoperability of computer and Web-based training software. Interoperability is important for organizations that plan to integrate off-the-shelf courses with courses authored in-house and tools for testing and training management.

Table 2.3. Comparison of Roles of Champion Versus Project Leader

Components of Role	Champion	Project Leader
Function	BU or dept manager	Training professional
Skills	Functional business skills	Skilled in filling knowledge gaps and WBT
Goals	Establishes WBT program goal	Creates project plan to meet program goal
Tasks	Secures resources Drives cross-functional teams Makes final decisions	Manages cross-functional team on a day-to-day basis Escalates appropriate issues
Communication	Communicates corporate-wide	Communicates with champion and team

The second area in which standards can be useful is in the adoption of software for creating and managing e-learning. Organizations should agree to adopt a select collection of software for all organizations, rather than allowing each division to select its own e-learning software. As a result of using a standard set of software, organizations can reduce their information systems (IS) support costs. It is more cost-efficient for IS organizations to master the nuances of installing, maintaining, and trouble shooting a limited number of software applications. In addition, when programs are created with a standard set of software applications, organizations can share and reuse modules.

Agreeing to a limited standard set of software tools for developing Web-based training is challenging. Choose software applications that offer the greatest flexibility and software that can grow and scale as your needs change. Often an application that is perfect for a specific project is not the best application for the broader range of programs the organization must develop. When group members insist on using software applications that are not part of the agreed-on standard set, question the exceptions. If applications are selected that do not adhere to standards such as the AICC, consider the impact of obsolescence and the problems of migrating the courses developed using these applications.

Standardizing on a limited number of software applications is also of benefit to learners. Using standard software packages can reduce the cognitive burden for learners. Learners find it easier to focus on the content if they are required to master a single software package and its navigation systems, icons, and passwords, rather than learning a new e-learning interface for each course.

The third kind of standardization is the standardization of process. Organizations benefit from standardizing on processes, such as creating a method for developing storyboards, creating flow charts, structuring directories, and using agreed-on naming conventions. Standardization is an important issue for organizations creating reusable learning objects and for organizations that are creating a large number of courses.

Projects that involve two or more people should establish agreed-on ways for communicating things, such as symbols for navigation, how to indicate what text is going to be hypertext, and how the learners will move forward and backward in a remediation sequence. Establishing standards will allow team members to hand off plans without needing to be involved in the detailed execution of those plans. At a more general level, there is a need to agree on what is considered a learning object versus a media asset. Later the ability to swap learning objects will be enhanced or hindered, consistent with standards for learning objects.

Comparing Standards for Learning Objects Worksheet

Directions: If you would like to explore how other organizations have defined standards, use the following links to locate white papers on learning objects. If you want to explore what the standards bodies have to say about learning objects, check out ADL, AICC, and IMS. Use the questions below to reflect on the experience.

White Papers on Learning Objects	Organizations That Define Standards for E-Learning
NETg *The NETg Learning Object Architecture* (www.netg.com/us/)	**ADL** *Advanced Distributed Learning* (www.adlnet.org)
Cisco *Cisco Systems Reusable Information Strategy* (www.cisco.com/warp/public/10/wwtraining/ elearning/learn/whitepaper.html)	**AICC** *The Aviation Industry CBT (Computer-Based Training) Committee* (www.aicc.org) **IMS** *IMS Global Learning Consortium, Inc.* (www.imsproject.org/)

REFLECTION QUESTIONS

- How are the strategies similar and different?

- Could the objects be swapped?

- How would you define learning objects in your organization?

- What other steps in the design process are impacted by learning objects?

- What assumptions are being made about how courses are developed?

6. Avoid a "Big Bang" All at Once Implementation

When implementing a program, it is best to roll out programs one curriculum and one audience at a time. Working on small-scale initiatives allows the training organization to make corrections without massive negative attention. Small programs allow the training organization to obtain feedback quickly and to learn from the mistakes. After a few successful implementations, organizations can build on the momentum of their success and the positive word of mouth.

It is also important to choose your initial implementation sites with care. Organizations are most successful when they "fish where the fish are"! Look for initial implementation sites that have the following characteristics:

- *Learners with a Need for Training.* Choose to develop curriculums for groups that need training. When possible, select audiences who need training to be successful.

- *Learners with Computer and Internet Skills.* Select audiences with strong computer and Internet skills. These audiences will have the energy to focus on the challenge of the new learning methodology and not become bogged down on the issues of basic computer skills.

- *Learners with Adequate Access to Technology.* Analyze the resources of potential audiences and choose those with good Internet connectivity, newer computers, and strong technical support. The better equipped and supported the learners are, the greater the odds for a successful implementation.

7. Measure Productivity Improvements

Organizations that develop Web-based training can easily lose sight of the business issues related to productivity. It is important to monitor costs and to strive for continuous improvements in cost and service. One of the best ways to improve productivity is to set cost and service targets. These targets can be quantitative or qualitative.

Examples of quantitative measures, that is, targets that you can associate number with are

- The number of calls to helpdesk per X users;
- The cost of program design, development, and delivery;
- The number of hours required to develop a WBT program; and
- The time it takes the average user to complete the course.

Examples of qualitative measures, that is, ratings that cannot be described with numbers are given below. These questions can be used to gather qualitative data:

- Did learners enjoy the program (high, level I evaluations)?
- Does the program supports the corporate mission?
- Does the program enhance training department's status?
- Is this program helping your company keep up with the competition?

8. Recognize WBT Is a Form of Software Development

Implementing Web-based training programs has a great deal in common with developing and implementing software. Like software, Web-based training requires the developers to think about things beyond audience and task analysis. There are issues that are new to many training professionals. The following list outlines the additional considerations:

- *Helpdesk.* Web-based training programs require technical support to deal with technical problems. The training organization is responsible for arranging support from the helpdesk.

- *Quality Assurance.* Learners expect Web-based training programs to be as reliable as the dial tone on the telephone. This means that programs must be tested to ensure that the interface is intuitive, the directions are clear, and there are no technical problems.

- *Legacy Programs.* Legacy programs are programs designed to be used for two to three years and then handed down or passed along to others in the organization. These legacy programs should be well-documented to make maintenance easy and developed using standards when possible. If tools and standards change dramatically, these legacy programs can become problematic to maintain.

- *Platforms.* Like any software program, a WBT program will need to address the issue of which platforms or operating systems it will support. Learners on Macintosh and UNIX systems may not be able to access programs or they may not be able to get plug-ins for all the interactive elements of a program. Authoring tools may also not be available for all operating systems. Many authoring packages are limited to Microsoft and Macintosh.

- *Infrastructure.* In an ideal world, training professionals can choose the online training strategies that best suit their needs. In reality, training professionals are constrained by the limits of the organization's infrastructure, such as modem speed, version of browser software, security rules, and organizational restrictions on plug-ins and streaming video.

9. Think Ahead and Anticipate Needs

Thinking ahead six, twelve, and eighteen months is essential when dealing with the Web. Things change quickly, so it is important to anticipate what an organization may want to do. When planning Web-based training, plan for some of these possibilities:

- *E-Business and E-Commerce.* Will the organization want to charge for training? Will training be part of a product mix for customers or for partners? Will the data from training classes be used for certification, lead generation, or prospecting?

- *Related E-Learning Tools.* Are there plans to purchase a learning or training management system (LMA/TMS)? Will Web-based training need to integrate with a knowledge management system or sales automation tool?

- *Application Program Interface (API).* Will the WBT program be expected to talk to other programs such as SAP or PeopleSoft? If so, does the program have APIs, that is, the ability to make requests of other programs?

- *Scalable Architecture.* Is the authoring tool capable of growing as the demand for WBT grows? How many students can it accommodate? How many users can be online at one time? Is the WBT server limited in the number of courses or sessions it can host?

10. Create an Instructional Technology-Smart Organization

Web-based training is a complex and expensive solution requiring managers to learn a great deal in order to make wise decisions. One of the best ways to ensure the successful implementation of WBT is to educate top management and line of business managers about the technology. The following list provides recommendations for educating managers:

- *Benchmark the Competition.* Make managers aware of what their competitors are doing regarding e-learning and Web-based training.

- *Monitor the External Environment.* Pass along information from magazines and professional publications for trends that will impact your industry. Point out ways in which e-learning can solve strategic problems.

- *Monitor the Internal Environment.* Identify decisions that will impact e-learning and WBT, such as new laptops for the salesforce, telecommuting programs, and partnerships with organizations that offer WBT.

Summary

Best practices for implementing WBT are simply lessons learned from people who have already implemented e-learning. Best practices do not offer directions, but rather they provide insights to shape decision making.

Implementing Web-based training is complex and demanding. For many training organizations, implementing an e-learning solution will be the most expensive and visible project they have ever undertaken. Success in e-learning is like a stool with three legs; e-learning will not be successful unless all three legs are of equal proportions. In this case the legs of the stool are *technology, business need*, and *education.* So far we have spent a great deal of time talking about the business need and the technology. It is now time to talk about learning. The next chapter looks at what is required to create an educationally effective program for adults in the workplace.

Suggested Readings

Barron, T. (March, 2000). Pioneering applications of learning objects. *LearningCircuits, 1*(3). [Online]. Available: www.learningcircuits.org/lc_index.html

Hall, B. (July, 1998). The cost of custom WBT: Are you getting your money's worth, or paying the price for poor planning. *Inside Technology Training Magazine,* pp. 12–13.

Golas, K.C. (1993). *Estimating time to develop interactive courseware in the 1990s.* Proceedings of the 15th Interservice/Industry Training Systems and Education Conference, Orlando, Florida, November 29–December 2, 1993.

Millison, D. (2001). Learning by the rules. *Knowledge Management, 4*(7), pp. 62–64.

Rosenberg, M.J. (2001). *E-learning: Strategies for delivering knowledge in the digital age.* New York: McGraw-Hill.

Chapter 3

Principles of Adult Education and Instructional Design

In the last chapter we explored the business issues critical to the success of e-learning programs. In many cases, the decision to implement Web-based training is made based on the business need to train workers using a methodology that is perceived to be better, faster, and cheaper than traditional training. In other cases, organizations choose Web-based training because it is trendy or because management mandates it. No matter how your organization arrives at the decision to deliver training via the Web, the most important key to the educational success of the program will be the application of principles of adult education and instructional design.

This chapter provides a foundation for designing programs and evaluating off-the-shelf courses. Training and development professionals often take for granted the skills and knowledge they have acquired through years of hands-on experience and formal education. These skills are a solid foundation on which to build an expertise in assessing Web-based training. Other professionals asked to manage and evaluate Web-based training programs will find the fundamentals in the chapter to be a solid starting foundation. The URLs and the exercises are provided to enable the reader to quickly find relevant examples that illustrate concepts.

What You Will Learn in This Chapter

After completing this chapter you will be able to

- Specify requirements when outsourcing a project or purchasing an off-the-shelf program;

- Explain the phases of instruction and the role of objectives;

- Identify what is unique about adult learners;

- List the skills required to facilitate adult learning; and

- Integrate the principles of adult education into a Web-based training program.

Guidelines for Assessing Programs: Phases of Interaction and Objectives

This section provides a high-level overview of what you should specify when outsourcing a project or considering the purchase of an off-the-shelf program. When assessing a program, there are two areas on which to focus. First, examine the overall course to ensure that it has all the phases of instruction needed to deliver an effective learning experience. If the phases are all there, drill down and examine the objectives to determine whether the course teaches what it claims to teach.

Phases of Instruction

Let's start by looking at the components of a Web-based course. There are four phases in any complete instructional interaction (see Figure 3.1). They are

- Presenting information;

- Guiding the student in practice;

- Practicing by the student; and

- Assessing the student's learning.

The informing/presenting phase is the foundation phase. In it, the instructional designer provides the student with content, information, and the method for achieving the instructional objectives. The guiding of the student phase provides the interaction needed to ensure that the learner has understood the concepts, principles, and procedures presented. It may include drill and practice or chaining or mnemonics (which will be discussed later in this section). The third phase requires recalling, manipulating, and applying new knowledge. Students must practice the

Figure 3.1. Four Phases of Instruction

PHASES OF INSTRUCTION

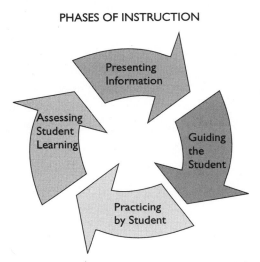

Source: Alessi, S. M., & Trollip, S. R. (1991). *Computer-based instruction: Methods and Development.* Englewood Cliffs, NJ: Prentice-Hall.

new skills and knowledge to move information from short-term to long-term memory and to develop mastery of the content. Finally, the cycle closes with an assessment phase that answers the questions: "Was the instruction effective?" "What is the next step for the learner?"

It is important to understand that Web-based training software packages allow organizations to create entire courses or put selected segments of their training programs online. Table 3.1 below provides links to examples focusing on selected phases, rather than offering complete lessons. Consider the possibility of using blended solutions combining live instructor-led training with Web-based training to achieve all four phases of instruction.

Objectives

Performance and content-based objectives are the foundation of effective programs. In the 1960s Robert Mager introduced training professionals to the concept of objectives and stressed the value of objectives in designing lessons and building assessments. Thousands of training professionals can write objectives using the essential ABCDs of Mager (audience, behavior, condition, and degree). Mager's influence continues to be evidenced in traditional classroom instruction and e-learning lessons.

Instructor talks about how a blended solution enables her to deliver all four phases

I used to teach a two-day course on interviewing skills for managers. The course is now a Web-based pre-course with a one-day classroom course. The Web-based course is used to present information about things like body language, open questions, surprise tactics, and active listening skills. Before attending the class, everyone reviews these concepts on the Web. When they do come to class, I expect them to be ready to start practicing interview exercises. The Web saves me having to lecture and enables me to focus on practice and assessing their skills.

Table 3.1. Examples of Phases of Instruction

Phase	What to Look For	Example
Presenting Information	This is a good example of information presentation. The practice of decorating a cake is left to the learner to do offline.	*Learn2 Decorate a Cake* (www.learn2.com/04/0412/0412.asp)
Guiding the Student	In this example, students are allowed to practice memorizing the names of state capitals and are given guidance in the practice and immediate feedback.	*U.S. State Capital* (www.quia.com/mc/4.html)
Practicing by the Student	This site allows learners to practice writing JAVA script and HTML code. The site provides minimal feedback, allowing the learner to develop self-correcting skills.	*UserActive* (Click on "The Learning Sandbox"; www.useractive.com/)
Assessing Student Learning	This site provides sample assessments from corporations, colleges, and kindergarten through 12th grade classes.	*Corporate, College, K-12 Assessments* (Click on "Try it Out"; www.questionmark.com/)

Note: Websites change frequently and pages move. If these sites are no longer operational, use a search engine and the following key words: "WBT, Web-based training: lecture, practice, and testing."

Mager-style objectives are a good starting point, but they don't take advantage of Dr. Merrill's more recent Component Display Theory (1994). This theory suggests that objectives should be classified according to two criteria: performance and content. Performance refers to the three types of performance possible: *remember, use* (apply), and *find* (create new instance). Content refers to four kinds of knowledge: *facts, concepts, procedures,* and *principles.* Based on a content-performance matrix, Merrill has identified optimal ways to present content, practice skills, and test knowledge.

Advancing Merrill's work, Dr. Ruth Clark has translated component display theory into an approach for developing classroom and computer-based instructional materials. Her work provides detailed prescriptions for the development of a wide variety of instructional materials and her book, *Developing Technical Training: A Structured Approach for Developing Classroom and Computer-Based Instructional Materials,* is an excellent reference for developers.

Since it is not the purpose of this book to teach detailed instructional design of Web-based materials (as Dr. Clark's book does so well), let me complete this section of the chapter by providing URL sites with instructional programs that illustrate teaching facts, concepts, procedures, and principles with varying performance objectives. You will find that the kind of knowledge being presented at these URL sites, as well as the desired level of performance (whether it's remembering, using/applying, or finding/creating) are clearly stated. You will also be guided by my comments in "What to look for and reflect on" to see how these instructional programs have incorporated the four phases of instruction, namely, the phases of presenting information, guiding students, providing opportunities for practice by the student, and assessing the student's learning.

This chapter is designed to prepare managers to specify projects to be outsourced, developed in-house, or purchased off the shelf. The first part of this chapter has focused on what it takes to develop a good program. Learning is a four-part process, and it doesn't matter whether all or only part of that process is completed on the Web. The important point to remember is that all the phases must be completed somewhere!

The next section looks at an often neglected aspect of online learning—the role of the learner. It is important not to lose sight of the learner and to take into consideration motivation for learning, techniques for facilitation, and factors that frustrate learners.

√ Teaching Facts Worksheet

Directions: Facts are bits of information for which there is a one-to-one correspondence. Facts are different from other types of content because there is only one thing learners can do with them—remember them. Use the URLs below to explore how facts are being taught, practiced, and assessed.

URLs	What to Look For and Reflect On
State Capitals (www.quia.com/mc/4.html)	These are examples of drill and practice exercises.
Body Parts (www.quia.com/jfc/305.html)	Think about how these examples could be improved.
Art History (www.quia.com/jg/823.html)	Use Quia's free tools to build your own drill and practice exercise.

Natural Resources and Environmental Conservation

Snakes of Massachusetts (www.umass. edu/umext/nrec/snake_pit/index.html)	Snakes of Massachusetts presents factual information in an interactive and engaging manner. Think about how practice exercises and assessment might be designed to complement this site.

Link Finder: If these links do not work, use combinations of the following key words to find new sites: quiz, test, e-learning, Web-based training, elearning demo, e-learning sample.

Teaching Is Only Half of the Instructional Transaction

Teaching online is a transaction between the program that teaches and the student who must do the learning. Despite the popularity of Web-based training and the claims that students enjoy online learning more than traditional classroom programs, online learning still requires work. Many WBT programs are simply self-paced learning online. A 1998 study by Georgia Tech found that most people had no experience with the Web for training and development, and that may have been the good news. Of the people who did have experience with training and development on the Web, the largest percentage responded that they somewhat or strongly disagreed with the statement: "My organization uses the Web effectively in training and development." The message to developers should be that putting training on the Web does not make training instantly better, nor does it make learners enjoy training more!

Teaching Concepts Worksheet

Directions: Concepts are groups of objects or events that share common characteristics and can be identified with the same name. Use the URLs below to explore how concepts are being taught, practiced, and assessed

URLs	What to Look For and Reflect On
Financial Concepts (www.dinkytown.net/) *Roche Pharm HIV Education* (www.roche-hiv.com/infoactive_static/infoactive_static.htm) *Physics Web: Virtual Laboratory* (http://physicsweb.org/TIPTOP/VLAB/) *MathDork: Interactive Math* (www.mathdork.com/)	Link to one or more of these sites to experience how multimedia helps deliver content. Consider the importance of interactivity in these examples.

Link Finder: If these links do not work, use combinations of the following key words to find new sites: elearning, e-learning, Web-based training, elearning demo, e-learning sample, concept.

Figure 3.2 shows a 1998 Georgia Tech Study asking end-users' opinions of how effective they perceived their organizations' use of the Web was for training and development.

Now let's look at how you can ensure that your Web-based training programs are effective.

Guidelines for Facilitating Programs for Adults

There is a significant body of research on adult learning and findings related to what works best when teaching in the workplace. While much of this literature predates the Web, the findings are worth considering because Web technology has simply altered the delivery medium.

Relevant and Problem-Centered Programs Are Best for Adults

Adult learners are unique in that they have more life and work experiences on which to draw. They are motivated to learn as a response to problems and changes. The special characteristics of adult learners have been described by authors such as

✓ Teaching Procedures Worksheet

Directions: Procedures are an ordered set of steps necessary to accomplish a task. Use the URLs below to explore how procedures are being taught, practiced, and assessed.

URLs	What to Look For and Reflect On
How to Drive a Stick Shift (www.learn2.com/06/0689/0689.asp) *How to Draw a Graph of a = X* (http://iln.go.com/html_p/c/453262/458832/453330/457593/55408.asp) *Web Monkey How to Library: Designing Websites for PDAs* (http://hotwired.lycos.com/webmonkey/) *SurfStatAustralian Statistics* (www.anu.edu.au/nceph/surfstat/surfstat-home/surfstat.html)	Consider how these sites use the Web to teach psychomotor and cognitive skills. How have sites used interactivity and multimedia to enhance the lesson? How could these sites be improved?

Link Finder: If these links do not work, use combinations of the following key words to find new sites: Web-based training, elearning demo, e-learning sample, steps, procedures, process.

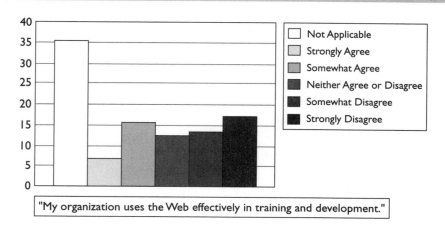

Figure 3.2.   Georgia Tech Study Results

Legend:
- Not Applicable
- Strongly Agree
- Somewhat Agree
- Neither Agree or Disagree
- Somewhat Disagree
- Strongly Disagree

"My organization uses the Web effectively in training and development."

Source: www.gvu.gatech.edu/gvu/user_surveys/survey-199810/graphs/use/q09.htm

✓ Teaching Principles Worksheet

Directions: Principles are explanations of why things happen or interpretations of how things work. Use the URLs below to explore how principles are being taught, practiced, and assessed.

URLs	What to Look For and Reflect On
The Particle Adventure (http://particleadventure.org/) *Virtual Economy* (http://ve.ifs.org.uk/) *The Physics Classroom* (www.glenbrook.k12.il.us/gbssci/phys/Class/BBoard.html) *The Net Economics Text Book Supply and Demand* (http://nova.umuc.edu/~black/pageg.html)	Sample the following sites to experience how information is presented. If practice using the principle is provided, how effective is it? How might these sites design an assessment?

Link Finder: If these links do not work, use combinations of the following key words to find new sites: principle, e-learning, Web-based training, elearning demo, e-learning sample.

Knowles (1998), Brookfield (1990), Kidd (1973), Freire (1970), and Merriam and Caffarella (1991).

Characteristics of adult learners are that they:

- Have real-life experiences;
- Prefer problem-centered learning;
- Are continuous learners;
- Have varied learning styles;
- Have responsibilities beyond the training situation;
- Expect learning to be meaningful; and
- Prefer to manage their own learning.

Figure 3.3 is an example of a WBT program, The Doctor's Dilemma, that provides relevant and problem-centered learning for medical professionals.

Structure Learners' Experience

Effective programs impose structure and limit learner control to a certain extent. The ability to surf the Internet is a much-publicized quality of the Web. Using the

Figure 3.3.   Relevant and Problem-Centered Content

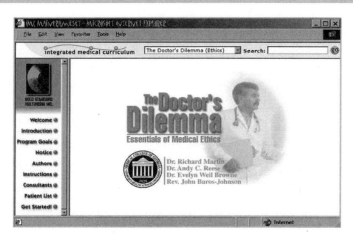

Source: The Doctor's Dilemma by the Medical College of Georgia, authors Dr. Richard Martin, Dr. Andy C. Reese, Dr. Evelyn Weil Browre, Rev. John Baros-Johnson, and Gold Standard Multimedia. www.gsm.com

Web as a learning environment requires that subject-matter experts and course developers impose structure. Learning is enhanced when programs are chunked, sequenced, and organized in a meaningful way. Well-structured programs reduce demands on short-term memory by organizing information into small pieces that are easy to remember and manipulate. For example, lessons can be organized based on

- Tasks;
- Job categories;
- Most common problems encountered;
- Basic, intermediate, and advanced skills; and
- Chronologically from first step to last.

The learner's skill level and the complexity of the content should dictate the amount of control granted a student.

All learners should have the ability to quit the program, create bookmarks to return later, replay audio and video segments, and review previously completed material. More advanced control, such as the ability to study lessons in nonlinear order and the ability to eliminate practice and assessment segments, should be determined as part of your needs assessment and formative evaluation. Experienced online learners may have the skills needed to move forward and backward in a program, learning the content in the order that pleases them. Learners who are familiar with the content may be able to find what they need and exit the program without practice or assessments. Keep in mind the success of a program should necessarily be measured by the number of learners who complete the program and pass the test.

Provide Meaningful Feedback That Improves Performance

Web-based training programs can provide rich and meaningful feedback during guided practice and student practice. In addition to simple test remediation explaining why an answer is wrong, graphics can illustrate solutions. Animation sequences can demonstrate steps, and audio can model correct responses. Feedback during guided practice should provide prompts that are more instructive than "please try again" or "correct." Effective programs use feedback to develop the learners' ability to self-diagnose their programs and eventually correct errors without prompts.

An excellent example of a program that provides rich feedback (even if it is smart-ass) is the trivia game "You Don't Know Jack." Pulse Learning, shown in Figure 3.4, offers a similar opportunity for rich feedback. This game models excellent examples of how feedback on wrong answers can be educational without giving away the right answer and how even feedback on right answers can be extended and expanded to deepen the learner's knowledge.

Figure 3.4.   Meaningful Feedback Improves Performance

Source: Pulse
www.pulse3d.com

Use Effective Assessments That Test What Has Been Taught

Use Merrill's performance-content matrix to be sure you are assessing the learners' mastery of the stated performance-content objective. For example, if the goal of the course is to teach learners how to calculate a standard deviation, then the test should assess whether students are able to apply the procedures required to calculate a standard deviation. That is, the test should avoid testing the definition of a standard deviation and it should not test the memorization of the steps in the calculation process. Rather, the test must determine whether a learner can use the procedure to calculate a standard deviation. Effective online learning programs match test items to stated objectives.

Provide Adequate Practice That Leads to Mastery

The phrase "practice makes perfect" may sound trite, but there is a great deal of research that supports this cliché. There must be adequate practice if students are to develop fluency and mastery of content. There is no magic number of interactions per lesson or ratio of exercises to pages of text. The only way to determine whether a program provides an adequate amount of practice is to conduct a formative evaluation and determine whether the target audience is getting too much practice, too little practice, or just enough. An example of this can be seen in ActiveUser's JavaScript Tutorial, which provides learners with deep and varied practice (see Figure 3.5).

Figure 3.5. Provide Adequate Practice

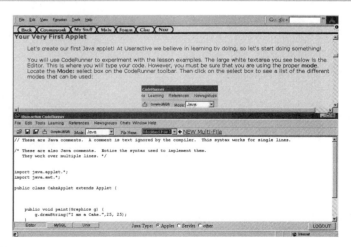

Source: Useractive, Inc.
www.useractive.com

Actively Engage the Learner to Increase Learning

Good WBT programs offer frequent interactions that probe the learners' understanding. Interactions should go beyond simple multiple-choice questions that provide linear branching (correct/incorrect). Ignore the old rule of thumb "provide an interaction every three screens." The number of interactions should be based on the complexity of the content and on the learners' motivation and experience with online learning. In the alpha phase of evaluation, while the program is still in development, the amount, quantity, and complexity of the practice should be evaluated. While the program is still in this formative stage, it is easiest to increase the number of practice examples, decrease the level of difficulty, or determine that too much practice has been provided.

Questions should offer the opportunity to move learners forward to new information, backward to review completed content, and sideways to provide supplemental information. Creating a program with meaningful probes and engagement requires more time and effort than a linear program offering a string of pages followed by a simple quiz. Figure 3.6 shows a sample interactive online program.

Figure 3.6. Engage the Learner

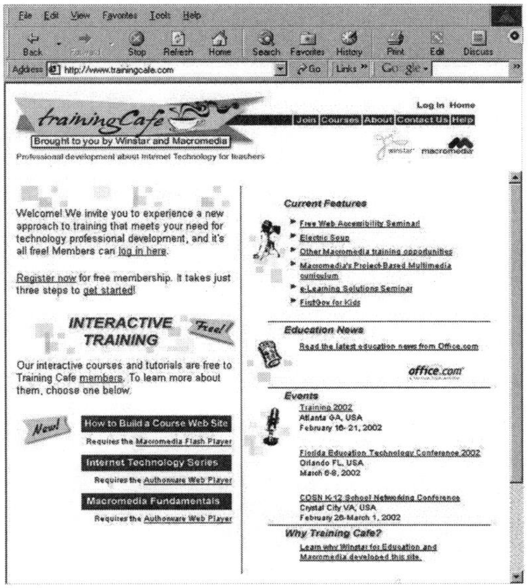

Source: Macromedia Training Cafe
www.trainingcafe.com

Use Multimedia Elements in Meaningful Ways

Multimedia can reduce the effort required to convey a message. When appropriate, WBT can take advantage of multiple media such as tests, graphics, animation, video, and audio to deliver instructional content. These media can improve instruction when they are used alone or in combination, reduce the effort required to convey a message, increase active engagement, and focus attention. The choice of media should be driven by the performance and content stated in the objectives. Avoid gratuitous multimedia such as sounds of cheering crowds for correct answers or animation sequences with a flashing "X" and thumbs-down symbol.

Figure 3.7 provides an example of a supplemental WBT program that uses streaming audio to teach English.

Figure 3.7.   Multimedia Uses to Enhance the Content

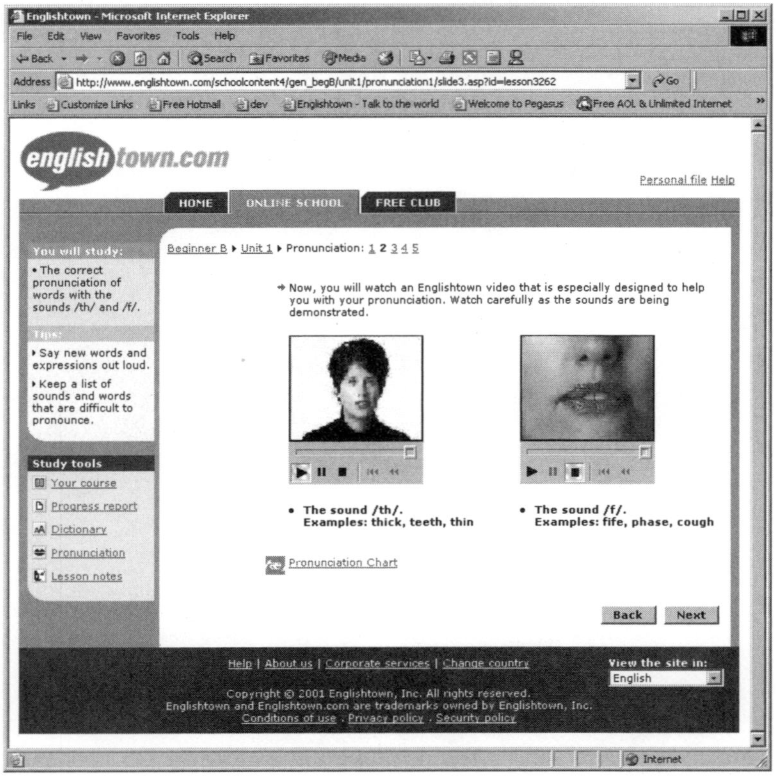

Source: EnglishTown, Inc.
www.englishtown.com

Create a Safe and Respectful Environment

Create an environment in which learners are valued as individuals and feel comfortable participating. Keep this principle in mind as you develop online forums, exercises, and feedback loops.

Encourage Exploration, Action, and Reflection

Encourage learners to explore new ideas and alternative ways of solving problems. Invite them to reflect on what they have learned by applying these ideas. Experiment with exercises that promote critical reflection. Design some individual and some group exercises.

Nurture Self-Directed Learning

Encourage learners to assume responsibility for continuing their education. Help them develop and apply skills for managing and assessing their own learning. Nurture the abilities and attitudes learners need to question their assumptions and to explore alternative ways of thinking.

What Frustrates Learners

Research (Hara & Kling, 2000) has shown that two kinds of problems frustrate learners: technical problems and pedagogical problems. The following summarizes some of the common problems adults encounter.

Technical Problems

The promise of WBT is "learning anywhere and any time." While this is one of the selling points of this technology, it is also a source of great frustration. Many employees are asked to take training after work hours, on weekends, and at night. This creates a problem for users who need technical support during those times. In many cases there is no one staffing the helpdesk. Even those working regular business hours may be frustrated by hardware and software problems that require a series of phone calls to resolve.

Inadequate Feedback

The role of the instructor or the role of the software in providing adequate feedback is essential for success. In a traditional classroom, students can gauge their performance based on the work of other students and the nonverbal gestures and facial expressions of the instructor. In addition, classroom feedback is immediate. WBT programs frustrate learners when the feedback does not provide enough information for the learners to understand what they have done wrong or how to correct a mistake. For example, responses such as "Please Try Again" and "That Is Incorrect" do not provide adequate feedback. In facilitated WBT programs in which instructors respond by e-mail, students express frustration when the facilitator fails to provide prompt feedback and when the feedback lacks detail.

Overwhelming E-Mail and Threaded Discussions

Many Web-based training programs make extensive use of e-mail for group work, feedback, question and answer sessions, and collaboration. Threaded discussions or forums are used to encourage dialogue and to post feedback, make assignments, and conduct class discussions. In workplace WBT programs, these tools can consume a great deal of time. Participants become frustrated when their mail accounts become cluttered with mail from WBT programs and notices regarding new postings to threaded discussions. Frustration can set in when students feel they cannot keep up or when there is so much material posted that the dialogue passes them by.

Lack of Navigation Skills and Metacognitive Skills

Learners can feel a deep sense of frustration if they lack the mental models and cognitive skills assumed by the developers. Some of the most common sources of frustration are not understanding how to use search engines, lack of ability to follow hypertext links, and inability to manage pop-up windows. Learners often report feeling lost in hyperspace. Unlike a book, in which learners know how to determine where they are, how much they have accomplished, and how to move forward and backward, the Web is a new environment and learners have few clues.

Ambiguous Instructions

Instructors experienced in traditional classroom teaching are familiar with the challenge of giving clear instructions. This challenge is amplified on the Web because directions are primarily given in written form. Learners may have difficulty understanding directions and require additional clarification. The need to clarify directions places the added burden of sending the instructor e-mail and waiting for a reply. There are also special challenges for instructors learning how to give directions in a live virtual classroom where the students have no visual clues.

Domination by One Group of Learner

The WBT classroom is a community of learners, and like any society it can have a good or bad sense of community. Learners engaged in group learning experience frustration if one group or person dominates the forum. Instructors should monitor threaded discussions and online forums to ensure the environment is conducive to e-learning.

Veteran of a Web/virtual synchronous classroom program

This summer, I was in a class [live virtual classroom] where the instructor kept acting like she was in front of a real classroom. She would say things like "Click here." We couldn't see where "here" was, so we didn't know what she wanted. She also would also tell us to do things like send her a question and mark items on a whiteboard, before she explained where they were or how to use them.

Things got better after about the third session. We knew where everything was and she also got better at giving directions. If I had one piece of advice for instructors, it would be "Give very careful instructions."

Physical Fatigue

Working for hours on a computer can be tiring and physically demanding. Learners can experience eyestrain from reading long documents online, and back and neck fatigue from sitting for long periods of time. When possible, long documents should be available to be read online and in hard copy. Lessons should be chunked in small bites to encourage learners to take breaks.

Figure 3.8 is an example of the kind of resource sites available online to help learners and facilitators.

Summary

In this chapter we have examined both sides of the educational coin, teaching and learning. The educational effectiveness of a program depends on many factors. Some of them are within your control, such as making sure the program presents

✓ Best Practices Regarding Facilitating Online Learning Worksheet

Directions: Explore what others have to say about teaching online. Read FAQs, join a threaded discussion, or just bookmark sites to share with colleagues. Visit the following sites for more information on teaching and learning online. Use the questions below to reflect on the experience.

Teaching/Facilitating	Facilitating Online Learning
Michael Coghlan's site (www.chariot.net.au/~michaelc/olfac.html#top)	Innovation in Distance Education
PennState (www.cde.psu.edu/de/ide/guiding_principles/)	Pedagogy in Practice
The Node (www.node.on.ca/)	Teaching Online Best Practices and Tips
Ohio State (http://courseinfo.jjay.cuny.edu/faculty/ teachonline.html)	

Learning	Learning on the Web
TeleEducation NB (http://telecampus.edu/)	What Makes a Successful Online Student?
Illinois Online Network (http://illinois.online.uillinois.edu/IONresources/ onlineoverview/StudentProfile.html)	

Link Finder: If these links do not work, use combinations of the following key words to find new sites "best practices, facilitation, online learning, students, instructors, guidelines, elearning, Web-based training, teaching adults."

REFLECTION QUESTIONS

- What best practices for instructors are common to all sites?

- What factors lead to success for learners?

- What factors detract from a learner's success?

Comparing Learning for Children Versus Adults Worksheet

Directions: Sample e-learning programs for children and adults using the URLs provided on this worksheet. Use the questions below to reflect on the experience.

Audience	Site URL
Children	*MaMaMedia.com* (www.mamamedia.com) Use this URL to access MaMaMedia.com's site. This is a site with games and learning activities for children. Sample some of these activities by clicking on the "For Grown-Ups" link. *Junior Net* (www.juniornet.com/) Use this URL to access Junior Net, an online environment where children can safely learn and grow through interactions with games, activities, and stories.
Adults	*Vanguard University* (www.vanguard.com) Use this URL to access the Vanguard site. Look for a link to "Education. Planning, & Advice" and learn the basics of investing in a series of simple one-page lessons. *CyberTravel Specialist* (http://cybertravelspecialist.com) Use this URL to access the demo lesson on the CyberTravel Specialist site. The course is designed primarily for agents and agency owners; the course is tailored for their needs.

Note: In an effort to make the learning experience as cost-effective as possible, every effort has been made to find sites providing free or sample lessons. In some cases you will be asked to register and you may get unwanted solicitations such as e-mail or faxes. In other cases, URLs are proved for award-winning sites that require a fee.

REFLECTION QUESTIONS

- How does the design of programs for children differ from those designed for adults?

- How do the programs differ in presentation, practice, and assessment?

- What assumptions have the course developers made about the learners' motivation, need for feedback, and application of new knowledge?

- What assumptions have been made regarding how people learn?

Figure 3.8. What Makes a Successful Online Student

Source: Illinois Online Network
www.illinois.online.uillinois.edu/IONresources/onlineoverview/StudentProfile.html

information well, enables adequate practice, and provides effective assessment. The type of content and the performance you need will dictate the optimal presentation of format, the practice activities, and the testing strategy.

While the course developer cannot learn *for* students, there is a great deal that can be done to motivate students. Based on what we know about adult learning, every effort should be made to optimize programs. Strategies that focus on making learning relevant and problem-based will go a long way toward motivating learners. Likewise, programs can avoid known pitfalls related to technology and instructional design.

The exercises in Chapters 1, 2, and 3 should be making you aware of the range of possibilities that exist for rich media, interaction, tracking, navigation, branching, and feedback. The next chapter will provide a technical overview of the tools used to create these programs.

Suggested Readings

Alessi, S.M., & Trollip, S.R. (1991). *Computer-based instruction: Methods and development.* Englewood Cliffs, NJ: Prentice Hall.

Brookfield, S.D. (1990). *The skillful teacher.* San Francisco: Jossey-Bass.

Clark, R. (1999). *Developing technical training: A structured approach for developing classroom and computer-based instructional materials.* Alexandria, VA: ISPI Press.

Dick, W., & Carey, L. (1995). *The systematic design of instruction.* New York: HarperCollins College Division.

Gagne, R.M. (1985). *The conditions of learning and the theory of instruction* (4th ed.). New York: Holt, Rinehart and Winston.

Glynn, S.M. (1995). Conceptual bridges: Using analogies to explain scientific concepts. *The Science Teacher, 62*(9), 25–27.

Hara, N., & Kling, R. (2000, March). *Students' distress in a Web-based distance education course.* [Online] Available: www.slis.indiana.edu/SCI/wp00–01.html

Kidd, J.R. (1975). *How adults learn.* New York: Associated Press.

Knowles, M.S. (1989). *The modern practice of adult education: From pedagogy to andragogy.* Englewood Cliffs, NJ: Prentice Hall.

Mager, R. (1997). *Preparing instructional objectives: A critical tool in the development of effective instruction.* Los Angeles: Center for Effective Performance.

Merriam, S.B., & Caffarella, R.S. (1991). *Learning in adulthood.* San Francisco: Jossey-Bass.

Merrill, M.S. (1994). *Instructional design theory.* Englewood Cliffs, NJ: Educational Technology Publications.

Moore, M.G., & Kearsley, G. (1996). *Distance education: A systems view.* Belmont, CA: Wadsworth.

Satran, A., & Kristof, R. (1995). *Interactivity by design: Creating & communicating with new media.* San Francisco: Adobe Press.

Tapscott, D. (1999). *Growing up digital: The rise of the net generation.* New York: McGraw-Hill.

Tough, A. (1971). *Adult learning projects.* Toronto, Ontario: Institute for Studies in Education.

Chapter 4

Tools of the Trade

The last chapter explored principles of adult education and learning as building blocks for effective programs. Facilitating learning and supporting learners are important activities, but in e-learning they are of little value if they are not reflected in the final product. The challenge of choosing software applications for e-learning is that the software you choose dictates the educational objectives you can and cannot accomplish. The term "tool" is used to refer to any software application, technology, or program that provides Internet-based online learning.

This chapter is devoted to making sense of the hundreds of software applications, technologies, and solutions available for Web-based e-learning. While it is impossible to provide a complete list of tools, it is possible to provide a framework for thinking about the categories of tools and to provide guidelines for evaluating these tools.

A challenge in writing this chapter has been the fragmentation of the e-learning market. It is hard to define clear product categories because there are large areas of overlapping functionality among products and a lack of agreed-on definitions. The number of mergers, acquisitions, and new vendors entering the market further complicates the process of understanding the options. The last section of this chapter provides a simple overview of hosting options, which are becoming increasingly important as a factor in selecting tools.

What You Will Learn in This Chapter

After completing this chapter, you will be able to

- Apply basic e-learning vocabulary;
- Place products in broad categories;
- Identify four kinds of Web-based e-learning environments;
- Explain the benefits and limitations of a hosted solution; and
- Understand the role of standards.

These foundation points will round out your understanding of the e-learning environment and basic e-learning definitions. It will help human resource managers put Web-based training into the larger context of learning management systems. It will also help educate all parties involved in making basic e-learning decisions on applications and implementation options that are appropriate to their specific training needs.

Categories of E-Learning Products

There are few agreed-on categories of products because the online learning industry is new. Economic forces are driving vendors to merge and acquire complementary technologies that further blur the lines among categories. Despite the fragmentation in the market, there is a need for categories in which to group tools for comparison. Having clear categories of products makes it easier to identify classes of products that can meet your needs.

A little background: There are three broad categories of e-learning products and each category serves a different purpose. Table 4.1 provides a summary of each category and examples of products that are representative of that category.

E-Learning Delivery Platforms. This is the oldest e-learning technology category. Software applications in this category are primarily focused on the design, delivery, and tracking of Web-based training courses. Organizations that want to get started quickly and inexpensively should consider this as the starting point. Software in this category ranges in price from less than $100 to $50,000, and generally these programs are easy to install. The differences in price among programs reflect the functionality of the application and the level of customer support you will receive. Making a business case for this category of software is relatively straightforward. Organizations justify the cost of the software by showing how much cost they will avoid related to travel and lodging for learners.

Table 4.1. Categories of E-Learning Products	
Category and Function	**Price Range**
E-learning delivery platforms are software applications that enable you to create, deliver, and manage e-learning programs.	Shareware up to $50K
Learning management systems (LMS) are software applications that embrace just about any use of Web technology to plan, organize, implement, and control aspects of the learning process.	$20K to $900K
Learning content management systems (LCMS) are software applications that label, track, and manage learning objects (PowerPoint slides, quiz questions, video clips, illustration, course modules) and then organize them for delivery in infinite combinations.	$90K to $1M

Learning Management Systems (LMSs).   These systems have been described as ERP-like (enterprise resource planning) applications; but rather than planning for the entire enterprise, they offer complete and deep planning for training. These programs embrace just about any use of Web technology to plan, organize, implement, and control aspects of the learning process. In some cases, these programs include e-learning platform functionality. All of this functionality comes at a cost. LMS systems range in cost from $20K to $900K and full-scale implementations require twelve to eighteen months. The long implementation cycle is related to the organization work that must be done to define and document rules, to establish processes for how things will work, and to integrate these systems into accounting and human resource applications such as PeopleSoft, SAP, or the company's general ledger.

Learning Content Management Systems (LCMSs).   The newest software application for e-learning is the LCMS. These systems label, track, and manage learning objects (PowerPoint slides, quiz questions, video clips, illustration, course modules) and then organize them for delivery in infinite combinations. These systems are purchased in addition to e-learning delivery platforms and as a complement to a learning management system. This is a fledgling industry and there is little data available, but a report by Bryan Chapman at Brandon-Hall.com sheds some light on this software category. His early research indicates that a five-year implementation of an LCMS for eight thousand employees averages about $585,000, compared with a similar implementation for an LMS, which averages $280,000. Organizations that create and deliver hundreds of hours of e-learning content will benefit from the ability to reuse content and to customize the look and feel of programs with ease.

A training director talks about how to make sense of the technology

Recently, three of my managers and I attended a training conference with a large trade show floor. I asked the managers to report back to the group on the technology they saw and how we might use it. The report-out session was eye-opening. We were awash in jargon, and we were hard-pressed to even figure out how to categorize and compare products. The funniest thing was that even people who saw the same demo could not agree on exactly what the product did.

In the end, we made a list of the things we really needed an e-learning solution to provide and revisited our notes. We then called a short list of vendors to come in and demo to the entire team. If we had it to do again, we would go with a clear list and ask vendors to explain how they would address our needs.

A Closer Look

This section takes a closer look at each of the three categories and provides you with additional information. You will also find a set of questions at the end of each section to help you think about these tools in the context of your organization.

E-Learning Delivery Platforms

If your starting point is e-learning delivery platforms, it's a good idea to drill down and understand the options. There are four kinds of platforms, and vendors offer them as standalone products, or some vendors offer products that combine two or more types.

The four kinds of e-learning delivery platforms are

- *Web/Computer-Based (W/CBT).* Individual learning that features drill and practice, simulations, reading, questioning, and answering.

E-Learning Platform Options Worksheet

Directions: Explore the vendors in each category of e-learning by linking to the listed URLs. Visit each of these sites and determine what the product does and how it differs from other products. If the site offers a demo, try it. Then use the questions below to reflect on the experience.

E-Learning Environment	Platform Options
Web/computer-based training (W/CBT)	*QuelSys: SocratEase* (www.socratease.com)
	Convene.com IZIO (www.convene.com)
	Serf (www.serfsoft.com/)
Web/Electronic Performance Support Systems (W/EPSS)	*XHLP* (www.xhlp.com)
	DomainKnowledge: ProCarta (www.domainknowledge.com/)
	Information Mapping: Formatting Solutions™ (www.infomap.com/)
Web/Virtual Asynchronous Classrooms (W/VAC)	*IMB/Lotus: Learning Space®* (www.lotus.com)
	Blackboard (www.blackboard.com)
	WebCT (www.webct.com)
Web/Virtual Synchronous Classrooms (W/VSC)	*Centra* (www.centra.com)
	InterWise (www.interwise.com)
	Placeware (www.placeware.com)

REFLECTION QUESTIONS

• How do the benefits of each category of products differ?

• What terms did you find confusing? Were terms used inconsistently from site to site?

• What do these sites assume to be the motivation for adopting e-learning?

- *Web/Electronic Performance Support Systems (W/EPSS).* Just-in-time training focused on problem solving. This is similar to an online job aid.

- *Web/Virtual Asynchronous Classrooms (W/VAC).* Non-real-time group learning using experimental tasks, discussions, and team projects.

- *Web/Virtual Synchronous Classrooms (W/VSC).* Real-time collaboration using group learning techniques such as discussions, problem solving, and reflection.

The ability to differentiate among the unique characteristics and capabilities of each environment is essential. It is highly recommended that you visit the sites of several vendors in each e-learning environment to gain first-hand experience. It is well worth investing time to understand the technical benefits and limitations. Chapter 6, Selecting the Most Appropriate E-Learning Method, also discusses each of these delivery platforms in detail.

Dressing Up the E-Learning Delivery Platform: Multimedia Development Tools

Most of the e-learning platforms allow you to create the pages from within the software application. That means if you want the learner to read ten pages of text and answer some questions, you can create the text with simple text and graphics tools. When you want to get fancy and do things such as add animation, create complex graphics, or edit video clips, you are going to need to use additional tools. You should read this section if you think the tools built into the e-learning platform are too basic or if you would like to see what is possible.

There are literally hundreds of tools used by course developers to create media elements such as video, audio, animation, graphics, and text. Multimedia development tools are generic Web creation tools used to build media elements for e-commerce sites, entertainment pages, and computer-based training. Using these tools, course developers can create attention-getting media elements that add production value or sizzle to a program. These tools work equally well in creating computer-based training and Web-based e-learning.

This is probably the largest product category because it is made up of several subcategories. Table 4.2 provides a small sampling of the tools available to course developers. The tools range in price from free to hundreds of dollars, and mastering the skills required to use the tools can take hours or weeks. Shareware sites provide access to free or nominal cost tools and they are well worth exploring.

Table 4.2. Multimedia Tools	
Multimedia Development Tools	**URLs**
Animation is software applications giving images, drawings, models, and objects the illusion of movement or life.	*Animation Online: Free Animated Banner Creation Software* (www.animationonline.com/) *MainConcept: MainActor* (www.mainconcept.com/) *MindWorkshop: GIF Construction Set* (www.mindworkshop.com/) *MacroMedia: Flash* (www.macromedia.com)
Audio software applications enable the capture, encoding, manipulation, and editing of narration, music, and sound effects into a file format for use in computer-based training.	*Sonic Foundry: Sound Forge* (www.sonicfoundry.com/) *Microsoft: Player 7* (www.microsoft.com/windows/windowsmedia/en/software/Playerv7.asp) *Voice Logistics™ Suite* (www.voxware.com/)
Graphic/image manipulation software programs enable the creation and editing of original drawing as well as the manipulation of existing images such as photos and scanned art.	*Adobe Photoshop* (www.adobe.com/) *Macromedia Freehand* (www.macromedia.com/) *Fractal Design Painter* (www.fractal.com/)
HTML editors and site design software programs make creating a Web page and sites as simple as typing in text on a word processor because they are WYSIWYG.	*Adobe Page Mill* (www.adobe.com) *Macromedia Dream Weaver* (www.dreamweaver) *Microsoft FrontPage* (www.microsoft.com)
Video software programs enable the encoding of videotape into a digital format and provide the tools for editing and enhancing the footage.	*Avid ePublisher* (www.avid.com/products/epublisher/index.html) *Apple FireWire* (www.apple.com/firewire/) *RealNetworks Real Producer* (www.RealNetworks.com)
Shareware is software available on a try it before you buy it basis.	*Pass the Shareware* (www.passtheshareware.com/c-grafix.htm) *ZDNet.com Downloads* (www.zdnet.com/downloads/specials/free.html) *Mac Download.com* (www.zdnet.com/downloads/mac/download.html)

More Tools to Enhance the E-Learning Platform: Specialized Tools for Educational Development

Developing education or training programs sometimes requires functions that are highly specialized, such as creating adaptive tests, simulating a software application, or allowing students to gain experience in a virtual lab. Just like the highly specialized tools for creating animation or video clips, there are tools for creating very special educational segments. These specialized educational tools are used three ways. They can be used as standalone learning programs; they can be used as part of a blended solution that integrates traditional classrooms and the Internet; and they can be used in combination with site design software or learning authoring software.

Choosing when and how to use these specialized tools for developing educational segments can be confusing. It is important to remember that these tools are designed to save hours of development time because they relieve the developer of re-creating the wheel. For example, rather than writing code or using authoring tools to develop a sophisticated adaptive test, a developer would purchase a program that could do that for him or her. The segments of instruction created by these special programs can then be integrated into the larger course. Table 4.3 provides a sampling of tools that are specific to course developers creating educational programs. This is a very small sample of specialized tools. There is no central repository or listing of these tools. Frequently, the challenge is simply finding the tools.

Making Courses Outside the E-Learning Delivery Platform: Course Authoring Tools

If you don't want to develop courses by moving back and forth between the e-learning platform and the multimedia tools and special education tools, there is another option. There are software packages that will allow you to create the entire course outside of the e-learning platform or the LMS. These tools are called authoring tools because you can author or write a course using them. Authoring tools are based on industry standards, and this ensures you can move the course you develop to any e-learning delivery platform or LMS with minimal effort.

Course authoring tools are very similar to HTML editors and site design, with one difference: They provide elements specific to instruction. These tools are designed for creating Web-based training and offer elements such as templates for creating courses, features for building tests and quizzes, and schemes for chunking

Table 4.3.   Specialized Tools for Educational Development

Function	URLs
Software for creating simulation: full-screen software simulations allowing learners to interact with the program in a controlled environment.	*X.HLP: elab* (www.xhlp.com/) *Xstream* (www.xstreamsoftware.com) *Network Emulation Software* (www.topology.org/sim.html)
Adaptive testing assessment authoring software enabling developers to create tests with adaptive branching based on how questions are answered and customized learning.	*QuestionMark: Perception for Web* (www.questionmark.com/) *RIVA* (www.riva.com)
Virtual labs: Provide Internet access to live networking equipment and applications any time, anywhere.	*Mentor Technologies: vLab Technology* (www.ccci.com/vlab/index.shtml) *Productivity Point: eLab* (www.e-lab.propoint.com)

pages into educational units such as lessons, courses, and modules. These tools are helpful to course developers because they eliminate the need to reinvent the wheel by creating navigation devices and site structure specific for learning, and they provide site management utilities. Course authoring tools are designed specifically to develop educational sites, so they have a lot of features that are not found in generic website development software.

E-learning software is really confusing, but let's add a little more complexity. Students can access e-learning courses designed using course authoring tools two ways. The least complex way to access the course is simply to put the course on the Web and allow the student to take the course. This method eliminates the need for an e-learning platform or LMS. This is s good solution if you have ten or fewer courses.

Once you have more than ten courses, you will want to have some way to allow learners to enroll and sign in from a single point—an e-learning delivery platform or LMS. Having a single point is good because the learner has one password and one student transcript and one URL links the learner to all the courses. An e-learning platform or LMS benefits the training department because enrollment, reports, and courses can be managed from a single software application. More information is provided about LMS in the next section. See the boxed list below for some sample sources for course authoring tools.

Click2Learn.com: ToolBook II (http://home.click2learn.com/products/instructor.html)

Macromedia CourseBuilder Extension for Dreamweaver 4 and UltraDev 4 (www.macromedia.com/software/coursebuilder/)

ReadyGo: Web Course Builder (www.readygo.com)

TrainerSoft: Professional Edition (www.trainersoft.com)

VizionFactory: Producer (www.vizionfactory.com/)

Learning Management Systems

The term "learning management system" (LMS) embraces just about any use of Web technology to plan, organize, implement, and control aspects of the learning process. Organizations purchase LMS systems to manage e-learning courses and traditional classroom training programs. Learning management systems are enterprise resource planning (ERP) tools for training and development. The category is still evolving, and it is also referred to as training management systems (TMS), instructional management systems (IMS), integrated learning solutions (ILS), and integrated training solutions (ITS).

The problem with this classification of LMS systems is that it includes everything. Larger LMS system vendors such as TEDS, Docent, IBM, Isopia, and Saba provide management systems that include course authoring tools, records management functions, competency assessment features, virtual classrooms, physical classrooms, and e-commerce capabilities. The box below provides a list of links to popular learning management systems (LMS).

Learning management systems can be deployed in two ways: Organizations can buy them outright and have them installed on their corporate intranets or they can have the system hosted by application service providers. More on hosted solutions later in this chapter.

CBM Technologies: TEDS (www.teds.com)

Docent Enterprise (www.docent.com)

IBM/Lotus: Mindspan (www.IBM.com/mindspan/)

Plateau Enterprise (www.plateausystems.com)

Saba Human Capital Development and Management System (www.saba.com)

Reviewing Table 4.4 below should highlight the fact that there is a lot of overlap between the LMS category and other categories of tools. In some cases the tools included in the LMS may eliminate the need for course authoring tools or specialized learning development tools and in other cases the LMS tools are not as fully functional as tools in a given category. For example, an LMS may offer a tool for giving tests, but the tool may have limited functionality. Organizations that want the ability to provide adaptive testing, to adjust the reliability and validity coefficient, and

Table 4.4. Primary Functions of a Learning Management System

Role	Functions
Using an LMS system, a *course developer* can	Author courses and tests
	Assemble a series of courses into a curriculum
Using an LMS system, a *learner* (employee, customer, partner) can	Enroll in courses or curriculums
	Search the course catalog
	Review his or her transcript
	Access a personalized training plan
	Take a course or online assessment
	Participate in a 360-degree review
	Complete a competency evaluation or gap analysis instrument
	Participate in an online community/collaborate
	Access an online tutor
	E-mail other students, the instructor, or administrators
	Submit assignments
	Work offline or online
	Locate additional resources such as a virtual library or virtual labs

(Continued)

Table 4.4.　Primary Functions of a Learning Management System (*Continued*)

Role	Functions
Using an LMS system, an *administrator* can	Schedule and manage classes and instructors for • Traditional physical classroom programs • E-learning courses • Self-paced kits • Events such as conferences or hotel offerings • Blended solutions Manage curriculum • Build and maintain a course catalog • Schedule courses • Manage level I, II, and III evaluations Manage enrollment • Send notifications regarding cancellation or enrollments • Establish, maintain, and clear waiting lists • Assign instructors and resources such as rooms and AV equipment • Use CSR and telecenter enrollment Generate reports (endless number) Create development plans for each job classification Market courses • Use affinity group and learner profiles to target marketing efforts E-commerce • Sell courses online • Bill online • Apply volume discounts Manage royalties and copyrights • Track usage and royalty fees due on off-the-shelf programs • Manage inventory of materials • Track copyright release info Connect to • HR systems • General ledger • Performance review systems • E-business sites Track tuition reimbursement to colleges and universities Manage compliance and certification documentation Manage a content repository of learning objects

Table 4.4. Primary Functions of a Learning Management System (*Continued*)

Role	Functions
	Manage hotel bookings
	Provide offering management
	Account management
	Certifications
	Records management
	Accounting
	Launch third-party and custom e-learning programs
Using an LMS system, an *instructor* can	Deliver live, real-time virtual classes
	Deliver asynchronous classes
	Support self-paced learners
	Give tests and quizzes
	Provide pre-course or post-class material for physical classroom
	Archive classes
	Manage virtual communities
	Keep a grade book

to provide analytic scoring will need a more specialized tool for developing tests. This tool can be integrated into the LMS to replace the existing testing function. The bottom line is, depending on what you want to do, you may still want to purchase other tools to achieve your goals.

Programs That Run on Both an E-Learning Delivery Platform and a Learning Management System
Off-the-Shelf Programs
Off-the-shelf programs are courses developed by vendors who sell their courses to many organizations. These course are called off-the-self because they don't require customization, they can be used right "off the shelf." The courses generally address topics that have broad appeal, such as teaching office workers to use desktop applications such as spreadsheets, word processing, or e-mail. There are also a number of highly specialized off-the-shelf program vendors who make programs dealing with topics such as OSHA compliance, sexual harassment, and English as a second language.

Off-the-shelf (OTS) programs generally need no customization and they are much less expensive than developing e-learning courses in-house. Most OTS vendors have libraries with hundreds of titles that can be mixed and matched to meet specific demands. Because the development costs are spread over a large number of customers, the program costs are low and the quality is usually good. For many organizations that want to offer e-learning but cannot afford the staff or resources

NETg (www.netg.com)

SkillSoft (www.skillsoft.com)

SmartForce (www.smartforce.com)

WebLearning (www.weblearning.com/)

English Town (www.englishtown.com/)

to develop their own programs, off-the-shelf programs are an excellent option. The listing above provides links to vendors who provide off-the-shelf courseware.

Off-the-shelf programs can be accessed in any of three ways. The easiest way to access a course is as standalone programs running on the off-the-shelf vendors' intranet sites. A second option is to integrate the OTS program into your e-learning delivery platform. Many of the e-learning delivery platform vendors have partnerships and agreements with OTS vendors. Examples of this integration are SmartForce and Centra or NETg and IBM Mindspan. A third way to access these courses is through a learning management system. Organizations that have LMS systems can easily launch and track OTS programs that are standards-based.

Human resource manager talks about why she choose to start with off-the-shelf content

One of the company's goals this year was to introduce e-learning to reduce training costs. We looked at all the options—doing it ourselves, outsourcing the work, and buying off-the-shelf content. We made the decision to use off-the-shelf content to start with because it was easy and low risk. We shopped around and purchased a regulatory compliance program. We knew exactly what we were getting, the quality, and the cost. We are now hiring an e-learning manager and a development team. Next year we will be making our own programs, but this year we got a fast start with off-the-shelf content.

Learning Content Management Systems (LCMS)

Learning content management systems are the newest category of software and the most expensive. These systems provide a way for training organizations to author, label, track, and manage learning objects (PowerPoint slides, quiz questions, video clips, illustration, course modules) and then organize them for delivery in infinite combinations. LCMS systems can be purchased as standalone software or are offered as an add-on to a learning management system (see boxed listing below).

Organizations that hope to build a case for purchasing a system need to make sure that the basic assumptions on which these systems are sold hold true. Here are some examples of the assumptions:

- The organization is developing enough learning objects/content that the database has adequate material to be reused.

- If traditional courses are going to be produced, the learning objects need to be designed based on agreed-on standards. Each organization will need to develop its own standards. (Currently, there is no agreed-on standard for the size, characteristics, or components in a learning object.) The standard must be enforced with internal developers and communicated when work is outsourced.

- The LCMS must be easy enough for all developers to use or the system will not have the critical mass needed to build a rich library of objects.

- The cost of LCMS systems will require many organizations with fragmented training divisions to join together to afford these systems and to justify the cost of purchase.

Learning content management systems hold great promise for organizations that develop large amounts of content, have strong internal processes, and teach material that is stable enough to benefit from reuse. Organizations that are just

---

Avaltus (www.paybacktraining.com/)

Global Knowledge (http://kp.globalknowledge.com/)

Knowledge Mechanics (www.knowledgemechanics.com/)

LeadingWay Knowledge Systems (www.leadingway.com/)

WBT Systems (www.wbtsystems.com/)

starting out should consider starting with an e-learning delivery platform or a learning management system.

Sorting Out the Options: Hosting or Owning E-Learning Software

Acquiring e-learning technology is a lot like acquiring a car. You have the option to buy or rent. In software, the term for renting is "hosting" and the hosting service is provided by an ASP (application service provider). Application service providers set up the software, make the software available to users, manage access to the software, and deliver services such as upgrades and an end-user helpdesk.

This is where it gets messy—again. The Internet is so new that the job of trying to figure out pricing models is evolving. In order to make this explanation simple, let's look at the two extremes: owning the e-learning application and having it hosted by an ASP.

You can outright buy the software, install it on your hardware, and manage the application with your own staff. This is an easy-to-understand model. The people who manage your e-learning application are accountable to your organization. Once you have purchased the systems, future costs should be low. The down side of owning the software is that you own it. Your organization is responsible for keeping it running. In addition, you will need a significant initial budget to get started. The large initial price tag is due to the one-time expense of buying the software, hardware, and the services needed to get your staff up-to-speed and ready to assume responsibility for running the application. There will be small additional costs related to maintenance agreements and possible upgrades, but in general the large costs are part of the initial purchase.

Hosting is a fancy name for a service in which the software and computer systems are supplied and managed by a vendor. This service is also referred to as application out-sourcing and rent-an-app. The advantage of having your application hosted by a vendor is that the vendor's staff can keep your e-learning program running 365 days a year, and they specialize in fixing problems, doing maintenance, and providing support for learners and administrative staff.

In e-learning, most categories of software are offered as hosted solutions; the challenge is that not every product in a given category may be available. Hosting is available for the following categories:

- Off-the-shelf courses;
- Learning management systems;

- Specialized educational development tools; and
- Learning environments, such as
  - Web/computer-based training;
  - Web/virtual asynchronous classrooms; and
  - Web/virtual synchronous classrooms.

The other extreme is to rent the software using a hosted ASP model. A hosted solution provided by an application service provider (ASP) is an excellent choice for training organizations that cannot get the IS resources they need to bring e-learning in-house. It is also a good choice for small organizations that cannot justify the headcount and specialized skills needed to implement and maintain an e-learning system.

Hosted solutions have special considerations related to price, length of contract commitment, and transferability of data. The price of an ASP solution is usually less at the start because the up-front costs of hiring a staff and buying hardware and software are eliminated. That doesn't mean that hosted solutions cost less; it means that the costs are more evenly spread over a number of years. ASP agreements usually last for three to five years, and the contract prohibits ending the agreement early or imposes penalties. There is also the issue of the data and information collected in e-learning. Changing from one ASP to another ASP or choosing a different e-learning system at the end of a contract may mean the data will not easily transfer. Talk to the application service provider about how you will retrieve the data if they go out of business or if you want to change ASPs or change e-learning platforms. Table 4.5 compares owning a solution to having a solution hosted.

Now let's look at the options between owning and renting. Cost may be a key consideration, but not because one option will cost less than the other. The cost issue is related to cash flow and how an organization would like to invest, all up-front or spread over time. The second consideration is the cost of staffing and training the people needed to run a system. A related issue will be your relationship with the information systems group. If the application is outsourced, you are the customer and you can anticipate excellent service. If your firm owns the application, you may have to wait your turn for service if the IS group is busy. In some cases training applications are considered low priority next to moneymaking applications such as sales automation and ERP systems. A final consideration should be the ability to scale the application, that is, bring on more seats if needed. A solution that is hosted can simply add users. If you own the solution, it may take time to order additional licenses, to buy servers to run the new and expanded application on, and to bring on additional staff to support the increased number of users.

Table 4.5.   Comparison Between Hosting and Owning

	Host E-Learning Solution	**Own E-Learning Solution**
Cost	Costs are evenly spread over term of contract	Large up-front costs for hardware, software, and staff
	Predictable	Costs decrease over time
	Contractually committed to for x number of years	Organization owns the software and hardware
	The software and hardware are leased or rented	
Staff	The ASP deals with hiring, training, and paying the staff	Additional headcount must be trained and managed
IS Relationship	Employees link to e-learning via the Internet, eliminating a burden on your IS group	An e-learning application has to compete for the IS group's limited resources to be assessed, installed, and maintained
Scaling Solution	The hosting service can provide e-learning for small or large firms	Some organizations are too small to justify an e-learning solution
	If needed, the ASP can increase the number of users it supports	Scaling or increasing the size of an e-learning application can be complex because of adding staff and acquiring more hardware and software

Vendors are trying a lot of different models to see what sells best. In an effort to appeal to customers, there are models that allow you to mix and match what you own, what you rent, and who is responsible for what part of the service. Be prepared to be creative in your negotiations because hybrid deals are possible. For example, you may be able to buy the software application, rent a server, and hire an ASP to install the application at their site and manage it.

Summary

If this chapter has left you overwhelmed by the choices, don't be too concerned. In general, the applications within each category are commodities. They all do about the same thing, so your decision should not be driven by the technology. The key to choosing the right software application is to understand the gap in skills and knowledge you are trying to fill and, at the same time, to understand the business issues that are driving the need for an e-learning solution. Knowing the educational and the business case will help you narrow down your options.

The next chapter will explore the process for developing e-learning programs. The ADDIE model (analyze, design, develop, implement, and evaluate) is used to help you move through the process. The analysis step in the model will provide useful information for selecting an e-learning application.

Suggested Readings

A day in the life of a learning management system. [Online] Available: www.fastrak-consulting.co.uk/tactix/features/lms/lms.htm

Barron, T. (2000). *The LMS guess: Learning circuits.* Retrieved January 8, 2001. [Online] Available: www.learningcircuits.org/apr2000/barron.html

Brown, J.S., & Duguid, P. (1991). *Organizational learning and communities of practice: Toward a unified view of working, learning, and innovation.* [Online] Available: www.parc.xerox.com/ops/members/brown/papers/orglearning.html

Hall, B. (2000). *Learning management systems: How to choose the right system for your organization.* Sunnyvale, CA: www. Brandon-hall.com publishing.

Hall, B. (2001). *News flash: LCMS and LMS technology converge.* Retrieved July 21, 2001. [Online] Available: www.brandon-hall.net/dispatch/index.html

Jones, C. (2001). Rules of the game. *Online Learning, 6*(6), pp. 20–22, 24–25.

Rosenberg, M.J. (2000). *Learning: Strategies for delivering knowledge in the digital age.* New York: McGraw-Hill.

Williams. R., & Tollett, J. (1997). *The non-designer's web book: An easy guide to creating, designing, and posting your own website.* Minneapolis, MN: Peachpit Press.

Chapter 5

Analyzing Needs and Selecting Delivery Methods

The last chapter provided a framework for understanding the categories of e-learning tools and how the categories related to each other. This chapter also features a framework or model for managing an e-learning project. The ADDIE model (analyze, design, develop, implement, and evaluate) provides an easy to follow organizing structure for teams. The bare-bones nature of the model may oversimplify the work required to produce an e-learning program, but for those just starting out, this model is a good starting point.

Managers will find this chapter provides a good overview of the ADDIE model and an explanation of the tasks related to the analysis phase: analyzing the learning goals, environment, audience, infrastructure, and culture. Instructional designers and course developers will be able to identify the differences between the tasks required to analyze traditional classroom programs and those required to produce e-learning programs.

Two notes of caution must be stated before reading the ADDIE chapters. First, each phase is not as discrete or as linear as it appears in the diagram. It is not unusual to be working on issues related to implementing the e-learning program while in the middle of designing and developing the program. Second, each phase of ADDIE is presented at a macro level, that is, there is not a lot of detail. There are entire books on the subjects of needs analysis, design, and evaluation. For readers seeking more details related to analysis, design, development, implementation, and evaluation, the end of each chapter provides references and recommended websites.

What You Will Learn in This Chapter

After completing this chapter, you will be able to

- Define ADDIE and locate alternative instructional systems design models;
- Determine whether training is needed;
- Define the program goals, audience, environment, and infrastructure; and
- Distinguish between instructional strategies and delivery methods.

Instructional Systems Design and ADDIE

Instructional systems design (ISD) is a process for developing instruction. The ISD approach acknowledges a relationship among three factors: learner, instructor, and materials. Many instructional system design models exist, ranging from simple to complex. All provide step-by-step guidance for developing training.

A quick review of recent books on instructional design for Web-based training, handouts from conferences, and websites offering guidance on developing e-learning programs point to the range of models. Frequently cited models are those offered by Dick and Carey in *The Systematic Design of Instruction*, Rothwell and Kazanas in *Mastering the Instructional Design Process*, and Alessi and Trollip in *Multimedia for Learning: Methods and Development*. These rich models offer instructional designers excellent guidance, but they are often too complex for teams that don't have a background in training and development.

An alternative model is ADDIE. The acronym stands for analyze, design, develop, implement, and evaluate. ADDIE is a simplistic model for developing any kind of training. Simplicity is important when explaining what needs to be accomplished by a cross-functional team who may not have educational or instructional technology background. ADDIE can create a shared vision of the process for developing the program and for understanding the relationship among phases in the process.

Each phase in the ADDIE model is comprised of a number of subtasks. Because this is a generic model, it should be modified to reflect the kind of Web-based program you plan to develop. The level of detail in the model will be influenced by decisions regarding which tasks will be outsourced, the experience level of the team, and the size and scope of a project. Now let's look at the model in more detail.

An Overview of the ADDIE Phases

Analyze

In the analysis phase for Web-based training, there are three areas to be analyzed: the audience, the task (skill and knowledge), and the environment. The analysis of these three can be done in parallel:

- *Audience.* When developing training to be delivered using the Web, there are two dimensions to the analysis: the learners' prerequisite knowledge of the skills or knowledge to be mastered and the learners' comfort and skill level working as self-directed learners using the computer.

- *Task.* The skill or knowledge should be examined to determine whether this is a subject that can be taught entirely on the Web or a subject that would be better suited to a blended solution of Web and traditional classroom.

- *Environment.* When delivering e-learning solutions, it is advisable to determine the physical and technical limitation of the environment in which the training will be delivered. Will there be enough bandwidth for streaming video? Do learners have access to computers with headsets and audio sound cards? and Will the use of sound bother others working in the area? Often organizations choose to adopt the lowest common denominator and the specification for the systems. This can mean that the solution must run on a 28.8 modem, even though corporate headquarters has a much better connectivity.

Design

Web-based e-learning programs come in many varieties. Some programs use streaming video, others rely on simulations, and others involve live audio for collaboration. It is essential to know the authoring tool and delivery environment before designing a program. A great deal of time can be wasted if a lesson is designed that is not supported by an authoring tool or delivery environment.

In the design phase, the work is confined to paper-and-pencil activities. The subtasks in this phase require creating design documents that specify the program's objectives; determining the skills learners must have prior to enrolling in a program; and creating a detailed outline of the presentation, practice, and assessment activities.

Develop

In the development phase, the blueprints for information presentation, practice, and assessment are authored or programmed. The activities taking place during the actual development depend on the authoring tools and delivery environment chosen. In some cases, the development will be simply creating a set of PowerPoint slides that will accompany a recorded audio track. In other cases, the interaction will require programming and screen captures to mimic the functionality of a system. And in yet other cases, development will be a simple outline for a videoconference broadcast with a few support images or an application to share.

Implement and Evaluate

Implementation and evaluation are shown on the ADDIE model to be two separate and linear steps. In reality, this is a messy process in which evaluation happens at a number of points. At each step of the ADDIE process, it is important to check back to determine whether the analysis is still accurate, design is appropriate, and the development consistent with the program's goals and objectives.

During the implementation phase, there is particular attention paid to the implementation of the pilot. During the pilot implementation, the program is evaluated with real learners. After the corrections are made, the program is then implemented enterprise-wide. The interwoven nature of the implementation and evaluation phases is more fully discussed in Chapter 10, Implementing and Evaluating WBT Programs.

Things to Note When Using the ADDIE Model

Estimating Cost.   Estimating the cost of customized Web-based training is challenging because it involves many variables. In the ADDIE model, shown in Figure 5.1, the cost of training is estimated during the analysis phase. The cost estimate will become more refined as the project becomes more defined. The choice of one authoring tool or delivery environment over another or a decision to implement worldwide versus a phased rollout can impact the costs. More on costs later in Chapter 9, Developing Blueprints.

Outsourcing.   If you are considering using external resources rather than internal staff for your project, the ADDIE model is a very useful tool. Using this model

Figure 5.1. The ADDIE Model

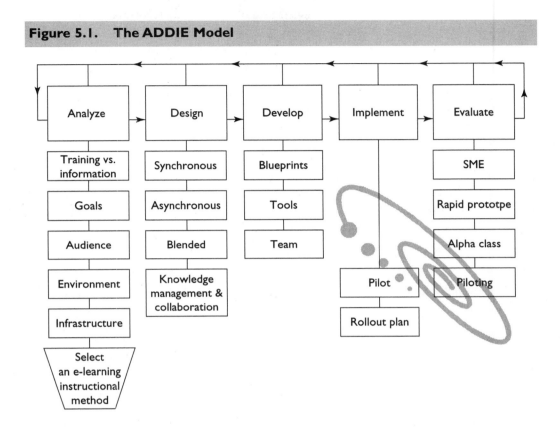

you will be able to identify key tasks or entire phases that can be done by people outside of your organization. As you break down the tasks in the ADDIE model, ask questions to identify places where it makes sense to outsource. The following questions can help you reflect on the pros and cons of outsourcing:

- Are there tasks for which your staff lacks the skills?

- Will this skill be used frequently enough to justify the cost and time required to teach a member of your team?

- Are there skills required in such small proportions that it would not be cost-effective to develop internal resources to deal with them, such as digital video editing?

- Will your timeline allow you to do all the work in-house?

- Could your staff be put to better use if some of the tasks were outsourced?

A Detailed Look at the Analysis Phase in ADDIE

Like building a house, the key to a good Web-based training program is a solid foundation. In the ADDIE model, the analysis phase is your foundation. Begin your project with an analysis of the goal, the audience, the environment, and the infrastructure. Figure 5.1 illustrates the subtasks that are part of the analysis phase of ADDIE for e-learning.

Now let's review the steps in the analysis phase.

1. Determine Whether Training Is Needed

Start with the most basic question, "Is training required?" To determine whether training is required, ask questions to discover whether poor employee performance is caused by a gap in skills or knowledge. Consider factors such as poor work environment, lack of employee motivation, and the absence of incentives.

- *Environment.* Do employees have the equipment they need, and is it reasonable to expect them to perform the required tasks with the given staffing levels?

- *Motivation.* Are there extrinsic rewards such as bonuses or recognition programs, and are workers intrinsically motivated by the work itself or by contact with customers?

- *Incentive/Compensation.* Is the compensation equitable when compared to that of employees in other divisions? When compared to people doing the same job at other companies? Are sales quotas and margins adequate to prompt the desired outcome?

Problems that are related to poor work environments, lack of motivation, and the absence of incentives will not be resolved by training. Conducting training programs rather than correcting environmental issues, improving motivation, and providing adequate compensation can result in greater worker dissatisfaction by inferring that the problems are related to lack of skill and knowledge.

Assuming There Is a Need.   In an ideal world, training professionals would start every project by determining whether the problem is caused by a genuine gap in skills and knowledge. In reality, e-learning projects often start with a predefined statement of need from the client. For example, a senior manager may demand that an e-learning program be created for sales representatives to bolster falling sales; or an e-learning program may be mandated for supervisors as a reaction to a sexual harassment lawsuit. In these cases, there might be a gap in skills and knowledge or there might not be, but the client has mandated training. In these cases you will still want to go through the remaining steps in the needs assessment process. If you write a project plan as described in Chapter 7, you will want to include a statement in the risks and dependencies section explaining the possibility that the program may not bolster sales or eliminate the risk of litigation if a lack of skills and knowledge is not the root cause of the problem.

2. Defining Goals

Define the goals of a training program by writing a brief statement that describes what learners will be able to do after their instruction. The goal statement should describe how the gap in skills and knowledge identified earlier will be remedied.

Be clear about what learners will be able to do. You will use the goal statement later during the evaluation stage to measure the success of the program. If the training has been successful, learners will be able to do what the goal statement says. Use the following questions to help define the goal:

- Why is training being offered?
- What should learners be able to do after completing training?
- How will you know that learners have mastered the skills and knowledge?

Writing the goals statement is an important task. The sample goal statements in the box below give specific goals that should result from training. Notice that all of the statements related to the Series 5000 laser printer, but what the learners will be able to do is different in each goal statement.

- Field service engineers will be able to identify the most common technical problems in the Series 5000 laser printer.
- Field service engineers will be able to use the six-step diagnosis process to resolve problems with the Series 5000 laser printer.
- Field service engineers will be able to write (create) new device drivers for the Series 5000 laser printer.

Informational Goals. If you find that words like aware, know, understand, and appreciate genuinely describe what you are being asked to do, don't worry. A challenge faced by many training professionals in both the e-learning world and the traditional classroom world is the gray area between training and documenta-tion. If you have a problem that can be solved without the four phases of (1) pre-sentation, (2) guided practice, (3) practice by the learners, and (4) assessment, then you probably need a documentation solution. Many times a document or reference manual can be the right solution. When users simply need step-by-step directions, a definition, or a demonstration, don't over-engineer the solution by turning direc-tions into a class.

3. Defining the Audience

The audience should be profiled or defined from three perspectives:

- Knowledge of the topic;
- Level of computer skills; and
- Attitude and aptitude for computer-based learning.

Knowledge of the Topic.   Gather information regarding how much learners already know about the topic being presented. Be careful not to train people to do things they already know how to do. On the other hand, do not assume they know the basics. Material that is too basic will bore learners; material that is too advanced will discourage them.

Like traditional classroom courses, e-learning courses should not be one-size-fits-all. The ability to give universal access to everyone in the organization does not

---

Instructional designer suggests ways to get around one-size-fits-all programs

Last year we revised a live classroom program that taught employees how to protect intellectual property. This was an annual mandatory program for everyone—and no one liked it. The classroom program was one-size-fits-all, it was too basic for some job classifications and somewhat irrelevant for others. When we moved it to the Web, things changed. We were able to put in a pre-test, allowing people to test out of what they could demonstrate they knew. We were also able to chunk the content into three versions so we could deliver a more tailored version based on job classifications. People also liked being able to take it at their convenience. It took some people longer than the half-day classroom program, but most people finished faster because they were able to test out of part of the program.

translate into a universally relevant learning experience. Consider a negotiations skills course for newly hired North American salespeople. This course would not be appropriate for senior salespeople working on international deals because the senior people know the fundamentals of negotiation and they need a program that addresses cultural issues as they relate to negotiating.

Level of Computer Skills.   Determine how much knowledge learners have about computers. Do not make assumptions about their skill levels. Learners can have Internet and browser experience and still require help to use certain functions.

Gather information on learners' levels of computer skills by interviewing a representative sample of learners, interviewing the learners' managers, or conducting focus groups. Do your homework. Prepare questions that will help you probe for a detailed description of the learners' proficiency levels. For example, to determine how computer-literate learners are, ask questions such as:

- Have you ever installed software on your computer? If yes, tell me about any challenges you faced during the installation and how you dealt with them.

- Which of the settings in the Microsoft Windows® control panel do you feel confident in your ability to adjust or change?

- Complete the following sentence: "When I have to use online help to solve a problem I . . ."

- Have you ever changed the default printer?

- Have you ever sent a fax from your desktop?

If assessing the skills of learners from a distance, use a survey or conduct a telephone interview. Be sure to make learners feel comfortable so that you obtain accurate information. Use the following questions to assess computer knowledge:

- Can you log on to the systems, to the service provider, to the Internet, and to the Web-based training site?

- Do you feel comfortable using the computer keyboard? Mouse?

- Have you used a Web browser?

- Which of the following browsers have you used: Netscape Navigator®, Microsoft Internet Explorer®, America Online®?

Learners are sometimes unaware of what they don't know. If possible, create a simple checklist and ask a representative sample to complete the checklist over the phone. The checklist below is a sample of items to test computer skills through a hands-on exercise. Call a representative sample of learners and ask them to do the following while they are on the phone with you:

1. Surf to a website and describe what they see.

2. Create a bookmark or favorite place for a given uniform resource locator (URL).

3. Download the plug-in for RealAudio® and install it.

4. Use the bookmark or favorite place to return to the URL saved earlier.

5. Follow a series of hyperlinks and then use the tool bar or mouse to return to the initial page.

6. Send an e-mail.

Ask questions or conduct a hands-on assessment to document the skill level of learners. The basic questions are essential. In some cases you must teach computer skills before beginning your Web-based training program.

Attitude and Aptitude for Computer-Based Learning.   Another consideration is learner preferences and attitudes toward computer- or Web-based training. If learners are veterans of programs that were text-intensive and difficult to navigate, they may not be enthusiastic about e-learning. Many learners have experienced boring "page turners" that lacked interaction. Some learners do not like using self-paced programs. They may prefer the interaction and social aspects of a live classroom program. Learning about learners' attitudes and preferences will help you plan effective programs.

Use the following questions to assess learners' attitudes toward e-learning:

• Have you ever used a computer-based training program (CD-ROM, multimedia, videodisk)? If yes, what did you like or dislike about it? What made the program enjoyable? What made the program effective?

• When learning new skills, do you prefer to learn by yourself or do you like to be part of a group? Describe the best experience you have had learning new skills.

• Have you ever taken a Web-based training course? Was the experience good or bad? In what way?

• Would you like to participate in a Web-based training course? Why or why not?

4. Defining the Environment

The most attractive feature of e-learning is that it is delivered at the learner's desk. This feature is also one of the biggest challenges to designing training. Ask about the delivery environment before designing Web-based training. It is also helpful to understand issues related to workplace rules and the level of supervisory-level support. All of these factors will influence the degree of success.

Start with the physical environment, as it is the easiest to assess. Consider the following factors:

Roles of Telephones. Evaluate the use of telephones in the organization by spending forty-five to sixty minutes observing. What is the lag time between calls? Do people forward their messages or use voice mail when they need to accomplish something? If people are continually interrupted with telephone calls, think about how this will influence lesson length.

Office Acoustics. Survey the office acoustics. If you plan to include sound in your training program, think about how it will affect others. Plan programs that will not compete with the office paging system and telephones. Determine the impact an audio track will have on co-workers who are answering phones or trying to concentrate.

Social Interactions. Notice the social interactions of the office, the nature of the teams, and the physical setup. Is this the kind of office in which workers are continually interacting and sharing information, or is it a place in which people make appointments to meet? Does the office feature open work space and clusters of cubes, or long hallways lined with individual offices? The social interactions tell a great deal about how the program will be used. In an open environment, a Web-based training program might be used by teams or pairs of workers. In organizations with individual offices, learners may be more likely to work alone in a quiet atmosphere.

Home Office. Ask where employees will really be taking Web-based training. In many cases the expectation is that learning will take place evenings or weekends. You will need to ask about the kind of systems that employees will be using from home. Are they using an older model home computer? What kind of modem connection will they have? A 28.8 modem, cable connection, or a high speed DSL line? Is the browser on the home machine AOL, or are they using an older version of Netscape Navigator or Microsoft Internet Explorer? Does the computer at home have the required plug-ins?

Learn More About Eliminating Barriers That Exclude People with Disabilities Worksheet

Directions: These URLs are a good starting point for learning more about designing for access. The reflection questions at the end can help you reflect on the experience.

Guidelines

AWARE Center Homepage: This is a site that encourages and instructs in accessible Web design, written by the HTML Writers Guild. (http://aware.hwg.org/)

ERIC Digest: Accessible Web Design: This article provides a brief overview of accessibility challenges and some basic Hypertext Markup Language version 4.0 (HTML 4.0) coding solutions for these challenges, and it provides an introduction to some of the legal requirements and considerations for Web accessibility. (www.ed.gov/databases/ERIC_Digests/ed435384.html)

NC State University: Accessible Web Design: Accessible web design is universal Web design. NC State's nationally recognized Center for Universal Design provides a rich set of resources. (www.ncsu.edu/it/dss/webaccess.html)

WebABLE: WebABLE is a provider of Web accessibility technology, consulting, and training. Their site offers articles, guidelines, and links to other relevant websites. (www.webable.com/index.html)

Americans with Disabilities and Section 508. Section 508 (www.section508.gov/buy_accessible/main.cfm)

The Access Board (www.access-board.gov/sec508/508standards.htm)

Organizations

Bobby: Web page authors identify and repair significant barriers to access by individuals with disabilities. (www.cast.org/bobby/)

Center for Applied Special Technology (CAST): CAST is an educational, not-for-profit organization that uses technology to expand opportunities for all people, including those with disabilities. (www.cast.org)

Web Accessibility Initiative (WAI): WAI, in coordination with organizations around the world, pursues accessibility of the Web through five primary areas of work: technology, guidelines, tools, education and outreach, and research and development. (www.w3.org/WAI/)

REFLECTION QUESTIONS

- Does your organization make accommodations for learners with disabilities in the traditional classroom?

- Are there official polices or guidelines? What guidelines exist for your organization's website?

- Go to "Bobby" at www.cast.org/bobby/ and enter a Web page to assess its accessibility for disabled users. What recommendations for corrections were made in your Bobby report? What implications would these kinds of recommendations have on your WBT program?

- How might these guidelines change your design or influence the specifications you issue for outsourced work?

Americans with Disabilities Act and 508. One more thing—keep in mind the Americans with Disabilities Act and Section 508 as you design and as you analyze your goal, audience, environment, and infrastructure. Section 508 of the Rehabilitation Act is intended to establish a "level playing field" by eliminating barriers that exclude persons with disabilities. If you are currently serving learners who have disabilities or if in the future someone with disabilities may be a learner, this is the time to consider how you will eliminate barriers.

A more difficult and equally important set of factors in the environment is related to workplace rules and the management support for Web-based training.

Management Support of Web-Based Training. Schedule interviews with managers to learn about their attitudes toward Web-based training. Do the managers plan to schedule time for workers to take training? Do the managers value Web-based training as highly as they value traditional, instructor-led training? Take steps to ensure the success of the program. Inform and educate managers on the value of Web-based training.

Manager at a financial services company recommends assessing the political environment

I could give you a list of the things we have done to make the learning environment better; we had signs printed that you put on top of your computer like those signs for Domino's pizza delivery vehicles, indicating that you're in training. We had carrels put in the training center to free learners from managers who couldn't bear to see people sitting in their cubes "not working." We even had a loaner laptop to take home. But what really worked was making the manager, as well as the employees, accountable for learning. All of a sudden the manager knew he would have to explain why someone didn't complete a course. After adjusting the accountability policy, people were allowed to set their phones to do not disturb, and time was allocated on the schedule just like any other task.

Pace of Work. Assess the pace of work by talking to managers and learners about peaks and valleys in the business cycle. Improve the odds that your program will be used and that it will be viewed as effective by creating a program that fits into the business environment. Avoid introducing Web-based training during the closing week of a fiscal period when everyone is rushing to process orders or close sales. Create lessons that are short enough to be taken between phone calls or before lunch. Understanding the pace of your learners' work environment makes implementation easier and the instruction more effective.

Workplace Rules.   Consideration must also be given to work rules for exempt, nonexempt, and union workers. Determine whether there are any issues related to asking hourly workers to take training after hours or on weekends. Will there be overtime and compensation issues? Do you have union workers or contracts with restriction regarding training and testing?

5. Surveying the Infrastructure

Understanding the technical limitations of your computer network will be important when choosing the tools to develop and design programs. A high-level survey of the infrastructure to identify key issues early in the ADDIE process will alert you to major issues. Later, in the design and development stages, you will revisit infrastructure issues and work with your information systems group to choose the best tools.

Operating Systems.   It is important to know what kind of computers are in use and the versions of operating systems they run. This is relevant because, the more operating systems upon which the e-learning program runs, the more systems the helpdesk must be trained to support. Consider the number of operating systems available for a PC, for example, Windows 3.x, Windows 98, Windows 2000, and Windows NT.

Browsers and Plug-Ins.   Many organizations have settled on a single standard for browser software to ensure that there is uniformity and it is easier to provide support. Standardization on a browser such as Internet Explorer or Netscape Navigator often includes standardizing on a particular version of the browser. Because many organizations do not want the hassle of supporting early releases of browser software, the standard browser will often lag behind the latest release of Netscape Navigator and Microsoft Internet Explorer. If you are counting on taking advantage of the soon-to-be-released versions, be sure to check with your IS group. It is also a good idea to ask which plug-ins the organization allows and what version is typically installed. In some organizations plug-ins are discouraged or disallowed.

Technical Capacity of the Network.   Assess the general technical capabilities of the organization's network by meeting with the information systems group that supports your learners. Understanding the network and computer system will help you understand the demands a Web-based training program can put on the network. Training programs can slow networks to a crawl because of large graphic and media files. Inquire as to rules related to use of streaming media and any policies that you should be aware of related to obtaining approval for an application to be placed on a server. Ask how the system deals with idle processes. Will the system disconnect if a learner leaves for ten minutes to attend to a customer? Be sure to double-check your assumptions regarding the capacity of your learners' computers, for example, does everyone have a color monitor and sound card?

Firewalls.   A firewall is a system that enforces an access control policy between networks. The firewall uses rules to allow e-mail and files to pass between systems, protects the system against unauthorized log-ins, and provides an audit trail. In some cases the files that a Web-based training system sends may violate a firewall's access control policies and result in the Web-based training system not working. It is important to consult with your IS group when you are narrowing your selection of tools.

Modem Speed.   If programs are going to be taken from home or delivered to salespeople on the road, be sure to find out about modem speed. The faster the modem speed, the more quickly the e-learning program will respond and the better the level of interaction with the program.

Home Phone and Modem.   Ask about the home users' access to two lines, one for the computer and one for an analog telephone line. If employees have two lines in their home offices, it will be possible to use Web-based software that allows a presentation to be shared over the Internet while participants are on a conference call. In some cases it may be most cost-effective to offer Web-based training programs that have IP audio, the ability to use a single Internet connection to talk and to share a presentation.

If there is one phone but the cost of telephone calls is very expensive, you may want to look for software that allows the learner to log on, download the application, and work offline. This is called disconnected use. After completing the training, users reconnect and upload their work. This is a good solution for learners who are working in locations with poor or unreliable Internet connections.

6. Selecting Training Methods

The initial decision in the analysis phase is whether or not there is a training need. The second decision is to choose a training or instructional method for

✓ Monitoring the Technical Side of E-Learning Worksheet

Directions: Visit the following links to learn more about the technical considerations, new products, trends, and issues related to Web-based training. These sites frequently have stories about products, case studies, product comparisons, and interviews with thought leaders. Then use the questions below to reflect on the experience.

Brandon-Hall.com Dispatch (www.brandon-hall.com/). Brandon Hall is the author of an e-mail newsletter called the Dispatch. The Dispatch and Brandon's site are strictly focused on e-learning technology and topics. The newsletter is free, and copies of old issues are archived on the site.

How It Works (www.howstuffworks.com/). This is an excellent site that explains even the most difficult concept in simple terms using lots of graphics and clear steps. For those who want more details, there are hyperlinks to additional material.

Computer World (www.computerworld.com/). Computer World is a new technology site. It offers a very special search engine that locates whitepapers, technical documents that explain the technical details, future directions, and strategies of products and services. These are written by vendors so they have a clear point of view, but they also offer more detail than a magazine ad or the vendor's website.

TechRepublic (www.techrepublic.com/). TechRepublic is also a general technology site, but it often has e-learning stories. This is the place to get technical articles and updates on what industry experts are saying. The site can be searched or you can sign up to become a site member and receive a newsletter called TechMails sent to your e-mail account.

Link Finder: If these URLs are broken, use the following terms in different combinations to find similar sites: hardware reviews, software reviews, consumer electronics, latest prices, tech news, free downloads, programming, networking, databases, and web.

REFLECTION QUESTIONS

- Which sites were most helpful? What assumptions do these articles make about learning, the process for purchasing software, and the challenges faced by trainers?

- If you signed up for e-mail newsletters, are they useful?

reaching the goal. The training methods should be the optimal way to close the knowledge gap, based on the goal, the audience, the environment, and the infrastructure. Examples of training or instructional strategies are lectures, case studies, hands-on labs, small group work, and discussions. Once the instructional strategies are defined, the delivery method(s) should be chosen. It is not a foregone conclusion that Web-based training is the delivery method.

Developers have a range of training and delivery methods from which to choose. Traditional classroom instructional strategies such as lectures, demonstrations, and questioning and answering can be used, along with many other delivery modes. The following list is just a small sample of training and delivery methods:

- Traditional classroom instruction;
- Educational satellite television;
- Self-paced workbooks;
- Videocassette programs;
- Videoconference programs;
- Audiocassette programs; and
- Web-based training.

A single training method or a combination of methods can be used. Obviously, Web-based training is not the solution to every training problem, but it is an appropriate delivery method for supporting many instructional strategies. If Web-based training is not the best delivery method, based on your analysis of needs-assessment data, be firm with clients and managers about your reasons for not recommending it.

Summary

This chapter has provided an overview of the ADDIE model and a review of the steps in the analysis phase. This is the foundation upon which your program will be developed. The analysis phase should not be eliminated nor treated lightly. It is cost-effective to find the factors that will facilitate and those that will present obstacles as early as possible.

The analysis phase can take 20 to 30 percent of the time allotted to an initial e-learning project. Consider the time it takes to deliver a needs assessment for a traditional instructor-led course. Additional time will be required for collecting data related to your organization's infrastructure and gathering technical and learner data from remote offices. This is time well-spent, and it is important to communicate with the team and your client during this phase. If the team members understand how the phases of the ADDIE model are related, they will appreciate receiving data from the analysis phase because it will inform their involvement in the next phases.

The next chapter is devoted to looking more closely at the types of Web-based training that are available. Selecting a specific e-learning instructional method is the last step in the analysis phase. If Web-based training is the best delivery method, there are four methods to choose from. Some are better suited to some instructional strategies and teaching methods than others.

Suggested Readings

Goals and Objectives

Clark, R. (1999). *Developing technical training: A structured approach for developing classroom and computer-based instructional materials.* Washington, DC: Society for Performance Improvement.

Mager, R.F. (1992). *Preparing instructional objectives: A critical tool in the development of effective instruction.* Los Angeles, CA: Center for Effective Performance.

Merrill, D. (1994). *Instructional design theory.* Englewood Cliffs, NJ: Educational Technology Publications.

Infrastructure/Technology

Derfler, F.J., Freed, L., & Derfler, F. (2000). *How networks work.* New York: Que Press.

Levine, J.R., Baroudi, C., & Young, M.L. (2000). *The Internet for dummies®.* New York: Hungry Minds.

Lowe, D. (1999). *Networking for dummies®.* New York: Hungry Minds.

Instructional Design Models

Alessi, S.M., & Trollip, S.R. (2000). *Multimedia for learning: Methods and development.* Boston, MA: Allyn & Bacon.

Dick, W., Carey, L., & Carey, J.O. (2000). *The systematic design of instruction.* Reading, MA: Addison-Wesley.

Rothwell, W.J., & Kazans, H.C. (1996). *Mastering the instructional design process: A systematic approach.* San Francisco: Jossey-Bass.

Needs Assessment

Rossett, A. (1987). *Training needs assessment.* Englewood Cliffs, NJ: Educational Technology Publications.

Rossett, A. (1998). *First things fast: A handbook for performance analysis.* San Francisco: Jossey-Bass/Pfeiffer.

Zemke, R., & Kramlinger, T. (1982). *Figuring things out: A trainer's guide to task, needs, and organizational analysis.* New York: Perseus Press.

Chapter 6

Selecting the Most Appropriate E-Learning Method

One of the most difficult things to understand about e-learning is that the term e-learning does not refer to a single recognizable form of learning. There are hundreds of paper, articles, and online sites that attempt to create order, but like any evolving technology, it is difficult to reach agreement on something that is technically changing every few months.

This chapter is designed to help you sort out the four major kinds of e-learning and to review the decisions to be made before your selection, namely, determining types or domains of learning—cognitive, psychomotor, or attitudinal—the level of skill to be taught, and the degree of structure necessary for the learning experience.

The last chapter helped prepare you for this last step in the analysis phase of ADDIE by reviewing the analysis of the learning task, environment, audience, infrastructure, and culture. Having detailed knowledge of these facts makes selecting an e-learning delivery method(s) easier. If you feel you are spending significant time in the analysis phase, you are right! It is the foundation of the entire WBT program and demands a high level of detail to ensure the program's success. Let's begin this selection analysis!

This is the last step in the analysis phase of ADDIE (see Figure 6.1).

Figure 6.1. The ADDIE Model

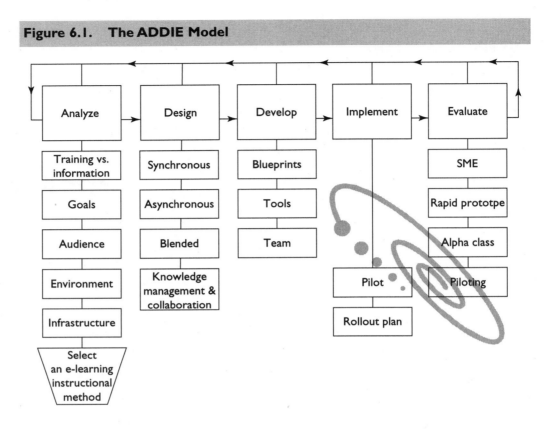

What You Will Learn in This Chapter

After completing this chapter, you will be able to

- Determine the kind of learning to be achieved;
- Evaluate options for a blended solution;
- Differentiate among four types of Web-based training; and
- Select the appropriate type of Web-based training for your purposes.

Step One in the Selection Process
Determining the Types of Learning

The goal statement developed during the analysis phase is the starting point for determining the types of learning your program must accomplish. It is worth revisiting the idea of classifying objectives discussed in Chapter 3. All goals and objects belong to one of three domains: cognitive, psychomotor, and attitudinal.

Classifying objectives is an important concept because it is the foundation for choosing the optimal instructional strategy and delivery methods. Instructional strategies are plans for taking learners through the four phases of instruction explained in Chapter 3: information presentation, guided practice, practicing by student, and testing. For example, a strategy might be to lecture and demonstrate how to calculate net present value, then to provide the student with guided practice, additional practice problems for after class, and an exam at the end of the module. Delivery methods are the means for teaching the lesson and include things such as videoconferencing, WBT, traditional classroom instruction, on-the-job training, and self-paced manuals. In some examples, like the lesson on calculating net present value, the instructional strategy could be used in either a traditional classroom or in an e-learning environment.

The classification process is also the foundation for a blended solution. The concept of using a mixture of instructional strategies and delivery methods to achieve a program goal is known as creating a *blended* solution. Later in this chapter, we will talk about blended solutions and the implications for the design and delivery of a program.

Domains of Learning

In real training situations, it is rare to find a goal that can be defined exclusively as one type of learning. Most situations require learning in two or more domains. For example, learning to sell life insurance may require both cognitive and attitudinal skills or learning how to assemble and use a meat slicer may require both cognitive and psychomotor skills. The key to identifying the types of learning required is to divide the goal into distinct parts. Classify the skills needed for each part as cognitive, psychomotor, or attitudinal and then develop optimal instructional strategies and choose the best delivery methods.

Table 6.1 gives examples of the three domains and questions to help you classify your goals.

Psychomotor. Psychomotor skills require repeated practice and feedback for mastery. They are not well-suited for delivery exclusively via Web-based training. If a goal calls for a combination of cognitive and psychomotor skills (such as teaching a diabetic patient to give himself or herself an insulin injection), you may want to use a combination of Web-based training and face-to-face tutorial sessions. Cognitive skills (such as procedures for preparing the injection and disposing of used syringes) could be delivered via the Web. Psychomotor skills required for

Table 6.1.   Indicators of Types of Learning

Types of Learning	Indicators

Cognitive Skills
Examples:
 	
   Completing travel expense forms
 	
   Memorizing and applying mutual fund terms and concepts
	Does the goal require the learner to
	   Memorize terms and concepts?
	   Apply rules?
	   Distinguish among items?
	   Analyze or synthesize data?
	   Evaluate information?
	   Solve problems?

Psychomotor Skills
Examples:
 	
   Giving an insulin injection
   Using a table saw
	Does the goal require the learner to
	   Engage in mental and physical activity?
	   Use muscular action?
	   Practice a skill with hand-eye coordination?

Attitudinal Skills
Examples:
 	
   Choosing to value diversity
   Sensitizing employees to sexual harassment issues
	Does the goal require the learner to
	   Change attitudes?
	   Reflect on his or her values?
	   Explore alternative perspectives?
	Will the goal require time to be achieved?
	Is the goal difficult to observe or measure in behavioral terms?

giving an injection would be taught in a face-to-face tutorial session that provided opportunities for practice, coaching, and feedback.

Attitudinal.   Teaching learners new attitudes requires the instructor to build on what the learners already know, both directly and indirectly. Neither direct methods, such as giving praise, rewards, and recognition, nor indirect methods, such as modeling appropriate behavior, is well-suited for Web-based training. Again, a combination of methods might be appropriate, for example, to teach managers to value diversity in the workplace, Web-based training and a mentoring program could be combined. The Web could be used to teach information about cultural differences, equal-opportunity regulations, and the company's philosophy about diversity. A mentor in a face-to-face situation could use direct methods, such as praise, rewards, and recognition. Indirect methods, such as role modeling and leading by example, would require identifying local managers to serve as role models. (See Table 6.2 for examples of programs that teach attitudinal skills.)

Cognitive. Cognitive skills are best suited for delivery via Web-based training because they can be communicated to learners using language, text, numbers, and symbols. The cognitive domain includes intellectual skills such as memorizing terms and concepts, problem solving, applying rules, distinguishing among items, analyzing and synthesizing data, and evaluating information. If the skills and knowledge you seek to teach require these intellectual skills, Web-based training is appropriate. (See Table 6.2 examples of programs that teach cognitive skills.)

What You Can and Cannot Teach: The Great Debate

There is a great deal of debate over the issue of what kind of things can and cannot be taught using e-learning. Vendors, conference presenters, and some educators

Table 6.2. Programs That Teach Attitudinal, Psychomotor, and Cognitive Skills

Attitudinal Skills	
Negotiate Your Success	*YouAcheive.Com* (www.youacheive.com/testdrive/default.asp)
Increasing Your Emotional Intelligence	*SkillSoft.com* (www.skillsoft.com)
Psychomotor Skills	
Driving a stick shift 2torial #0689: Drive a Stick Shift	*Learn2.com* (www.learn2.com/learn2_everyday.asp)
Build It/Install It	*Home Depot.com* (www.homedepot.com/)
Cognitive Skills	
Balance a Checkbook	*How to Balance a Checkbook* (www.ianr.unl.edu/pubs/homemgt/nf4.HTM)
Write a Resume	*LearnThat.com* (www.learnthat.com/courses/business/resume/)

argue that the Web can be used to teach anything and everything. Currently there is little research available to support claims of the efficacy of teaching psychomotor skills such as skiing, sailing, or learning to bake bread with e-learning.

It is debatable if the Web is an optimal medium in which to teach attitudinal skills such as choosing to obey the software license agreements, choosing to practice safe sex, and adopting a low cholesterol diet using a course metaphor. Some practitioners would argue that these topics couldn't be taught well in a traditional classroom either. There is great promise and even some early research findings (Tate, 2001) on the effectiveness of Web-based programs for dietary change, smoking cessation, and exercise. The question educators must debate is where the line between education and counseling should be drawn. The Web is simply a medium; the question is really about the strategies that are considered educational and those that are related to clinical psychology and counseling.

Teaching cognitive skills is a different story; there is no shortage of research on the effectiveness of teaching cognitive skills using computer-based training methods (Kuilik & Kulik, 1986, 1991). There is a rich body of research (Gagne, 1985; Merrill, 1994) documenting the value of creating optimal conditions for learning. While people may be able to learn under less than optimal conditions, it is not recommended. There are methods, such as Merrill's (1994) Component Display Theory, that prescribe optimal methods for fast, effective, and efficient skills and knowledge transfer. The motivation for using optimal methods is straightforward. Effective methods remove unnecessary obstacles and reduce learner frustration; therefore these methods are faster and yield greater skills transfer.

Creating Blended Solutions

Blended solutions combine Web-based instruction with traditional classroom teaching to create courses that mix instructional strategies and delivery methods. Blended solutions have gained popularity because they reduce training costs and the time learners spend away from their jobs by offloading classroom learning to the Web. In blended solutions, participants are asked to learn the cognitive content, such as negotiation concepts, mentoring roles, or effective communication tactics, online. The class time is then used for practice, coaching, feedback, and dialogue. A second kind of blended solution involves mixing the four modes of online learning delivery and varying the instructional strategies. This section will examine both kinds of blended solutions.

Blending Traditional Classroom Teaching with WBT

The key to creating a blended solution is to optimize the design by clarifying the goals, selecting effective instructional strategies, and choosing the best delivery modes.

The first step in crafting this kind of blended solution is to break the goal into manageable pieces. For example, if the goal is to teach learners how to write a newsletter, it can be broken into objectives such as the following. Learners will be able to

- Develop a profile of reader interests;
- Describe three strategies for finding story leads;
- Interview someone for a story;
- Write a feature story free of spelling and grammatical errors; and
- Lay out a newsletter using desktop publishing software.

Once the goal has been broken down into a number of objectives, it is a good idea to identify the cognitive objectives that can be taught via e-learning and the attitudinal and psychomotor skills that are best delivered using methods such as face-to-face instruction, mentoring, and on-the-job training. The combination of Web-based training and one or more of these delivery methods is an example of a blended solution.

Refining Objectives

In e-learning it is important to further categorize the objectives because program developers need to know more about the kinds of cognitive skills that must be taught. A more granular understanding will help designers choose the right instructional strategy, then choose between classroom and Web-based training, and finally choose the best mode of Web-based training.

There are six kinds of cognitive skills, and each requires a different kind of presentation of information, practice for the student, and assessments. Bloom, Hastings, and Madaus (1971) identified six levels of intellectual abilities and skills that could be used to classify cognitive objectives (see Figure 6.2). The levels range from simple knowledge to complex evaluation. Understanding the different levels is important because the intellectual skills and abilities required influence the selection of a Web-based training method.

Knowledge.   Knowledge can be defined as the recall of specific and isolated bits of information, methods, sequences, and principles. Teaching couriers the map

Figure 6.2.   Bloom's Taxonomy of Educational Objectives in the Cognitive Domain

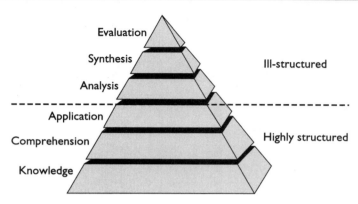

Source: B.S. Bloom, J.T. Hastings, & G.F. Madaus, *Handbook on Formative and Summative Evaluation of Student Learning.* New York: McGraw-Hill, 1997.

symbols, such as icons for interstates, railroads, airports, and bridges, is an example of teaching knowledge.

Comprehension.   Comprehension is the ability to use knowledge without necessarily relating it to other material or seeing its fullest impact at the time. Teaching a field technician to assemble a computer without helping him or her to understand how the power supply, CPU, operating system, and other components are related is an example of teaching comprehension.

Application.   Application is the ability to abstract information, such as rules, general methods, and procedures, and to apply them. Teaching telephone representatives to use checklists of questions to resolve simple problems without scheduling a repairperson to visit a customer is an example of teaching application.

Analysis.   Analysis is the ability to break-down an item into its constituent elements or parts. Teaching loan officers to examine a loan applicant's financial data and to identify the applicant's financial liabilities and assets is an example of teaching analysis.

Synthesis.   Synthesis is the ability to put together elements and parts to form a whole. Teaching product managers to develop marketing plans that incorporate market data, competitive information, and personal experience is an example of teaching synthesis.

Evaluation.   Evaluation is the ability to apply judgment about the value of materials or methods for a given purpose. Teaching college admissions officers to determine which courses are granted transfer credit is an example of teaching evaluation.

Highly Structured and Ill-Structured Problems

A second way to analyze objectives is to look at them as being either highly structured or ill-structured. The dotted line shown in Figure 6.2 divides learning opportunities into structured or ill-structured. The skills associated with knowledge, comprehension, and application can be characterized as structured. There are clear right and wrong answers, performance is observable and measurable, and the application of knowledge varies little from situation to situation. Examples of structured situations are teaching learners how to use word processing software, apply a 15 percent discount, and withdraw money from an automatic teller machine.

Analysis, synthesis, and evaluation are characterized as ill-structured learning opportunities. They involve applying skills and knowledge to problems that are complex and require a combination of concepts, principles, and theories to resolve. The application of ill-structured knowledge also requires that learners apply knowledge to situations that differ from case to case and to problems for which there is no single right answer. Examples of ill-structured problems are analyzing the benefits and limitations of outsourcing work, designing a Website for e-commerce, and developing a treatment plan to manage HIV.

Training problems can be envisioned as falling along a continuum ranging from structured to ill-structured. Where a training problem falls along this continuum will influence the choice of WBT delivery methods and the design of blended solutions.

Choosing an Instructional Strategy

Once the objectives have been analyzed and categorized, it is time to think about creating a lesson plan to teach the objectives. An instructional strategy provides a plan for taking learners through the four phases of instruction: information presentation, guided practice, practicing by the student, and testing. If you have the option of creating a blended solution, think broadly about your options. Create the strategy first and then decide whether that segment of the lesson is better delivered in a traditional classroom or on the Web. Choosing between traditional classroom and Web-based training delivery is more art than science. At this point in the process, you must return to the data collected earlier in the ADDIE model and balance among competing factors such as learning needs, time limits, budget constraints, technical factors, and the training goals. There is no single right answer, and what is best for one division of an organization may not be optimal for another.

Step Two in the Selection Process
Selecting the Most Appropriate Type of Web-Based Training

When educational considerations discussed above or business imperatives lead you to choose to deliver all or some of your program online, decisions still need to be made regarding what mode of online learning is best. Understanding the four modes of Web-based training will help you smoothly integrate classroom training and WBT or deliver completely online. If you choose to deliver the program exclusively via the Web, a clear understanding of the WBT options will also enable you to take full advantage of the delivery method.

To get started in selecting among the four kinds of Web-based training, first determine the learning domain that best describes the goal, that is, cognitive, psychomotor, or attitudinal. If the goal is in the cognitive domain, determine the level of intellectual skills, and characterize it as being a structured or ill-structured problem.

Then use the following questions to help refine the instructional needs of your program and the most appropriate type of Web-based training:

- Are the instructional goals and objectives measurable?

- Will the learners benefit from working alone or in teams, groups, or pairs?

- Is there a single right answer to the problems?

- Will the learners' experience be a resource for the lesson?

- Do the learners need to interact with one another?

Finally, review each of the four kinds of Web-based training and make your selection based on the learning domain and purpose of the instruction. Table 6.3 summarizes the purpose and types of learning associated with the four kinds of Web-based training. Appendix E, Matrix of Web-Based Training Types, has more details on the roles of facilitators, students, and interactions based in each the four modes of Web-based training.

Let's now look at each of these WBT options.

Table 6.3.	Four Kinds of Web-Based Training			
Characteristics	**Web/Computer-Based Training**	**Web/Electronic Performance Support Systems**	**Web/Virtual Asynchronous Classroom**	**Web/Virtual Synchronous Classroom**
Purpose	To provide learners performance-based training with measurable goals and objectives	To provide learners practical knowledge and problem-solving skills in a just-in-time format	To provide group learning and communication in an asynchronous environment	To provide collaborative learning in a real-time environment
Types of Learning	Highly structured problems that require transferring knowledge, building comprehension, and practicing application of skills	Ill-structured problems that require analysis and synthesis of elements, relationships, and organizational principles	Less structured problems that require application, analysis, synthesis, and evaluation	Ill-structured problems that require the synthesis and evaluation of information and shared experience

Establishing a shared vision regarding Web-based training can be a challenge

I was asked to initiate a pilot program [Web-based training] for my company. At the first meeting, I was getting directions from everybody. It was clear we were not talking about the same things. Some people were describing "information" or "reference material" online; other people were talking about desktop videoconferencing; and others were talking about just putting CD-ROMS on the internet. It was clear that unless we could all look at some concrete examples we would never share a vision about the program.

Web/Computer-Based Training

Web/computer-based training (W/CBT) is similar to traditional multimedia computer-based training (CBT) programs. In W/CBT learners engage in self-paced programs that use multimedia. Interactions take the form of branching decisions that are either controlled by the learner or by the program, based on responses. These programs are most frequently used to meet structured learning goals related to transferring knowledge, building comprehension, and practicing the application of skills.

Characteristics of W/CBT. Table 6.4 provides a summary of the learning characteristics of Web/computer-based training. The hallmark of this kind of training is the design of the program. Individual learners working at their own pace take Web/computer-based training. The programs address structured problems and are designed to teach knowledge, comprehension, and application skills that can be assessed by observation of measurable outcomes. Because W/CBT programs teach subjects with measurable objectives, it is expected that learners will complete the learning nugget related to a given objective.

Comparison of W/CBT to Traditional CBT. Web/computer-based training is similar to traditional computer-based training in many ways. Both delivery methods are designed for individual learners and both are well-suited for teaching

Table 6.4. Learning Characteristics of W/CBT

Characteristic	Description
Self-Paced	Learners engage in learning at convenient times and set their own pace for completing lessons and module.
Individual Learning	Learners work alone to master skills. W/CBT is well-suited to drill and practice of repetitious skills.
Highly Structured	Topics with clear right and wrong answers are well-suited to W/CBT. Developers can predict the answers and provide feedback, reinforcement, and remediation.
Discrete Units of Instruction	Teaching measurable objectives makes it desirable to divide the content into lessons and modules. Learners are expected to complete discrete units of materials to demonstrate mastery of the objectives.

✓ Web/Computer-Based Training Worksheet

Directions: The best way to understand the qualities of a Web/computer-based training program is to enroll in a program and complete a lesson. Try at least two of the following programs. Be sure to read all the directions regarding system requirements and plug-ins. Because these sites are updated frequently, the demo course(s) may change or the site may have moved. Use the questions at the end of this exercise to reflect on the experience.

NETg (www.netg.com)
Test Drive the Course: Microsoft Word 97 Proficient User

Mindleaders (www.mindleaderscom)
DEMO COURSE: Office 2000

SkillSoft (www.skillsoft.com)
DEMO COURSE: Call Center Communication Skill

BitLearning (www.bitlearning.com/)
DEMO COURSE: Computer Hardware

Link Finder: If the URLs are no longer working, use a search engine to find other sites using combinations of these terms: e-learning, Web-based training, demo, test drive, sample, free course, trial.

REFLECTION QUESTIONS

- What did you like about the courses?

- What did these demonstration classes have in common? How did they differ?

- What assumptions are being made regarding the learner's motivation and entry-level skills and the need for feedback?

- If appropriate, what strategies were used to address ill-structured learning objectives?

cognitive skills related to knowledge, comprehension, and application. Table 6.5 summarizes the key differences between the two delivery methods.

The two can only be contrasted when comparing a standalone (not connected to a network) CD-ROM and an e-learning program. The two mediums are becoming more alike due to advances in technology and a blending of the two media. In some situations, programs are delivered using a combination of CD-ROM and Web technology. This trend is best seen in today's authoring tools. Many of the authoring tools allow the same program to be mastered as a CD-ROM and put on a server for use as a Web-based training program.

Web/computer-based training differs from traditional computer-based training because W/CBT draws on the resources of the World Wide Web and proprietary information found in company databases. In addition, information located on the company's intranet can be used. In traditional CBT programs the resources are limited to those included on the CD-ROM.

Another difference is the number of options for communications between the learner and the instructor. Web/computer-based training offers tools such as e-mail to communicate with the instructor or link to an online bulletin board. Some

Table 6.5. Comparison Between Traditional Standalone CBT and Web/CBT

Traditional CBT	Web/CBT
Resources are limited to what is included on the CD-ROM.	Resources can include proprietary company databases as well as information on the World Wide Web.
Communication between the learner and the instructor is not highly integrated.	Communication between learners and instructor can be seamlessly integrated.
Updates and modifications require the CD-ROM or disks to be revised, mastered, pressed, and distributed.	Program can easily be updated and modified.
Rich multimedia options for video, audio, and images are available. Robust tools for creating sophisticated interactions and exercises and tracking learners are available.	Rich media such as video, audio, and images can cause congestion on networks or can be blocked by firewalls. Tools are improving for creating interactions and tracking learners.

Web-based training software programs track learners' progress. They inform the instructor of learners' quiz scores and notify him or her if a learner fails to log in for an extended period of time. In general, traditional CBT programs offer better tools for scoring the learners' performance, but these programs lack the network connections required to send that information back to a central database for tracking purposes.

Web/computer-based training offers developers the ability to update programs easily instead of creating a new CD-ROM master, scheduling a press run, or distributing a revised disk. Web tools and technology can be used to create rich media such as video, audio, and images. Additionally, the computers used by learners are being upgraded continually, making it possible for developers to create sophisticated programs for powerful multimedia computers.

Current Web tools and technology are constrained by bandwidth limitations that prohibit developers from using rich media such as video, audio, or graphics that require large files. Large files cause network congestion and take a long time to download or paint on the learner's screen. But this situation is improving as new tools are created to compress large files, as greater bandwidth becomes available, as faster modems are installed, and as old computers are replaced. These improvements will make it possible for Web-based training developers to create more sophisticated programs with rich media.

Web/EPS Systems

The Web and Internet make it possible to use high-tech job aids. Using the Web, a learner can find a Web page that provides step-by-step instructions for completing a travel expense form or directions to replace a computer motherboard. Electronic performance support system (EPSS) applications offer several advantages over paper-based job aids. The most obvious is that they are available worldwide through the Internet and its communication links. Learners can access instruction just in time, avoiding what they do not need. Well-designed programs can link learners to experts, colleagues, threaded discussions, step-by-step instructions, training modules, and reference materials.

Characteristics of W/EPS Systems. Table 6.6 provides a summary of the characteristics of Web/computer-based training.

The ability to provide learners with training and information when and where it is needed distinguishes W/EPS systems from Web/computer-based training. In the latter, the learner is expected to complete all of the lessons and modules and

Table 6.6. Characteristics of Web/EPS Systems	
Characteristic	**Description**
Learner-Determined	Learners determine how, when, and at what level of detail they will use the Web/EPS systems.
Individual Learning	Learners work alone to solve problems.
Ill-Structured	Used to solve problems that require analysis, synthesis, and evaluation. Problems lack a clear right or wrong answer.
Just in Time	Learners use Web/EPS systems when and where needed, rather than in anticipation of future needs.

hold the skills and knowledge for later use. Using a Web/EPS system, the learner does not access the system until the skills or knowledge are required, and then he or she decides how much information or training is necessary. There is a broad range. For example, a first-time learner may complete a lesson, read the documentation, and review tips posted to an online bulletin board before starting the task. On the other hand, a learner who has done the task previously may choose to scan the steps in the procedure to refresh his or her memory.

Web/EPS systems are ideal for helping learners with ill-structured problems that do not have simple right or wrong answers and problems that involve so many variables that it is impossible to anticipate all of the possible solutions.

Comparison.   Table 6.7 summarizes the differences between traditional EPS systems and Web/EPS systems.

Table 6.7. Comparison of Traditional and Web/EPS Systems	
Traditional EPS Systems	**Web/EPS Systems**
Updates require distribution of new software or media.	Updates from a central point are available immediately.
Communication with other learners requires separate software.	Communications with others can be integrated into the system.

Web/EPS Worksheet

Directions: W/EPS systems are difficult to find because they are often designed for internal use or are viewed as proprietary. The list below provides two kinds of URLs; the first two URLs are links to sites that host EPS forums and the last two links are examples of W/EPS tools. Keep in mind that EPS tools are simply online job aids, and they can be as basic as a set of directions or smoothly integrated into a sophisticated application. Use the reflection questions to think about your experience.

EPSS Info Site: Excellent meta resources for EPS (www.epssinfosite.com/)

EPSS World: Great collection of EPSS examples (www.epssworld.com/)

Colorado Pre-Hospital Care Program: An Electronic Performance Support System for EMT-Basic Instructors (www.cdphe.state.co.us/em/home.htm)

Quicken: Retirement Planner (www.quicken.com/retirement/planner/)

Calgary Homes: Floor Planner (www.calgaryhomes.com/html/interactive/floorplanner.html)

Amazon.com: This is not a training-based site, but it does offer a glimpse of what is possible with W/EPSS. Search for an electronic item such as a digital camera or a DVD. Use the searching tools, and read the customer reviews to experience what performance support for making a purchasing decision is like. Consider how some of these features might be transferred to a workplace task. (www.amazon.com)

REFLECTION QUESTIONS

- What are the differences and similarities between W/EPS systems and the W/CBT systems?

- How might the W/EPSS solutions discussed at EPSSInfoSite.com and EPSSWorld be used in your organization?

- What are the challenges to building a W/EPSS solution?

- Have you used W/EPS systems in your job? At retail websites?

One of the key differences between traditional EPS systems and Web/EPS systems is the technical implementation and use of networks. Traditional systems depend on software on the learner's computer to find steps, procedures, tips, definitions, checklists, and glossaries. In contrast, Web/EPS systems link learners to a central server, where information is easily updated and made available.

Integrated tools and the ability to connect learners to peers and experts are unique to this environment. Information contained in threaded discussions, online forums, news groups, and notes files is the equivalent of an electronic bulletin board. Users can post requests for information, recommendations, and answers to questions posted by others, creating a resource that grows over time.

Web/Virtual Asynchronous Classrooms

Like a traditional classroom, an asynchronous virtual classroom brings learners and instructors together to learn new skills and knowledge. The learners and instructor log on to the Internet at various times to work on assignments, read, and work on projects. The learners share a group learning experience but do not meet in real time. This application blends a variety of Web technologies, such as hypertext documents, online quizzes, multimedia, notes files, and e-mail to produce programs. The complexity and sophistication of the program are largely determined by the design and the hardware limitations of the learners.

Asynchronous virtual classroom programs are distinguished by their reliance on a variety of communication tools that allow peer-to-peer learning, group learning, and learner-instructor coaching. As a result of extensive communication and shared goals, a geographically dispersed class develops a sense of community, complete with norms for acceptable communication outside the virtual classroom.

Characteristics.   Table 6.8 summarizes the characteristics that set Web/virtual asynchronous classrooms apart from other type of Web-based training.

The most important characteristic of Web/virtual asynchronous classrooms is the focus on group learning. Unlike Web/CBT and Web/EPS systems, which are designed for individual learners, Web/virtual asynchronous classroom programs are designed for groups. Organizations use this form of Web-based training because their goal is best achieved in a group learning environment. Learners work together to brainstorm ideas, analyze case studies, and solve problems, but they are not necessarily online at the same time. Learners log in at any hour of the day or night to contribute ideas, add insights to case studies, and present alternative solutions to problems.

Table 6.8. Characteristics of Web/Virtual Asynchronous Classrooms

Characteristics	Description
Group learning	Involves learners working with one another on projects, case studies, and exercises. Learners are encouraged to learn from one another as well as from the instructor, using collaborative learning strategies such as brainstorming, discussions, and problem solving.
Accessed at different times of day and night	Learners and instructor independently access the Web. Although learners and instructor are not online together, they participate in group learning activities such as projects, brainstorming, and case studies.
Problems/topics are somewhat structured	Topics best for this type of Web-based training are those for which the instructor and course developers can define the outcomes and anticipate most of the resources learners need. The role of the instructor is to provide flexible facilitation that supports learners' exploration of additional topics or new problems as they explore the subject.
Learning is done in anticipation of need	Learners take training to fill a current or anticipated gap in skills and knowledge.
Requires more than one class meeting	Group work and projects require several sessions to complete.

Web/virtual asynchronous classrooms are well-suited to problems or topics that are ill-structured. They teach learners to apply guidelines, theories, and concepts to problems that are complex and varied and for which there is no single right answer. For example, a program to teach store managers how to increase sales, a program to teach human resource managers how to recruit and screen seasonal employees, or a program to teach physicians how to take a patient's medical history are appropriate for Web/VAC programs because they can be taught by providing learners with established guidelines, steps, procedures, and practices for real-world situations. The skills and knowledge taught require analysis, synthesis, and evaluation, and there is a range of correct or acceptable answers.

Web/Virtual Asynchronous Classroom Worksheet

Directions: This exercise requires a time commitment. Unlike self-paced courses that you complete at your own pace, the Web virtual asynchronous classroom is a group activity. You will need to participate in the program over the course of several days or weeks to experience the sense of community and collaboration. It is also important to take advantage of opportunities to engage in group projects such as case studies, brainstorming, and dialogues. Try at least two of the following W/VAC to get a sense of how communities and activities differ. Use the questions below to reflect on the experience.

Athenium: Free demo session (www.athenium.com/html/home/home.html)

Blackboard: Course developed by faculty are open by request to guests (www.blackboard.com/)

ElementK: Fee-based instructor-led online classes (www.elementk.com/home.asp)

WebCT: Free demo course (www.webct.com)

REFLECTION QUESTIONS

- Did the program you sampled take advantage of having a group of learners online?

- Did you share your experience? Was there collaboration on assignments?

- How did the time commitment differ from the W/CBT?

- What role did the facilitator play? What tactics and strategies were effective for encouraging collaboration?

- What assumptions are made when designing a W/VAC regarding the learner's level of motivation? Ability to collaborate in a virtual environment?

- If you did not complete the course, why? If you did, what motivated you?

Learners participate in Web/VAC programs to fill a current gap in skills and knowledge or an anticipated need for new skills and knowledge. For example, a store manager faced with hiring summer workers may enroll in a Web-based class to improve his or her current recruitment practices. An assistant store manager may enroll in the same class because he or she anticipates the need for this knowledge. Conducting a Web/VAC program usually requires more than one meeting. Because learners log in at their convenience to contribute, the program must be conducted over a period of time long enough to allow interaction, reflection, and feedback.

Comparison. The primary advantage of Web/VAC programs is their ability to bring together a geographically diverse class. Traditional classes are bound by geography. A Web/VAC program can enroll learners across the country or around the world in highly specialized classes that would not attract enough local learners to be viable.

Web/virtual asynchronous classes are not fixed by time. Traditional classes require learners to meet at a set time. Web learners log on at a time that suits their schedules. Table 6.9 provides a summary of the differences between traditional classroom instruction and Web/VAC programs.

Web/Virtual Synchronous Classrooms

The most technically sophisticated Web-based training applications are virtual synchronous classrooms, in which the instructor and class are online at the same time (synchronously). Synchronous classroom tools consist of the following:

- Whiteboards
- Shared applications
- Videoconferencing
- Audioconferencing
- Chat rooms
- Breakout rooms

Table 6.9. Comparison of W/VAC to Traditional Classrooms

Traditional	Web/Virtual Asynchronous Class
Geographically bound	Geographically open
Fixed in time	Independent of time

Online whiteboards enable the entire class to write on them in turn. Shared applications, such as a spreadsheet, allow learners to work as a group to fill in cells, correct formulas, or modify column labels. Videoconferencing and audioconferencing are conceptually similar to traditional audio- and videoconferencing systems. Both allow learners to interact in real time and to hear and/or see the instructor and other class members. Chat rooms are a structured way for learners to carry on a dialogue by typing comments into a running discussion. Breakout rooms are virtual spaces to which the instructor can send students to work together with access to the whiteboard, applications sharing, and other tools.

Characteristics.   Web/virtual synchronous classrooms share some characteristics with Web/virtual asynchronous classrooms. Table 6.10 summarizes these.

Both synchronous and asynchronous Web programs bring learners together to learn as a group. Another similarity is the current or anticipated need for skills or knowledge that may not be as immediate as those that a Web/EPS system addresses.

A major difference between Web/virtual synchronous classrooms and all other types of Web-based training is the requirement that the learners and the instructor be online at the same time. Learners participate in a live, instructor-led class. This requires that time zone differences be considered when scheduling classes (see Figure 6.3). For example, a ninety-minute class that starts at 4:00 p.m.

Table 6.10.   Characteristics of Web/Virtual Synchronous Classrooms

Characteristic	Description
Group learning	Learners work together on projects, case studies, and exercises. They are encouraged to learn from one another as well as from the instructor.
Anticipated need for knowledge	Learners enroll because they have a current or anticipated need for skills and knowledge.
Meets at fixed time	Learners and the instructor meet online at an agreed-on time.
Ill-structured problems	Topics best suited to this type of training involve many variables and complex issues. The problems do not have clear right or wrong answers or are so complex that simple answers are not possible.

Figure 6.3.   Take Time Zones into Consideration

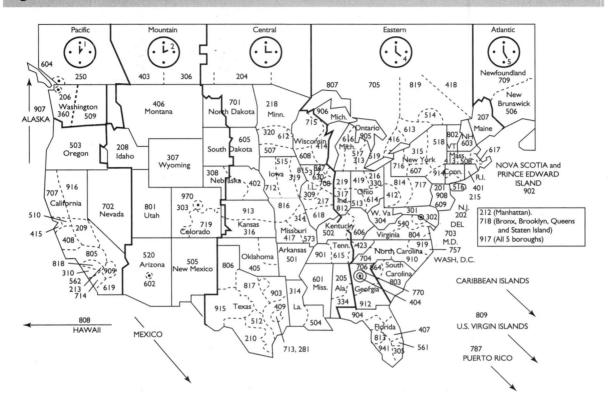

Eastern Standard Time requires that learners on the West Coast log in at 1:00 p.m. Pacific time. Once online, the learners participate in class and interact with one another in real-time.

Like Web/virtual asynchronous classes, Web/virtual synchronous classes are well-suited for ill-structured learning and complex problems that lack clear or simple answers. Web/virtual synchronous classroom programs enable learners to build new knowledge through active participation, dialogue with the instructor and other learners, and share experiences and knowledge. For example, sales representatives can learn to conduct a competitive analysis or identify decision makers during a sales call. As these topics do not have simple answers, they are well-suited for group learning.

Comparison.   Web/VSC programs can be very similar to traditional classroom instruction; Table 6.11 provides a comparison. How closely Web/VSC programs

Web/Virtual Synchronous Classrooms Worksheet

Directions: W/VSC programs must be sampled to be truly appreciated. They offer so many features and so many instructional possibilities that sampling the demo programs listed below would only scratch the surface. Get access to a computer with a sound card and reliable Internet connectivity and download the needed plug-ins. Be sure to ask for a demonstration of all the synchronous features such as shared whiteboard, application sharing, Web touring, polling, and breakout rooms. The more features you can experience, the more knowledgeable you will be regarding the possibilities for your organization.

Keep in mind these demos are marketing programs and may not evidence the hallmark of training. Use this opportunity to experience the technology and consider how it might be used in your organization. Try at least three examples of live Web-based training and keep notes regarding how the experiences are similar and different. Use the questions below to reflect on the experience.

Centra (www.centra.com)

IBM Mindspan (www.ibm.com/mindspan/)

InterWise (www.interwise.com)

KnowledgeNet (www.knowledgenet.com)

Mentergy: ILinc (www.mentergy.com/)

PlaceWare (www.placeware.com)

WhitePine (www.cuseeme.com/)

REFLECTION QUESTIONS

- What did you like or not like about the W/VSC experience?

- What content works best in this mode? Is there content that would not be optimal in this mode?

- What tactics and instructional strategies worked best? Why?

- How important is the skill of the facilitator? What qualities are most important?

- How might W/VSC be used as part of a blended solution?

Table 6.11. Comparison of W/VSC to Traditional Classroom	
Traditional Classroom	**Web/Virtual Synchronous Classroom**
Geographically bound	Geographically open
Resources limited	Vast resources

mimic a real classroom depends on the kind of software chosen. If the software allows learners to see and talk to one another and to share an application, it is very similar to a real classroom. Software that only allows learners to type messages back and forth is obviously not as closely related.

Two key differences between a traditional classroom and all forms of Web/virtual synchronous classrooms are (1) the ability to draw a class from anywhere and (2) the ability to use resources that are located on the Web and on corporate intranets.

 **A professor who teaches instructional design recommends that trainers become connoisseurs of Web-based training before developing their own**

It is outrageous to think that you can design training programs in a medium in which you have never learned anything. I ask all my students to choose a topic, any topic, and try to learn about it via the Web. After this experience they are sensitized to the design issues.

Summary

Getting the analysis (or A) in the ADDIE model right is essential. This is where the foundation is set and difficult decisions are made. Web-based training is simply a delivery method; the key to optimizing this delivery method is to understand the audience, the training goal, the environment, and the infrastructure. At this stage you must determine what you will teach and how. If you choose a blended solution, you will need to determine what is taught in the traditional classroom and what will be delivered via the Web. Web-based training solutions come in four modes. The four kinds of Web-based training have been presented as distinct and

Table 6.12.   Summary of Key Differences Among E-Learning Formats

	Learning Unit		Temporal	
	Individual	Group	Asynchronous	Synchronous
Web/Computer-Based Training	X		X	
Web/Electronic Performance Support Systems	X		X	
Web/Virtual Asynchronous Classrooms		X	X	
Web/Virtual Synchronous Classrooms		X		X

separate. In reality, there are many variations of these modes and many ways to use them in combination. Table 6.12 above highlights the key differences among the e-learning formats.

It is important to be aware that some e-learning formats are designed for learners working alone and other formats are best for group work. There is also a choice in selecting Web-based training programs that can be done at the learner's convenience asynchronously or programs that can be run at a set time for synchronous group learning. Instructional strategies are available for each e-learning format. The next chapter will provide you with the concepts and tools needed to design and document your training plan.

Suggested Readings

Bloom, B.S., Hastings, J.T., & Madams, G.F. (1971). *Handbook on formative and summative evaluation of student learning.* New York: McGraw-Hill.

Gagne, R.M. (1985). *Conditions for learning* (4th ed.). New York: Holt, Rinehart & Winston.

Gagne, R.M., Briggs, L.J., & Wagner, W.W. (1992). *Principles of instructional design.* Fort Worth, TX: Harcourt Brace.

Heinich, R., Molenda, M., & Russell, J. (1989). *Instructional media and the new technologies of instruction* (3rd ed.). New York: Macmillan.

Keegan, D. (1993). *Theoretical principles of distance education.* London: Routledge.

Kuilik, C., & Kuilik, J. (1986). Effectiveness of computer-based instruction in colleges. *AEDS Journal, 19,* 81–108.

Kuilik, C., & Kuilik, J. (1991). Effectiveness of computer-based instruction: An updated analysis. *Computers in Human Behavior, 7*(1 & 2), 75–94.

Kruse, K. (1999). *Technology-based training.* San Francisco: Jossey-Bass.

Lee, W.E., & Owens, D.L. (2000). *Multimedia-based instructional design: Computer-based training, Web-based training, and distance learning.* San Francisco: Jossey-Bass.

Mager, R.F. (1975). *Preparing instructional objectives.* Palo Alto, CA: Fearon.

Merrill, D. (1994). *Principles of instructional design.* Englewood Cliffs, NJ: Educational Technology Publications.

Moore, M.G., & Kearsley, G. (1996). *Distance education: A systems view.* Belmont, CA: Wadsworth.

Palloff, R.M., & Pratt, K. (1999). *Building learning communities in cyberspace: Effective strategies for the online classroom.* San Francisco: Jossey-Bass.

Tate, D., et al. (2001). Using Internet technology to deliver a behavioral weight-loss program. *Journal of the American Medical Association, 285,* 1172–1177.

Twitchell, D. (Eds.). (1991). *Robert M. Gagne and M. David Merrill—In conversation.* Englewood Cliffs, NJ: Educational Technology Publications.

Chapter 7

Designing Asynchronous Interactions

The title of this chapter, Designing Asynchronous Interactions, is challenging to decipher. "Asynchronous" in online learning terms refers to the delivery of training that is not presented in coordinated time, that is, asynchronous learning is taken at the learner's convenience. The facilitator and learners do not need to be online at the same time for the learning to take place. The term "interaction" refers to the give-and-take between the learner and the instructional medium. This chapter will look at the tools available to course developers who want to make programs for learners studying in asynchronous time.

The last chapter provided an overview of four distinct modes of Web-based training. Each mode has strengths and limitations, and there is clearly an optimal WBT mode for each goal in your program. In many cases you will want to use a blended solution, combining traditional face-to-face instruction with Web-based training as well as designing solutions that blend the four modes of Web-based training. Sorting out your options is easier if you understand the instructional tools (software applications) that are available for asynchronous and synchronous delivery.

This chapter provides an overview of activities and interactions that can take place in the asynchronous modes (Web/computer-based training, Web/EPSS, and Web/virtual asynchronous classroom).

What You Will Learn in This Chapter

After completing this chapter, you will be able to

- Distinguish among different types of interactivity;
- List examples of asynchronous interactions; and
- Design asynchronous assessments, tests, and quizzes.

Defining Interactivity

Interactivity is a term with a great deal of appeal to course developers and funders, but no agreed-on definition. Interactivity, as applied to Web-based training, is still an evolving concept. There are as many definitions as there are authors, as shown in the listing below:

- "Interaction: a cyclic process in which two actors alternately listen, think, and speak" (Crawford, 2000);
- "Interactivity refers to active learning, in which the learner acts on the information to transform it into new, personal meaning" (Campbell, 1999);
- "The ability to create a totally immersive experience" (Mok, 1996);
- "The ability to interact with words, numbers, and pictures" (Kristof & Satran, 1995); and
- "An instructional program which includes a variety of integrated sources in the instruction with a computer at the head of the systems" (Schwier & Misanchuk, 1993).

Given the variety of definitions, it is more useful for our purposes to identify the hallmarks of an interactive training program. Traditional interactive classroom programs and Web-based training programs have the ability to

- Encourage reflection;
- Provide control;
- Direct attention; and
- Add dimension to content.

Encourage Reflection. Traditional classroom programs encourage reflection by asking students to keep journals, critique the work of others, and consider alternative solutions. Web-based training programs can encourage learners to reflect on their experiences and question their assumptions. Plan a brainstorming session that requires learners to consider a wide range of solutions to a problem. Encourage learners to draw on their life experiences and not discount any possible solutions. Such interactions with course content and peers can create meaningful adult-learning experiences.

Provide Control. In traditional computer-based and classroom programs, learners have varying degrees of control. In simple CBT programs, learners may control the order in which they study the lessons. In traditional classroom programs, learners may control or influence the topics to be covered and how the class will be evaluated. Web-based training programs can offer learners a range of opportunities to control the learning experience. Therefore, develop interactions that enable learners to control the path, rate, and depth of content.

Direct Attention. Traditional classroom programs direct attention and motivate learners by making content relevant and meaningful. This strategy is also pertinent for Web-based training, but the tools available to the instructor are different. Create interactive programs that engage learners in topics that are important to them. Develop programs that are learner-centered rather than content-centered.

Add Dimension. In traditional classrooms, instructors add dimension to the topic by showing videos, inviting guest speakers, or taking field trips. The Web offers a range of tools to assist the instructor. Give learners opportunities to interact with multiple forms of media and to develop new perspectives.

Types of Interactions

Interactions make learning active rather than passive, and they provide learners and the instructor with feedback. It is important to develop a variety of interactions. Moore and Kearsley (1996) describe three kinds of interaction found in distance-education programs: learner-content interaction, learner-instructor interaction, and learner-learner interaction. Table 7.1 shows which types are associated with the various WBT methods.

All forms of Web-based training feature learner-content interactions, in which the learner is presented with material to study. This can be as simple as text to read, a video to watch, or a lecture.

Learner-learner interactions are communications among learners working asynchronously, as in W/EPS systems and W/VAC programs, or as part of a real-time

Table 7.1. Types of Interactions Associated with WBT Methods

	W/CBT	W/EPS	W/VAC	W/VSC
Learner with materials	X	X	X	X
Learner with learner		X	X	X
Learner with instructor	X		X	X

group in W/VAC programs. The interactions can be as simple as e-mail messages or postings to online discussion groups, or as complex as real-time audio-based conversations. Web/computer-based training does not use learner-to-learner interactions.

Learner-instructor interactions can include feedback on assignments, responses to questions, quizzes, suggestions, encouragement, and motivation. How this is accomplished depends on the type of Web-based training. In Web/CBT, interactions are usually e-mail exchanges between instructor and individual learner. In W/VAC and W/VSC programs, the interactions can be between individual learner and instructor or among groups of learners and the instructor. There is no learner-instructor interaction in W/EPS programs because, as the name suggests, it is an electronic performance support system designed to be used without an instructor.

Asynchronous Versus Synchronous Interactivity

It is important to remember that interactions can be synchronous or asynchronous. Synchronous interactions only happen in Web/VSC programs. They take place in real time, when the learners and instructor are online at the same time having direct contact. In contrast, asynchronous interactions take place at the learners' and instructor's convenience.

Other multimedia products, such as graphics, video, animation, and sound, can add richness to programs, but they do not add interaction. Simple text, graphics, images, animation, video, and sound meet only some of the criteria for interactive learning. They attract attention, but they are passive. A clever animation sequence or colorful graphics attracts the learners' attention, but does not engage them in making decisions or immerse them in the program. However, these elements can improve training programs when used in combination with asynchronous and synchronous interactions.

Asynchronous Options

An asynchronous interaction creates a reciprocal interchange between the learner and the instructional material, instructor, or other learners. Asynchronous interactions do not require the learners or instructor to be online at the same time. This section explores six kinds of asynchronous interactions: e-mail, discussion groups, community spaces, quizzes/tests, hypertext/media, and simulations.

Asynchronous interactions may result in both immediate and delayed feedback. Immediate feedback happens when programs automatically score quizzes or link the learner to documents. Learners may experience delay in learner-to-learner and learner-to-instructor feedback. These interactions require time for the instructor and other learners to respond to discussion group dialogue and e-mail messages.

E-Mail

Electronic mail enables learners to send messages over the Internet or intranet. Most e-learning software packages have e-mail built into the application. Having e-mail integrated means that learners can send e-mail while in the middle of a lesson; this means the learner can remain focused because he or she does not have to log out of the Web-based training program and log in to e-mail to send a message. E-mail is a powerful tool because it weaves instruction and feedback into the learner's daily routine of communication.

The advantages of e-mail can sometimes be overlooked because e-mail has becomes so ubiquitous, but it is a valuable exercise to think about the instructional possibilities and advantages. The most obvious advantage is that learners are familiar with e-mail and need little instruction. The low learning curve for e-mail is a real advantage because it enables the learners to focus on the content of lessons rather than on mastering tricky software. Like a private conversation, e-mail is an excellent way for the instructor and learner to communicate. This medium allows learners to ask questions that they might be too hesitant to ask if the entire class saw the question. The reverse is also true; a good question can also shared with others, if desired. See Figure 7.1 for some of the various possibilities.

In more complex e-mail interactions, an expert can reply to a question and the response can be shared with the entire class. For example, a learner may have a question that only an expert can answer. The learner can send an e-mail to the appropriate expert and copy his or her instructor (Figure 7.2). The instructor can also see a learner's question and the expert's reply, realize the answer is important

Figure 7.1. Possible E-Mail Interactions Between Instructor (I) and Learner (L)

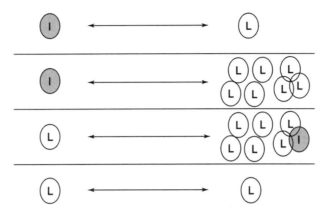

Figure 7.2. Example of an E-Mail Interaction with an Expert

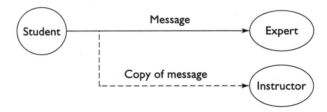

for all learners, and forward the reply to the entire class. Figure 7.3 shows the steps used in the process of sharing an expert's reply.

E-mail is an excellent tool for learners whose first language is not English because they can take whatever time they need to read and comprehend e-mail exchanges. E-mail does have two major disadvantages. First, learners must possess strong writing skills. Those who lack grammatical skill, spell badly, or cannot express themselves in writing are at a disadvantage. Exchanges can be rambling and hard to understand. Second, e-mail messages can be lost among learners' other e-mail correspondence from work, family, and interest groups. E-mail messages related to class can stack up, or worse, be stored and forgotten.

To address this issue, let learners know that e-mail should be used for items that require immediate attention or response. Establish expectations about how e-mail

Figure 7.3. Examples of E-Mail Interactions

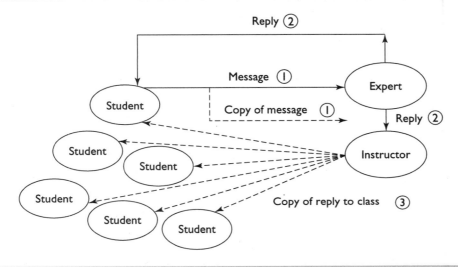

Figure 7.4. Checklist for E-Mail Usage

- ☑ Spelling and grammar.
- ☑ Response times.
- ☑ "Netiquette" rules.
- ☑ Message length.
- ☑ Type of interaction.
- ☑ Type of document.

should be used in the training program. See the checklist in Figure 7.4 above for some guidelines.

Spelling and Grammar. E-mail is often used as a quick, informal communication tool. If learners are responsible for using it in a more formal way, let them know that grammar and spelling are important.

Response Times. Set realistic expectations regarding how quickly e-mail messages will be answered. If instructors are traveling or teaching a traditional class, they may take several days to respond.

Netiquette Rules. Good manners on the Internet are not intuitive. Suggest that learners become familiar with netiquette (see Appendix F).

Message Length. Provide guidance regarding the length of messages and the kinds of information or questions that are appropriate for e-mail. Long e-mail messages are better posted to online bulletin boards or put into a directory and downloaded with file transfer protocol (FTP), which allows users to copy files to and from directories and to work around file size restrictions imposed by some e-mail systems.

Type of Interaction. Complicated questions can be sent to a subject-matter expert. Questions that require a broader response can be posted to members of a listserv. Questions that do not require an immediate answer or questions of general interest should be posted to an online forum.

Type of Document. E-mail can include more than text. Learners can e-mail sound, video, animation, and graphics files as an attachment to their messages (see Figure 7.5). Such attachments offer perspectives not possible with words alone.

Figure 7.5. Sample Attachments

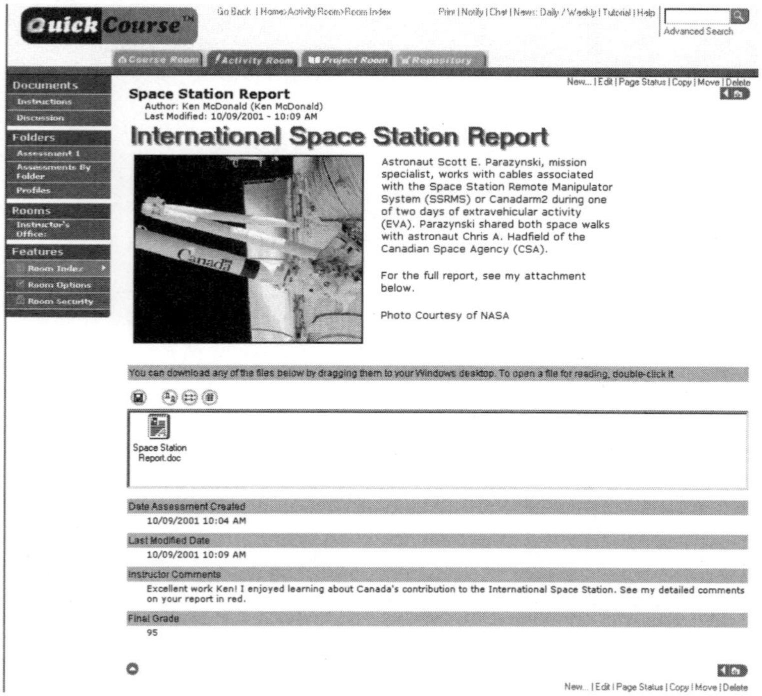

Source: QuickCourse by Collaorative Learning Network Inc.
www.Co-Learn.Net

Establish the kinds of files that are readable by the class, and be sensitive to the impact large files have on disk space and download times.

Discussion Groups and Community Spaces

In this section, discussion groups and community spaces are presented together because of their relationship. Discussion group software has been around a long time, and each generation of this software becomes better and more functional. An extension of discussion group software is a category of software called community space software. Community space software allows groups to do more than carry on a dialogue; it includes the ability to share documents, create a calendar, post photos, conduct polls, and other useful features. The asynchronous interactions and course design possibilities associated with this application can be created from within most e-learning software applications or it can be accessed via standalone applications that complement an e-learning program.

Discussion Groups

Talking about discussion group software is challenging because of the proliferation of applications for conducting online dialogues and the overlapping features among the different applications. In the last several years there has been a blurring of distinctions among online forums, bulletin boards, discussion groups, newsgroups, threaded discussion, and mailing lists. All of these applications serve a similar purpose: They provide a way for people to share information, ask questions, and provide answers. In the past, the distinctions among these applications were based on how the technology worked. In some cases applications required the user to go to the website in order to participate in the conversation; other applications automatically sent new postings to the user's e-mail account; and yet other applications provided a user with the ability to follow a single topic or thread within a discussion. Today these distinctions are blurred because the forums, bulletin boards, discussion groups, newsgroups, threaded discussion, and mailing lists have co-opted each other's features, making them hard to tell apart. In addition the usage of these terms is relatively lax.

In this book, the term "discussion group" refers to all variants of technology that enable group discussion. This technology can be found within e-learning software applications, that is, when you buy a product such as BlackBoard.com™ or LearningSpace™ discussion group capabilities are included. If the e-learning platform you are using does not provide these functions, it is possible to find applications that reside outside of your e-learning package to complement your program by providing these features.

Discussion groups are best suited for use with W/VAC and W/EPSS programs. The advantages and benefits of using discussion groups differ somewhat in W/VAC to W/EPSS learning platforms. In the case of the Web/virtual asynchronous class, using a discussion group can provide a sense of community and connectedness. Most W/VAC classes are conducted over the course of several weeks, and it is important to keep learners motivated and engaged. Discussion groups can be used to post questions related to the readings, the exercise, or the learners' experiences. In an active class, learners may receive postings every day or every few days. A dialogue centered on a reading or relevant topic can keep learners connected to the course and motivated to participate. Effective use of discussion groups is a factor that sets W/VAC programs apart from self-paced W/CBT programs.

Discussion groups are also useful as part of W/EPSS solutions. Although W/EPSS are generally designed to be used by an individual seeking performance support, discussion groups can be a valuable tool. Discussion groups can be used to create communities of practice. "A community of practice is a group of people who are are informally bound by what they do together—from engaging in lunchtime discussions to solving difficult problems—and by what they have learned through their mutual engagement in these activities. A community of practice is thus different from a community of interest or a geographical community, neither of which implies a shared practice" (Wenger, 1998).

Discussion groups are not without disadvantages. One of the biggest challenges is learning the application and figuring out how to join the group. Like e-mail, discussion groups are best suited for learners with good writing skills. Participating in an ongoing dialogue requires strong grammatical, spelling, and composition skills. The volume of messages generated by some discussion groups and the poor quality of responses can tire learners. If the discussion group lacks the ability to monitor topics or threads, conversations can become entwined. In a threadless discussion group, comments from one thread or topic can blend with another, causing confusion. It is also difficult to use the discussion group archive as a resource if the messages are not categorized. Figure 7.6 illustrates how threads provide organization for the dialogue.

There is also the challenge of keeping the conversation moving and on track. Discussion groups can be moderated or not. Either can be problematic. Highly moderated discussion groups stifle dialogue because learners feel edited. Moderating can also mean a great deal of work for the facilitator if he or she has to

Figure 7.6. Example of a Discussion Group with Threads

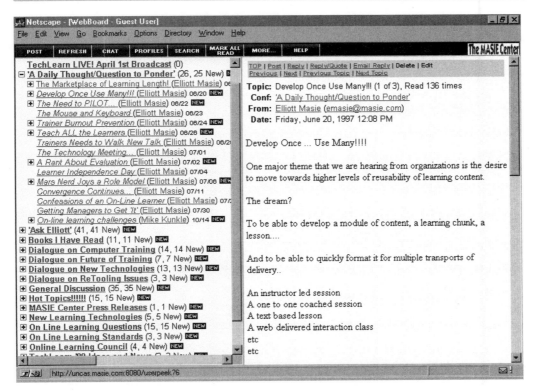

Credit: The Masie Center

approve all postings. The flip side is that discussion groups that are not moderated can become dominated by a few learners or fall into disuse because no one is responsible for keeping the conversation moving or on track.

Community Spaces

Community spaces take the concept of discussion groups and extend that concept by providing additional services. These services include the ability to post documents, share URLs, upload photos, review archives of the discussion group posting, annotate a group calendar, conduct polling, and access a directory of members. Community spaces are not exclusively designed for learning; rather, they support communities of interest. Examples of community spaces can be seen at Yahoo Groups and AOL. Like the features of a discussion group, the features of community spaces are built into many e-learning software applications such as WebCT™ and LearningSpace™. There are also products exclusively designed to provide community spaces, and they can be used to complement an e-learning program.

The initial advantage of a community space is its ability to provide an infrastructure for the community. Using features such as the calendar, a virtual daily bulletin, and broadcast messaging, a community space can provide a site at which learners can check in on the progress of class or gain a sense of how things operate.

Community spaces also encourage collaboration and interaction. The interaction and collaboration are delivered both actively and passively. Active participation takes place when learners go directly to the site and participate in the discussion group, post documents and photos, and share URLs. Passive participation is when messages, documents, and reminders are pushed to the learner's e-mail account.

These spaces can also be customized. Facilitators and learners can adjust the community space to their needs. The instructor is able to choose which features (calendar, polling, membership list) are enabled and can choose to moderate or not moderate the site. Learners can choose where and how they would like to receive postings, as well as defining which postings they wish to receive.

The disadvantage of community space applications is the complexity of the applications. The more features the community space software includes, the steeper the learning curve. There are also challenges related to community space applications that are not a part of an e-learning software application. If the community space is not built into the e-learning software application, the learners must move back and forth between two programs.

In short, use the interactive qualities of discussion groups and community spaces when you want to create an ongoing conversation and collaboration, and remember that many instructional design decisions must be made when using these applications to add interactivity to a Web-based training program. Figure 7.7 provides a checklist for some of them.

Figure 7.7. Checklist for Effective Discussion Groups and Community Space Usage

☑ Establish norms and standards.

☑ Determine whether to moderate.

☑ Determine who will be included.

☑ Decide whether to participate in a public discussion group.

☑ Determine whether to maintain after the class.

✓ Community Space Worksheet

Directions: The links below will take you to three places where you can access free community space applications. Choose one of these applications to create a community to complement a traditional or online course you are teaching. Use the questions below to reflect on the experience.

eRoom (www.eroom.com)

QuickPlace (www.lotus.com)

Topica (www.topica.com/)

Yahoo Groups (www.yahoo.com)

REFLECTION QUESTIONS

- How did the group use the community space? How might the space have been used differently?

- Who were the most active members of the community space? Why?

- Did activity in the community space increase, decrease, or stay the same after a face-to-face meeting?

- If people were hesitant to participate, what factors were barriers to participation?

- Would you use this kind of tool again? If yes, would you change anything? If not, why not?

Quizzes and Tests

Quizzes and tests are another type of asynchronous interaction. Online quizzes and tests enable the instructor and learners to assess progress or mastery of a topic. Designing online quizzes and assessments requires not only an understanding of how to design quizzes and tests but also an understanding of what is special about developing online quizzes and tests. Before looking at the issues related to designing test items, it is essential to understand the limitations and special considerations related to writing online assignments.

Technical Considerations for Developing Online Tests

How online tests and quizzes work is determined by the software package you use or by your ability to program. Unlike a paper-and-pencil test, in which you control every aspect of the experience and to which the learner brings a clear mental model regarding how to interact with the test, online tests are different. Each maker of quiz/test software has different ways of creating, organizing, delivering, and scoring tests. Before using all the bells or whistles, let's explore some of the common features that can influence the quality and effectiveness of your test or quiz.

Question Banks.   In some programs, there is an option to create question banks that list questions upon which the system draws to create tests. This can be a powerful feature if understood and used. Question banks can be created for each objective, for each course, or for each topic. In some cases, the questions in each bank can be rated from easy to difficult. The purpose of creating question banks is to provide learners with randomized tests, that is, not two learners receive the same test. This is a good idea in concept, but for it to be effective you must create and use the question banks in combination with principles of good test design. The question banks should present questions ranging from hard to easy, and like questions should be presented together and not all jumbled up. The use of question banks assumes that the course developer will create many more questions than the learner will see and that the same objective has multiple questions of equal difficulty.

Timing.   Testing software is getting more sophisticated. One of the features it offers is the ability to have a timed test. Ask yourself whether you really need a timed test. Does the evaluation suffer if learners fail to complete the test in a given period of time? There may be cases in which you want to give a timed test; if so, consider how a timed test is presented. There are a number of options for letting the student know how much time remains, such as a countdown clock on the screen, a time bar that diminishes, or auditory tones indicating the halfway point and three minutes remaining. If this is an important option, understand how the application works before you buy it.

Rich Media Questions.   The benefits of multimedia do not end with the presentation of content. Tests can also use rich media such as video, audio, and animation to show a scenario and ask the learners about what they observed. When using rich media in a test item, be sure the learner has the ability to replay these rich media elements as often as needed.

Submitting.   When completing a traditional test or quiz, the learner can complete the items he or she knows and then return to items not answered during the first pass. Not all software packages are created equally, so check out the options. Some packages present the questions one at a time and the learner must answer the question to move to the next item. Other packages put all the questions on a single page and the learners must scroll up and down a long page. The single-sheet test program can sometimes be tricky because the learner must locate and press the submit button, after scrolling up and down responding to questions.

Scrolling.   Scrolling is the process of moving the page up and down within the browser window. There will be times when scrolling is unavoidable, but in general it should be eliminated during testing because it adds to the learner's cognitive burden. Scrolling requires the learner to look away from the test item to move the screen, thus breaking concentration. When writing single test items, try to keep them on a single screen and eliminate scrolling.

Mixing Question Types.   Good online testing software offers you a large number of item types and ways to lay out an item, including options for responding, such as buttons, pull-down menus, and drag-and-drop targets. These options are fine, but keep cognitive burden to a minimum by using groups of like items. Cognitive burden is reduced if the learner does not have to shift gears every other question.

Feedback.   Testing software often doubles as software for creating practice exercises. In a practice exercise, you want the ability to give immediate feedback; not so in testing. A test is designed to assess the learner's mastery. The test should not be giving feedback for each item. Rather, the test should provide a final score and the ability for the learners to review the items and to receive feedback on what they had correct or incorrect.

Designing Tests for Adult Learners

Design quizzes and tests that demonstrate respect for adult learners. As you probably know from your own experience, tests can make adults feel anxious and stressed. Show respect for learners. Clearly explain the purpose for testing. State that test scores are intended to help the learner assess progress; that they will not be shared with managers; or that test scores are recorded anonymously and only class averages will be available to department heads.

In addition, provide feedback on tests quickly, and make the feedback positive and respectful. Use automatic scoring mechanisms to furnish immediate scores, and include a rationale of the test items that explains the right answers. Make feedback positive, identify the items learners scored high on, and provide the correct answers for incorrect items. Avoid using sound effects such as buzzers or cheering crowds as feedback. Give learners an unlimited amount of time to complete the test, unless time is a factor in assessing competence.

A consultant talks about the challenges of convincing a development team to rethink the tone of their program

I was asked to review the first couple of modules of a Web-based training program for a fast-growing manufacturing company. The corporate culture was young, confident, Web-savvy, and a little flippant. The development team was comprised of technically sophisticated trainers, subject-matter experts, and course developers. The program was technically outstanding—great graphics, wonderful tracking, and an easy-to-use interface. Despite the technical strengths of the program, the most noticeable characteristic was the tone. The program was sarcastic and patronizing of others. The tone was sarcastic when it reported out the learners' test scores. Learners who scored 0 to 30 on a quiz were told to "look for a new career." It was patronizing in an exercise when a box popped up that read "Come on, you can do it."

We talked about the intended audience and how these kinds of things might make those learners feel. The group said they liked learning from programs with this kind of feedback; it was funny. We talked more about how the intended audience would like attending an onsite class that was delivered with sarcastic feedback and patronizing support. The trainers were the first to acknowledge that it would not be a good idea. After more consideration and with some reluctance, the team modified the tone.

Several test formats can be used to add interactivity to asynchronous Web-based training. Table 7.2 shows some of the test variations and the advantages and disadvantages of each.

True/False Questions

True/false and yes/no answers are best for testing simple recall, sequences, or patterns. There are several advantages to using true/false in a WBT program. Questions are easy to develop; the answers can be scored by the system; and learners can receive immediate feedback on their performance. Learners can also obtain a detailed explanation of why an answer is right or wrong. In addition, learners understand how to take true/false tests, so the directions can be brief.

Table 7.2. Assessment Options for Web-Based Training

Format	Variation	Advantages	Disadvantages
True/False	Yes/No	Relatively easy to • construct • correct • administer	Guessing Not reliable indicator of depth of knowledge
Multiple Choice	Fill in the blank Matching column Drag and drop	Relatively easy to • construct • correct • administer	Not reliable indicator of depth of knowledge Choices may be too close in meaning Difficult to write plausible choices
Essay	Short answer Long answer	Relatively easy to • construct • administer Good indicator of depth of knowledge	Correction is subjective Penalizes weak writers Requires SME to correct
Application/ Job Task	InterConstructive	Measures job proficiency Good indicator of depth of knowledge	Time-consuming to • construct • complete • correct

The same disadvantages that apply to the use of true/false tests in a classroom are relevant for their use in Web-based training. A learner can answer many questions right by guessing. The depth of knowledge that can be tested by true/false questions is limited. They should be reserved for testing recall of simple knowledge or for assessing knowledge and concepts. The following section provides guidelines for developing test questions.

Provide Clear Directions.   Explain how learners are to indicate true or false. Figure 7.8 shows a click box, but other variations could include typing the words, selecting a pull-down menu item, or turning on radio buttons.

Make Statements Simple.   The statement (what learners are asked to evaluate as true or false) must be clear. Avoid asking about multiple items, some of which are true and some not. The question below is poorly designed.

____True   ____False   Computer input devices are keyboards, scanners, and printers.

Figure 7.8.   Directions Clarify How to Respond

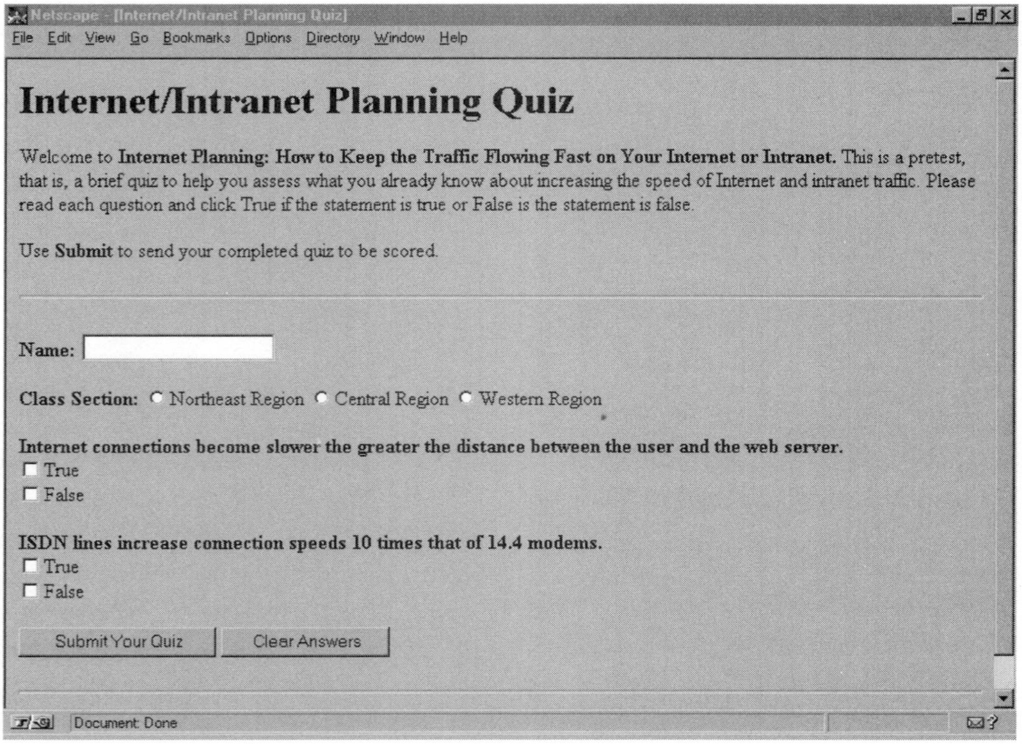

Asking learners to evaluate a single item requires that the learner evaluate each item as true or false. The learner is penalized because, even if the learner knows two of the three items, he or she will still be awarded no credit for the answer. The question below is a better test item because it tests for a single fact.

——True ——False   A keyboard is a computer input device.

Ask Questions in Logical Sequence. Ask questions in the order in which the content was presented in the lesson. Learners recall information better in a sequence similar to how it was learned.

Use Terminology from the Lesson. Use the same terminology in the quiz that was used in the lesson to avoid confusion. For example, if the lesson consistently used the term "Internet service provider," do not use the acronym "ISP."

Test Breadth of the Lesson. The quiz or test should assess the entire lesson; that is, test all the content you teach.

Allow Learners to Review Their Answers. Demonstrate respect for learners and be conscious of test anxiety. Allow learners to review their answers and change them, if necessary, before submitting them.

Provide Respectful and Meaningful Feedback. A score tells learners little. Develop feedback that provides more than the percentage right or wrong. Let learners know which answers were incorrect and why. Be respectful; proof any comments to guard against sarcasm.

Multiple Choice

Multiple-choice tests can take a number of forms, such as drag and drop, matching columns, and fill in the blank. These assessments are best for testing simple recall and for applying abstract concepts to a particular situation.

The advantage of multiple-choice tests is their ease of design and administration. It is relatively easy to develop questions that test learners' recall or to diagnose what learners have misunderstood. Like true/false tests, multiple-choice tests are a familiar format for learners, and the scoring and feedback can be done with a computer program.

The depth of knowledge indicated by a multiple-choice test is limited. Like true/false tests, these tests are best for assessing simple recall. The biggest challenge is in designing answers that are distinctive and plausible. Possible answers should not be too similar; each should be unique and meaningful, not silly. It is often difficult to come up with four wrong answers that are plausible. The easier it is to eliminate possible answers, the easier it is for learners to guess the right answer. The following section discuses considerations for creating Web-based multiple-choice tests.

Provide Directions.   Because multiple-choice tests can take many forms, such as drag and drop, pull-down menus, radio buttons, and click boxes, explain to learners how to indicate their answers (i.e., click, pull down, drag).

Put All Repeated Words into a Stem.   Write clear and easy-to-understand stem statements. If possible, start with words like where, when, and what, which make clear the kind of answer you are seeking. Reduce cognitive loading, the amount of information that learners must keep in their heads. Put repeated words in the stem and not in the answer. Compare the samples of poorly written and well-written multiple-choice questions below to see the effect of cognitive loading.

> Sample of a poorly written multiple-choice question:
> 1. Cyberbrand multimedia development tools
>   (a) enable designers to develop cross-platform applications
>   (b) enable designers to repurpose existing CD-ROM content
>   (c) enable designers to reduce disk pressing times
>   (d) enable designers to integrate legacy files

> Sample of a well-written multiple-choice question:
> 1. Cyberbrand multimedia development tools enable designers to
>   (a) develop cross-platform applications
>   (b) repurpose existing CD-ROM content
>   (c) reduce disk pressing times
>   (d) integrate legacy files

Test One Idea Per Question.   Develop test items that assess a single idea and avoid complex multi-faceted stems. Let's look at an example of a needlessly complex stem.

> "_____ is the network protocol used to _____."

The question shown above is confusing, it asks for two pieces of information, and it may not accurately assess what the learner knows. A better stem statement is shown below:

> "TCP/IP is the network protocol used to _____."

Use a Logical Sequence for Answers.   List answers in a logical sequence, such as numerical, alphabetical, or temporal. For example, list modem speed choices from lowest to highest. The following example shows how much easier it is to review the answers when they are presented in a logical sequence:

Poor Sequence	*Good Sequence*
3600	1200
9600	2400
2400	3600
1200	9600

Create Plausible Alternatives.   All answers should be plausible. When possible, create one correct and four incorrect answers. Learners' performance is more accurately measured when none of the answers can be eliminated because they are absurd. Review the following poor and good answers to see how many answers you can eliminate, even if you know nothing about backing up a production server:

How often should a production server be backed up?

Poor Answers	*Good Answers*
Once in a lifetime	Daily
Whenever you have time	Bi-weekly
Once a month	Weekly
Once a day	Monthly
After a disaster	Quarterly

Avoid "All" or "None."   There is little value in using "all of the above" or "none of the above." Learners who identify a single right or wrong answer can eliminate those alternatives. Using both items in the same list indicates that one of the answers is a throwaway and improves the odds for guessing.

Create Only One Answer Per Question.   Avoid creating items that have several right answers or questions that require learners to choose the best answer from several that are correct. In multiple-choice tests, learners do not have an opportunity to explain why they chose an answer. Without understanding the learner's rationale for choosing an answer, it is difficult to objectively assess his or her understanding.

Provide No Clues Inadvertently.   Review multiple-choice tests to identify any inadvertent clues you may have included, such as stem statements or answers that provide information that can be used to answer questions elsewhere in the test. Let me show you an example:

1. In 1975 Bill Gates and Paul Allen founded what company?
   IBM
   Compaq
   Gateway
   Microsoft
   Dell

2. Microsoft, the world's largest software company, was founded in what year?
   1970
   1972
   1975
   1978
   1979

Demonstrate Respect for the Learner.   Always demonstrate respect for learners. Provide scoring information that offers more than a score. Craft feedback that explains why an answer was not correct and provide recommendations for finding additional information. Deliver feedback in a tone and format that will not diminish the learners or make them feel bad.

Essay

Essay questions merely ask a question and provide directions for answering it. (See the sample in Figure 7.9.) Essays are powerful assessment tools and should be used only after careful consideration and design.

Essay questions can ask for short or long answers. The advantage of these questions is that essays allow learners to demonstrate a greater depth of knowledge than true/false or multiple-choice questions. Essay questions are easy to write, and the format is familiar to most learners.

The disadvantage of essay questions is the amount of work required to correct them. Answers cannot be machine scored, and automated feedback is not possible. A subject-matter expert capable of providing an objective evaluation must correct responses. The value of this kind of interaction is based on the feedback that results. Essay tests may penalize weak writers. If a learner is not able to write well enough to respond to an essay, the exam may not provide a true measure of what he or she knows. Because of the labor-intensive nature of essay tests, carefully craft the questions. This section provided guidance for developing essay questions.

Using Online Quiz Building Applications Worksheet

Directions: Use the URLs below to find applications for writing online tests and quizzes. Many of the URLs are K-12 oriented because these sites are free and easily accessible. Build the same quiz using two or more programs. Ask a friend or colleague to take the test and to give you feedback on his or her experience taking the test. Use the questions below to reflect on your experience.

DiscoverSchool.com (http://school.discovery.com/quizcenter/quizcenter.html)

FunBrain, Quiz Lab (www.funbrain.com/)

Kelly's Multiple-Choice HTML Quiz Generator (www.aitech.ac.jp/~iteslj/quizzes/help/write-mc.html)

Quia (www.quia.com/)

Quiz Factory (www.ianr.unl.edu/ianr/cit/quizzes/quizfactory.html)

Test.com (www.test.com/)

Zoomerang (www.zoomerang.com/)
This is survey software, but the idea of multiple choice is similar. Zoomerang offers a Level I course evaluation form.

E.L. Easton (http://eleaston.com/quizzes.html)
Meta Site for quiz links

Link Finder: If these sites are no longer reachable, try the following terms in different combinations: test, quiz, assessment, online learning, e-learning, Web-based training, survey, true, false, and multiple choice.

REFLECTION QUESTIONS

- What assumptions were designed into the test-building applications?

- How did building an online test differ from building a paper-and-pencil test?

- What did friends and colleagues experience when taking the test?

- What would you do differently in the future?

Figure 7.9. Sample Essay-Based Question

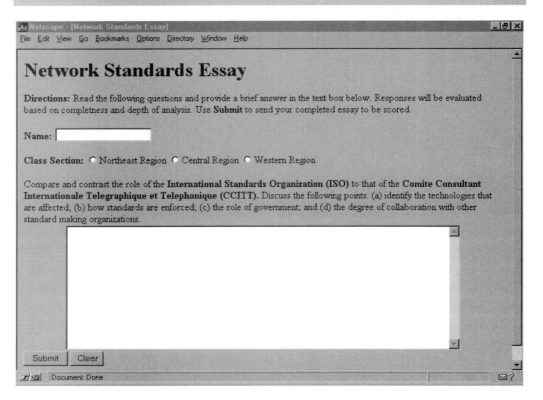

Provide Explicit Directions.   Make it clear what you expect from learners. Let them know what you want them to compare, contrast, identify, discuss, relate, or evaluate. The more detailed the directions, the more succinct and focused the answers will be. Indicate whether spelling, grammar, and composition are to be evaluated.

Encourage Learners to Respond to Long Essays with Alternative Tools.   Short answers (no more than one screen in length) can be solicited online, using the browser's text editor. If the essay is longer and the learner needs to work on it over a period of time, provide alternatives such as an e-mail address to send a word-processing file or a directory where learners can store responses.

Test Everything Being Taught.   Test the entire breadth of the course to determine learners' mastery of content. Essay questions should be broad enough to require learners to integrate all of the course content or there should be enough short-answer questions to sample the entire course.

Identify Subject-Matter Experts.   Essay tests are time-consuming to correct and require individualized feedback. If the course developer or facilitator is not a content expert, identify subject-matter experts and confirm that they will have time to correct tests. Ensure that evaluators share an objective standard for assessment. Create an answer key that outlines what should be included.

Plan Respectful and Timely Feedback.   Provide guidelines for responding in a respectful manner. Recommend turnaround time on exams (e.g., three working days), and suggest that feedback be informative. For example, an evaluator should suggest additional readings, videotapes, or Web-based training programs that will help the learner understand what he or she is missing.

Application/Job-Task Assessment

The last type of test is an application or job-task assessment. This is a form of performance-based testing that requires learners to exhibit the skills they learned in class by performing them on the job or on a task that mimics the job. There are many permutations of this kind of assessment, ranging from simple to complex. A complex example would be to ask programmers to create and post a Java applet to the class website. This is called "InterConstructive" testing. The Web is used as a repository, showcase, or arena for real-world testing or piloting. For example, a group of learners studying corporate communication can develop a "zine" (Web magazine) to demonstrate their ability to communicate with employees. Trainers learning to develop WBT programs can publish sample WBT modules on the Web.

Job-task assessment interactions are an effective way to test how well learners have integrated new skills and knowledge. The tasks should be closely related to the skills and knowledge required on the job in order to assess learners' depth of knowledge.

For traditional site-based training, an instructor can observe learners on the shop floor or at their terminals. In Web-based training, the assessment is limited to tasks that can be completed using the Internet or intranet. Because of the complex nature of the skills and knowledge being assessed, the tasks are often time-consuming to complete. Like the correction of essay questions, the evaluation of job-task performance is labor intensive. However, application tests can provide great value.

Use Only for Performance-Based Testing.   Not every WBT program is a candidate for job-task assessment. For example, it would not be an adequate way to determine whether a manager were able to conduct a performance review. Apply this kind of assessment only to skills and knowledge that can be demonstrated by using an application and sending a file. Consider blended solutions that rely on traditional on-the-job assessments for assessing other performance-based skills. In the case of assessing a manager's ability to conduct a performance review, the learner's manager may be asked to observe using a checklist outlining what he or she is looking for and providing room for comments.

Provide Detailed Directions.   Explain how you expect the learner to demonstrate mastery of the content. Describe the behavior accurately; use terms such as create, modify, incorporate, assess, compute, and diagnose. Inform learners of any special testing conditions, such as ability to refer to a textbook, use a diagnostic program, or work alone. Set performance expectations, that is, the degree of mastery expected (no errors, within ±5 percent, or free from spelling or grammatical errors).

Provide Adequate Time.   Application- and job-task-based assessment takes more time than true/false and multiple-choice tests. Allow learners adequate time to work on the task. If possible, suggest how much time it should take to complete the project. Some learners will wait until the last minute and not allow themselves enough time, and others will exceed what is expected.

Ask Subject-Matter Experts to Evaluate.   Identify subject-matter experts (SMEs) who are competent to evaluate projects.

Determine Criteria for Evaluation.   Provide detailed criteria to help the SMEs deliver objective and consistent feedback. Set expectations with evaluators for providing feedback. Brief comments like "well done" and "nice work" do not provide much value. Ask the evaluator to comment specifically on which aspects of the assessment were done well. In addition, ask SMEs to point out what could have been done better.

Develop Meaningful and Respectful Feedback.   Demonstrate that you appreciate learner efforts by providing adequate feedback. Suggest that SMEs explain the rationale for their comments and, when possible, direct learners to additional materials. Even learners who demonstrate a clear understanding of a task should be directed to more advanced or challenging readings, courses, or software.

Hypertext/Media

There is little agreement on the definition of hypermedia. In simplest terms, it is a product that connects media (text, audio, graphics, video, and animation) in a nonlinear manner. The terms "hypermedia" and "hypertext" are often used interchangeably. Hypermedia is used here because it more accurately describes the applications in Web-based training. It is a powerful tool that offers many opportunities for interaction, but also has the potential to confuse learners.

Hypermedia allows learners to control the pace, sequence, and depth of content. Learners choose what topics to examine and in what order. For example, learners can choose to review the introductory material quickly and then slow their pace to read a description or watch a narrated animation. Because the path through the content is not linear, each learner's path is unique. The unique path created by a learner is easier to remember because it is closer to the links in human memory. Hypermedia also creates links to rich resources within the organization's intranet and external links on the Internet.

The biggest problem with hypermedia is being "lost in hyperspace." Learners may get lost in complex hypermedia webs. Learners may find it difficult to orient themselves and may not be able to find their way back to the Web-based training. The second disadvantage is the unpredictable nature of how readers link to hypermedia elements. If essential information is located in a hypermedia link that is not selected, the learner will not master the objectives in that lesson. There is also a high degree of maintenance associated with links, especially external ones, because instructors have no control over when the information changes. Instructors cannot keep external websites current or guarantee that they will be available. Maintaining links on an intranet is also a problem when other groups own them and are responsible for keeping the information current.

Figure 7.10 is an example of a course that uses hypermedia to navigate among modules. The bulleted items in the left frame are hyperlinks. The right frame shows the first page of the Welcome module. The icons and text in the right panel provide hypermedia links to a page listing the objectives, a page displaying schematics, and a video discussing product features. Icons show the learner what type of media each page contains.

Hypermedia is a valuable interactive product that offers instructors many opportunities to engage learners with layers of information. This section provides guidelines and a checklist (Figure 7.11) for developing hypermedia interactions.

Figure 7.10.   Sample Hypermedia Interaction

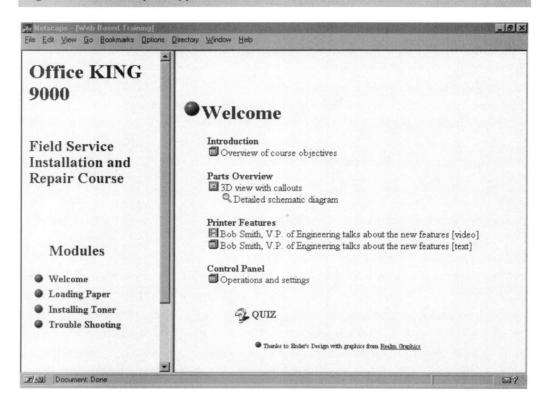

Figure 7.11.   Checklist for Designing Hypermedia Interactions

☑ Target and profile the audience.

☑ Educate users about hypermedia.

☑ Collect information and establish links.

☑ Develop hypermedia and pilot the product.

☑ Keep design simple.

Target and Profile the Audience. Determine how skilled the potential learners are in managing their learning in a nonlinear environment. Find out how familiar they are with navigating hypermedia during the analysis phase. Ask questions such as: Do they know what a hypertext link looks like? and Do they know how to use a link and how to return to the WBT program after following a series of links?

Educate Users About Hypermedia. If they are not skilled, provide a section in the training program that explains how to use links and what kind of information they can access via the links. For example, is hypermedia used as a way to navigate the program or is it used to provide enrichment material?

Collect Information and Establish Links. If a Web-based training program is organized by objectives, design the hypermedia to educate, providing links that are related to the objectives. Do not abdicate responsibility to learners by asking them to figure out which links are essential and which are merely nice to know.

Develop Hypermedia and Pilot the Product. It is the developer's responsibility to create links between different pieces of course content. Links are established using a two-step process. First, create links based on the experience of the developer or subject-matter expert. Then test the links with the target audience, when possible in collaboration with potential learners and their managers. Check the effectiveness of links and pilot a sample section of the program. Get feedback from the target audience to assess whether they understand the connections. Identify links that learners expect and add them if they are missing.

Keep Design Simple. Keep the design of hypermedia links simple. Put essential content in the body of the lesson; use hypermedia to provide enrichment or background information. Link information in logical groupings. Make the hypermedia structure clear to learners. When using icons or text clues, be consistent. Throughout the program, use the same symbol to represent help or indicate when an image is available, and use fonts and indents to suggest levels of detail. If hypermedia links take learners outside the Web-based training program, warn them that they are leaving the program and tell them how to get back. Figure 7.12 shows a simple linking model in which the learner moves back and forth between the lesson and the supporting hypermedia.

Figure 7.13 shows a more complex linking diagram. In this model, the learner moves back and forth between the lesson and the supporting hypermedia and among multiple links. With such complexity, the instructor should ensure that the learners do not become lost in hyperspace. Use navigation maps or color queuing

Figure 7.12.   Sample Simple Hypermedia Links

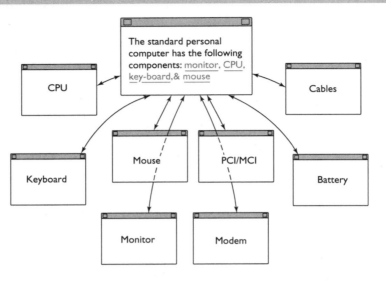

Figure 7.13.   Sample Complex Hypermedia Links

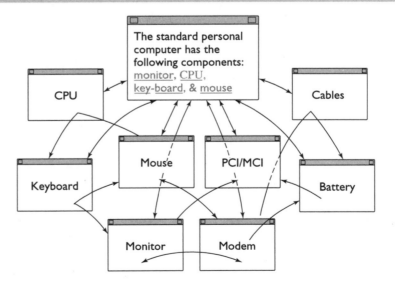

to help learners stay oriented. For example, create a colored button for each module in a course and use the color as a way to remind learners what lesson they are in. Figure 7.14 is an example of a navigation map that provides learners with information about the elements in the Periodic Table. Learners click on an element to navigate to a page with more information.

Simulations

Web-based training programs using simulations offer dramatic alternatives to page turners. Simulations are a means of motivating students working alone or working in groups. Simulations put learners in a setting and require them to apply new knowledge or skill. Outstanding examples of these kind of programs can be found in continuing professional education, commercial courses, and higher education. Complete the following exercise to gain a better understanding of the range of simulations available for Web-based training.

Figure 7.14. Sample Navigation Map

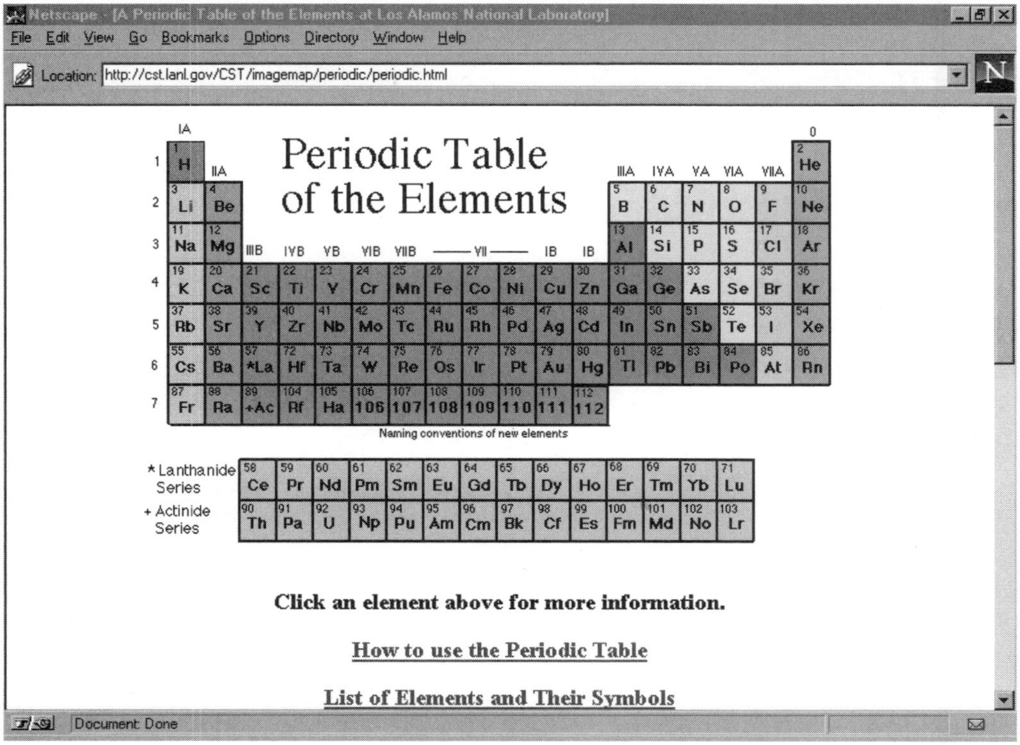

Simulations in Action Worksheet

Directions: The following examples demonstrate the range of production values, complexity, and the topics for which simulations can be used. Try one simulation from each category and reflect on the experince by using the questions below.

Continuing/Professional Education

MBAgames (www.mbagames.com/)
This site teaches management skills and strategies in a Web-enabled simulation, allowing teams or individuals to learn while engaging in scenario-based games.

The Doctor's Dilemma (http://imc.gsm.com/siteinfo/browse_sitemap.htm)
Ethics Education

Commercial Courses

SMGnet (http://www3.smginc.com/smgnet/simulation/)
SMGnet has developed a Java-based simulation allowing learners to experiment with running a business.

Soft Skills (www.skillsoft.com/)
Scenario-based learning for customer service, communications, and leadership skills.

K-12 and Higher Education

Geology Labs Online: Virtual Earthquake (http://vcourseware3.calstatela.edu/VirtualEarthquake/VQuakeIntro.html)
This interactive program helps students understand how the epicenters of earthquakes are located from seismograms and how their Richter magnitudes are determined.

InvestSmart Market Simulation (http://library.thinkquest.org/10326/market_simulation/index.html)
An educational stock and mutual fund simulation that uses real stock and mutual fund delayed quotes from the major U.S. exchanges such as NYSE, AMEX, and NASDAQ. All services are free to users.

Link Finder: If these sites are no longer reachable, try the following terms in different combinations: simulation, e-learning, elearning, online learning, java calculator, Web-based training, scenario based learning.

REFLECTION QUESTIONS

- Which simulations did you find most engaging? Why?

- How do simulations differ from other kinds of asynchronous interactions?

- Does the production value of "glitz" factor make a difference?

- How easy would it be to transfer the skills or apply your new knowledge to the real world?

After sampling some of these award-winning programs, the advantages of simulations are easy to understand. These programs force learners to select, organize, and integrate knowledge, and this results in greater motivation and enhanced transfer of learning. Unlike page turners, which require highly self-directed students who are ready to learn, simulations provide a means of motivating students by making them open and receptive to new information.

Other advantages include the ability to provide a substitute for access to difficult or hazardous environments. Consider the benefits that airlines enjoy through the use of flight simulators to train pilots. It is far safer and more cost-effective to use simulations than to use real planes. Simulations also offer the ability to overcome practical difficulties such as expense of materials, scale of experiment, and time scale. There are a number of scientific simulations, such as the Virtual Earthquake, or epidemiological studies that would not be practical in real life. These simulations provide large numbers of learners with experiences that would otherwise be too expensive or time-consuming. Other simulations offer the ability to introduce simplified concepts prior to developing complexity. Consider the advantages of using an online program to teach simple concepts related to gravity before attempting to teach more complex physics concepts. Simulations also promote an intuitive understanding of systems, through greater knowledge of how different factors interact. SMGnet has developed a simulation allowing learners to experiment with running a business and to observe how factors interact.

The disadvantages of simulations can be the cost, time, and level of creativity needed to develop simulations. The exercise above should have given you a sense of the range of production values (cost, time, money) of three simulations. Another risk of simulations is over-simplification. While it may be easier to build a simple simulation, it may not deliver meaningful results if the simulation fails to convey the complexity of a situation.

Summary

Asynchronous learning is often considered a poor cousin when compared to the glamorous, and highly technical, synchronous learning. This perception need not be the case if asynchronous interactions are well-designed. The power of asynchronous interactions is most clearly demonstrated when designing Web/virtual asynchronous classes. As we have seen in this chapter, group learning in the asynchronous mode offers benefits not possible in the time-constrained synchronous delivery mode. For example, in W/VAC programs that take place over the course of weeks or months, learners have the opportunity to reflect on what they are reading and experiencing by using interactions such as e-mail, discussion groups, and community spaces. They also have the opportunity to collaborate with others. And finally, many of the applications used for group learning become part of the learner's everyday set of tools for working on other virtual teams.

On the other hand, asynchronous interactions also offer robust design options for programs geared to the individual learners. Using the applications described in this chapter, W/EPSS and W/CBT users will be more engaged and connected. The power and reach of W/EPSS programs can be extended by using discussion groups and community spaces that foster communities of practice. These tools allow users to interact with experts, novices, and colleagues to create knowledge and to solve problems. A W/CBT program in which a learner works alone at his or her own pace can also benefit from asynchronous interactions that engage the learner with the materials and the instructor. Simple applications like e-mail can provide the support needed to get through a difficult lesson or the encouragement needed to complete an assignment. More complex tools such as quizzes, hypermedia, and simulations can add richness to the lesson.

In summary, the optimal use of these interactions requires an understanding of what you want to accomplish, knowledge of the possibilities of the asynchronous applications, and attention to the best design practices illustrated in this chapter.

Now let's move on to a discussion of synchronous interactions in the next chapter.

Suggested Readings

Campbell, K. (1999). *The web: Design for active learning.* [Online] Available: www.atl.ualberta.ca/articles/idesign/activel.cfm

Crawford, C. (2000). *Understanding interactivity.* [Online] Available: www.erasmatazz.com/book.html

Horton, W.K. (1990). *Designing and writing online documentation: Help files to hypertext.* New York: John Wiley & Sons.

Jategaonkar, V.A., & Babu, A.J. (1995). Interactive multimedia instructional systems: A conceptual framework. *Journal of Instruction Delivery Systems, 9*(4), 24–29.

Kenny, R.F. (1995). Interactive multimedia instruction to develop reflective decision-making among preservice teachers. *Journal of Technology and Teacher Education, 3*(2), 169–188.

Kristof, R., & Satran, A. (1995). *Interactivity by design: Creating & communicating with new media.* San Francisco: Hayden Books.

Malatesta, G. (2001). *Conformity rules in cyberspace.* [Online] Available: www.theaustralian.news.com.au/printpage/0,5942,2651185,00.html

Mok, C. (1996). *Designing business: Multiple media, multiple disciplines.* New York: Macmillan.

Parcel, B. (1997). *Testing 1, 2, 3.* Unpublished manuscript. Boston, MA: Boston University, School of Education.

Park, I., & Hannafin, M.J. (1993). Empirically based guidelines for the design of interactive multimedia. *Educational Technology, Research and Development, 41*(3), 63–85.

Schmucker, C. (1999). *A taxonomy of simulation software.* [Online] Available: www.apple.com/education/LTReview/spring99/simulation/

Schwier, R.A., & Misanchuk, E.R. (1993). *Interactive multimedia instruction.* Englewood Cliffs, NJ: Educational Technology Publications.

Wenger, E. (1998). *Communities of practice: Learning as a social system.* [Online] Available: www.co-i-l.com/coil/knowledge-garden/cop/lss.shtml

Wenger, E. (2001). *Supporting communities of practice: A survey of community oriented technologies.* [Online] Available: www.ewegner.com

Chapter 8

Designing Synchronous Interactions

When most people think of online learning, what usually comes to mind is the image popularized in television commercials and in movies. The popular images depict a learner dressed in pajamas and slippers participating in a live class from home or a group of grade school students interacting with an astronaut teaching a physics lesson from the Space Station. These images of synchronous learning have raised the bar regarding what people expect of the live synchronous classroom. These images, as superficial as they may seem, have provided decision makers, learners, and facilitators with models for how this type of learning works.

This chapter looks at the interactions that are possible in the synchronous classroom. It is important to understand the range of synchronous interactions, from simple real-time chat (where learners type back and forth) to sophisticated videoconferences where learners see one another and carry on a dialogue. Both synchronous and asynchronous applications have the potential to change how training is delivered. These technologies make it feasible to create new ways to deliver peer-to-peer collaboration, simulations, and coaching. In many cases, teaching strategies are literally transferred from the classroom to the Web. As you consider the synchronous applications, think about how these tools could change or extend your training programs though a pure Web-based synchronous delivery (W/VSC) or a blended solution.

What You Will Learn in This Chapter

After completing this chapter, you will be able to

- List the benefits of W/VSC programs;
- Define four kinds of synchronous interactions;
- Explain the advantages of each; and
- Integrate synchronous interactions into Web/VSC programs.

Web/synchronous virtual classroom programs are the most technically complex type of Web-based training to implement and maintain. Generally, the tools used to create and deliver them require computers with newer processors, dedicated servers, robust bandwidth, and adequate technical staff to support developers and end users. Observing a W/VSC program can be a challenge because it requires you to seek out a demonstration or real class being offered at a fixed time. It is not possible to judge the benefits of W/VSC by looking at a recorded session. With a recording, you cannot assess the value of students interacting in real time, asking questions and providing feedback, and it is hard to judge the synergy of sharing a whiteboard to develop a solution and the benefits of an impromptu debate.

Web/Virtual Synchronous Classroom Programs

Synchronous interactions are only possible when instructor and learners are working together in real time. It requires a set of tools that enable learners to see, hear, and/or share applications across the Internet. Because there is a great deal of overlap in what learners are able to accomplish in Web-based asynchronous (W/VAC) and Web-based synchronous (W/VSC) interactions, the following section points out the unique benefits and limitations of W/VSC. Then we will examine the tools and interactions possible in the synchronous environment.

Benefits

Live Group Learning and Immediate Feedback.   The opportunities for live group learning and the immediacy of feedback are unique strengths of the Web/virtual synchronous classroom. The ability to bring a group of learners together for discussions, brainstorming, case-study analysis, debates, and project work in real time is only possible in this form of Web-based training. W/VSC programs allow immediate feedback on ideas, extension of suggestions, and building of consensus. Real-time interactions reveal the tone and personality of learners and create a greater sense of presence. Learners become part of a community, complete with norms and netiquette.

Just-in-Time Development (JIT). The JIT development and delivery capabilities of W/VSC are ideal for providing skills and knowledge for which learners cannot wait. Using tools such as Web-based audioconferencing, Web videoconferencing, and application sharing, corporations can deliver programs without long development cycles. For example, a software company can quickly provide sales representatives with the skills and knowledge needed to sell a new product. Using application sharing and live two-way audio, a program can be created in a matter of hours to demonstrate software features and to offer subject-matter experts to answer questions.

Range of Tools. The range of tools available in W/VSC programs makes complex topics manageable. Complex topics can be explained by directly using tools such as whiteboards, application sharing, text-chat, real-time audio, and videoconferencing. These synchronous tools can be combined with asynchronous tools such as video clips, text, images, animation, polling, and quizzing. Instructors and learners can illustrate their ideas and take the class in unanticipated directions. If the instructor discovers that a class lacks basic skills, he or she can digress to review basics with a whiteboard or a visit to a website that provides fundamental skills. After all learners have the prerequisite skills, the instructor can begin teaching the topic.

Simple Classroom Metaphor. The simplicity of the classroom metaphor is a benefit of W/VSC programs. This form of Web-based training is most like a real classroom, where learners and the instructor gather at the same time to share a learning experience. Unlike other types of Web-based training that rely on learners to be self-directed and motivated to log on and work alone, the virtual synchronous classroom provides a structured meeting time and the support and encouragement of live peers. The class cannot be put off like self-paced training.

Limitations
Limitations in Web/VSC programs can be classified as educational, logistical, and technical.

Educational Limitations. The educational limitations of W/VSC programs are the flip side of their advantages. Programs designed for individual learning or that employ passive instructional strategies do not work well in the virtual synchronous classroom. There is little value in bringing learners together if they are working on their own. Using passive strategies such as reading or viewing a video are of little value in this environment. The effectiveness of this technology is limited to instructional strategies that build on the synergy of live group interactions.

Logistics.   Logistics can be a major limitation for organizations that want to offer programs to learners working in different time zones. For example, a class starting at 2:00 p.m. Pacific Standard Time would require learners in New York to log on at 5:00 p.m. Eastern Standard Time. Time-zone difference can become an even greater issue when learners in Europe or Asia are involved.

Technical.   W/VSC programs require powerful networks and servers, multimedia computers, layers of software, and substantial technical support. Many of the software tools require powerful servers to host the programs and substantial bandwidth to accommodate video, audio, and application sharing. In addition, the computers used by learners may require sound cards, microphones, and color monitors. Because the software required to participate in a W/VSC is layered on network software, browsers, and operating system software, substantial technical support may be required to install and troubleshoot programs.

The interactions described on the following pages are only possible in Web/ virtual synchronous programs. They are described in general terms, as the specific functions and features of each vendor's synchronous tool and/or software package differ slightly.

Types of Synchronous Interactions

W/VSC programs are used to teach learners to solve unstructured problems such as how to design a database, how to evaluate chemicals for process manufacturing, how to plan computer-telephone integration, and how to develop strategies to enter a new market. The problems presented do not have a single right answer; rather they require learners to draw on their experiences, question one another's assumptions, and consider alternatives. As a result, learners create plans, develop unique solutions, and improve products and services. The instructor's role is as a facilitator who helps the group stay focused.

Four categories of tools provide synchronous interactions. As shown in Table 8.1, synchronous tools are often used with the asynchronous tools discussed in Chapter 7.

Table 8.1. Tools Used in Group E-Learning	
Synchronous	**Asynchronous**
Internet Relay Chat/Instant Messaging	E-Mail
Real-Time Audio	Discussion Groups/Community Spaces
Application Sharing	Quizzes/Tests
Whiteboards/Videoconferencing	Hypertext/Hypermedia Simulations

Select synchronous tools based on what is to be accomplished, and balance that selection against what is technically reasonable for the organization. Let's look at each one.

Internet Relay Chat

Internet relay chat (IRC) is real-time, text-based conferencing via the Internet or an intranet, sometimes referred to as "chat." IRC "chat rooms" offer real-time communication between two or more people. They are similar to meetings or conference calls; the chats take place in the form of moderated discussions, private conversations, and question-and-answer forums. The IRC application shown in Figure 8.1 features a main menu in a panel on the left and the conversation on the right panel.

Advantages and Disadvantages

Consider the advantages and disadvantages of using IRC for synchronous interactions. Internet relay chat is an effective tool for creating peer-to-peer learning opportunities. Learners participate in discussion groups, brainstorming exercises, and problem-solving activities, and they learn from one another. IRC also levels the playing field. Participants are judged by their contributions and not by their physical traits. Try to select IRC software that allows learners to determine their online names rather than defaulting to using their login names. For example, some IRC programs use the learner's login name, such as "twood" and "zimm800," rather than Tom Wood or Zimmerman.

Because the conversation in an IRC scrolls onto the screen, it can be observed as it progresses. Learners are encouraged to think about the conversation and to reflect on its evolution. Depending on the IRC software functions, the instructor can

Figure 8.1.   Sample of Chat

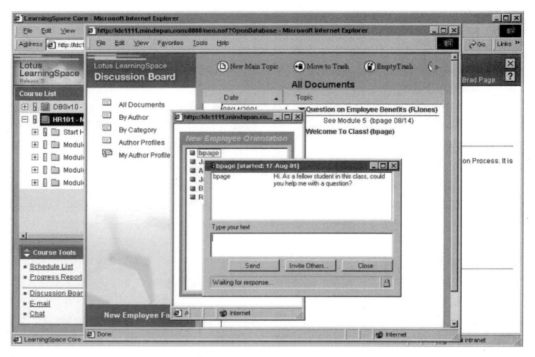

Source: Screen captures or other materials © 2001 Lotus Development Corporation. Copyright IBM Corporation. Used with permission of Lotus and IBM Corporation. LearningSpace is a trademark or registered trademark of Lotus Development Corporation and/or IBM Corporation, in the United States, other countries, or both.

An instructor talks about creating a safe environment and naming conventions

We used to let people choose any name they wanted. Then students voiced concern that they did not feel comfortable speaking up in class because they couldn't tell who was really in class. They didn't feel free to discuss their experiences or ask "dumb" questions because their boss or peers might be participating under a pseudonym. Now, to create a learner-friendly environment, we require students to use their real names.

store the text in an online archive and refer to it later. This gives learners who were unable to attend the opportunity to read the conversation they missed.

Like all text-based learning tools, IRCs penalize poor writers. Learners who are not capable of expressing themselves clearly in writing are at a disadvantage. Because IRC programs take place in real time, the interactions do not allow learners time to review their prose. Not only do learners have to be good writers, but they must also be fast typists, responding to a comment in a relatively short period of time; otherwise, the strands of conversation pass them by. Relay times—how long it takes a message to move across the Internet—can cause lags or delays and create disjointed conversations.

Internet chat rooms are not as much like real conversations as the name implies. There is a lack of context, as well as a lack of verbal and nonverbal clues. It is difficult to tell whether a chat room comment is meant to be funny, sarcastic, or serious. IRC comments do not benefit from an inflection of voice, a smile, or good timing.

Guidelines for Internet Relay Chat

This is a challenging technology to use as part of a live virtual class. Novice instructors find it distracting to have students "chatting" while they are delivering a lesson. Most e-learning platforms address the problem by providing the instructor with the ability to control chat by turning it off, by limiting it to instructor/learner conversations, or by enabling chat among pre-defined groups. IRC can be used as standalone applications and as part of blended solutions. Chat can be beneficial because it draws on the experience of learners, builds new knowledge, and can be useful in solving ill-structured problems. The following provide some guidance for using chat in your training program.

Provide Clear Directions.   Explain what you expect to result from the conversation. Provide a well-defined discussion topic, a brainstorming session with bounds, or a debate with clear expectations. Let learners know how long the IRC will last. (Will it take twenty or forty-five minutes?) Give every learner a chance to participate in the conversation. If possible, select the IRC group members to ensure that the group has a balance of participants. Mix experienced IRC participants with novices to create rooms that have a balance of senior managers and new hires; integrate staff from headquarters and the field.

Limit Number of Participants.   Create groups of five to seven learners to give everyone an opportunity to contribute. Too few people and the conversation lags; too many people and the conversation becomes chaotic. Create a respectful and safe environment for participation and encourage observation as well as active participation.

Keep the Conversation on Track.   Monitor the conversation or ask a learner to play the role of monitor. Keep the conversation on track by tabling items that become deadlocked. Capture issues for later that are sidetracking the conversation, and ask those who are observing passively what they think.

Ask for a Conversation Summary.   Appoint a scribe to summarize the IRC chat. The report can be posted to a threaded discussion or sent to a listserv for review by the group. Use these kinds of exercises to develop learners' skills of analysis and synthesis.

Involve Learners in Setting Norms.   Allow them to determine who should monitor and keep IRCs on track, what other IRCs should be created, and who should participate.

Instant Messaging

Instant messaging is a technology that serves a similar purpose to that of Internet relay chat. It enables real-time text-based chat. Using instant messaging, learners are able to create a contact list of fellow students and have the computer track their peers' status (i.e., online, busy, not online). If a fellow student is online, a learner can contact that person, and a small window will open for the participants to type messages. This is where things get messy. Some instant messaging programs even support the ability to "invite" additional people to join, making instant messaging similar to a chat room. As we discussed in Chapter 4, e-learning technologies are crossing boundaries and it is very hard to categorize software applications.

Instant messaging is a synchronous tool, but it is most often used in combination with asynchronous self-placed programs or asynchronous group learning programs to enable students to collaborate with the instructor and other students. Those interested in creating blended, Web-based solutions should consider tools such as instant messaging to create that blend.

Real-Time Audio with Visuals

Real-time audio is the ability to carry on a conversation with learners over the Internet or intranet. In most cases, real-time audio is used in combination with visuals. This enables the instructor and learners to talk to one another while sharing graphics, images, videos, and animation related to the topic. This kind of interaction

√ Internet Relay Chat Worksheet

Directions: If you have never participated in a chat session, this worksheet is a must!

Below are five Internet relay chat sites. These sites are not dedicated to training, but they offer you an opportunity to experience IRC. Try at least two of the sites and use the questions below to reflect on the experience.

AOL People & Chats (www.aol.com [members only])

If you are an AOL member, locate the People and Chat link. Find a chat room that interests you and join in the conversation.

Chathouse.com (www.chathouse.com/)

At chathouse.com you can either join an existing chat room or you can create your own free room.

Cybertown (www.cybertown.com/)

If you are an old hand at chat, try Cybertown and chat in 2D and 3D. This chat program requires some technical skills to access and to establish your avatar.

TalkCity (www.talkcity.com)

This site offers chat sessions on topic related to entertainment, commerce, travel and music. Pick a chat room and join a conversation.

Yahoo (http://chat.yahoo.com/)

Participation in chat rooms can be unreliable, that is, you may not find people chatting about a topic that interests you when you log on. An alternative is to join a scheduled chat session. Live chat events usually feature an expert or celebrity who will talk with chat room participants at a scheduled time. Check out the listings on Yahoo's Live Events Board and join a session that is guaranteed to be active at a listed time.

REFLECTION QUESTIONS

- Did you enjoy the experience? If not, why not? If yes, what did you like about it?

- How could you use this tool for training? What are its limitations? What are its benefits?

- Would it be beneficial to have a moderator in the chat?

is well-suited for round-table discussions, question-and-answer sessions, guest speakers, and debates.

The functions of the audio vary from product to product. In some applications, the audio works very much like a teleconference call. In others, the audio works like a call-in radio program in which the instructor acts as the host and puts learners on the air. In yet others, the instructor can talk to the audience and the audience can type questions to the instructor in real-time and receive answers immediately. Figure 8.2 is an example of a Web-based training program that uses live audio with visuals.

As Figure 8.3 shows, there are several permutations of real-time audio with visuals. Audio can be heard via the Internet in three ways, and visuals can be broadcast from a single source or multiple sources.

One-way audio is analogous to a radio show. Two-way audio is analogous to a walkie-talkie, and multipoint audio is similar to a teleconference.

Figure 8.2.   Example of Real-Time Audio and Visuals

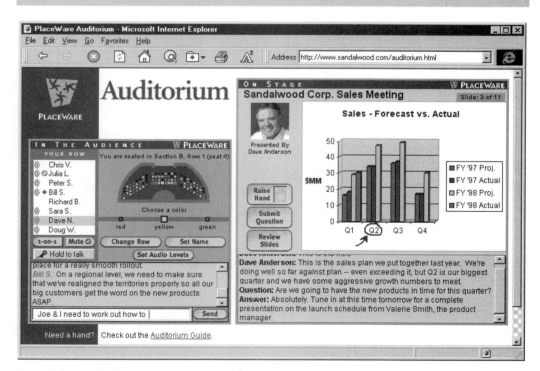

Source: Auditorium by Placeware
www.placeware.com

Figure 8.3.   Mix of Real-Time Audio and Visuals

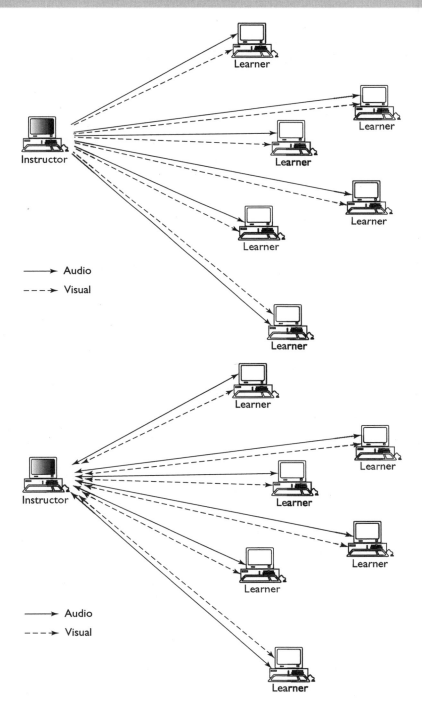

(Continued)

Figure 8.3.   Mix of Real-Time Audio and Visuals   *(Continued)*

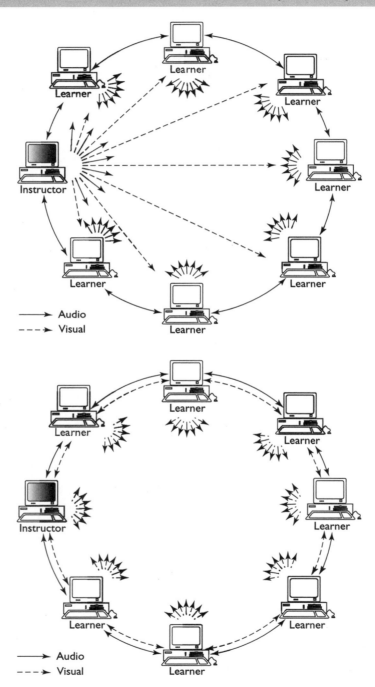

Generally, visuals are broadcast from the instructor to learners' computers. Sophisticated and powerful software packages allow visuals to be broadcast from multiple sources. A sophisticated Web videoconferencing package allows learners to broadcast images, graphics, animations, and text from their computers to the instructor and other class members. As the technology evolves, the permutations continue to grow and the distinctions blur.

Advantages and Disadvantages

Like other tools for synchronous interactions, real-time audio with visuals has advantages and disadvantages.

One of the advantages of real-time audio with visuals is robust communication. Learners gain a deeper understanding of a topic when the information is delivered on two channels (auditory and visual). In this type of synchronous interaction, visual information is supported with interactive verbal messages that benefit from inflection, tone, and pace. For example, learners can see how an order form has been redesigned and hear how the changes will make it easier to track backorders.

Real-time audio does not penalize learners who are weak writers or poor readers. There are many variations on this form of interaction, such as round-table discussions, guest speakers, and debates.

Finally, real-time audio with visuals enables speakers to use graphics, images, and videos from anywhere on the Internet or intranet. Speakers can change the visuals that support their lessons on relatively short notice. Because the materials need not be shipped to other`locations, they can be changed minutes before the course starts.

Real-time audio does have limitations. It requires a highly structured program format, such as radio programs with detailed scripts or outlines and the added complication of visuals. The instructor must be prepared to talk about the visuals, make transitions, monitor his or her timing, and manage interactions. Because visuals are usually sequenced in advance, it can be difficult to make changes during the program. Addressing new or unexpected issues can present a challenge because the program length is fixed and appropriate graphics to support unexpected topics may not be available. Again, the degree of structure or flexibility will depend on the software being used to deliver the program.

Managing learner-to-instructor and learner-to-learner interaction is not intuitive. In Web-based training there are no clues that a learner wants to ask a question or that a point was not clear. In a traditional classroom it is easy to see if a learner looks puzzled or to observe body language. It is an intuitive human response to stop and ask about the problem. The instructor must learn to proactively use tools built into the software to inquire about pacing, comprehension, and clarity of instruction.

Instructors must also be aware of other issues that can affect interactions, such as Internet lag times, learners who step away from their computers during class, and confusion caused by the interface. Learners may have a slow connection to the Internet and their responses may lag behind those of other learners. The instructor must be patient and not assume that the learner is not paying attention. Learners may log in to a class and then be called away, so be careful not to chastise a learner who is logged on and not responding. Also, the interface may confuse learners. Learners' interactions may be hampered by their inability to find the keys that control the microphone or volume or to signal the instructor that they wish to respond to a question.

If the software package being used does not offer tools to manage interactions and gather feedback, the instructor must continually seek this information by asking learners to summarize the points, provide examples, or provide non-examples as a means of gathering feedback.

Guidelines for Real-Time Audio with Visuals

Figure 8.4 provides a list of guidelines for creating a sound Web-based training program using real-time audio with visuals. Also see the template at the end of this chapter for scripting real-time audio with visuals.

Figure 8.4. Checklist for Creating Real-Time Audio with Visuals

☑ Create an advance organizer.

☑ Explain to learners how to interact.

☑ Plan five- to seven-minute segments.

☑ Use a variety of strategies.

☑ Have visuals support the audio.

☑ Create a respectful environment.

☑ Draw on audience experience.

☑ Limit length of program.

☑ Bring the program to a clear close.

Create an Advance Organizer.   Give learners an outline of what to expect. This can be an overview or list of objectives that helps learners anticipate what to expect. Agendas, program guides, and course maps help orient learners.

Explain How to Interact.   At the start of the program, review how interactions will take place, for example, how to use the "raise hand" button or yes/no buttons. Then ask learners to practice by signaling that they want to speak and introducing themselves. This is a good way to take roll call and to give learners a chance to interact in a safe environment. If you will call on learners randomly to respond to questions, make them aware of this.

Plan Five- to Seven-Minute Segments.   Plan segments that are no longer than five to seven minutes. Real-time audio with visuals is a demanding medium, and learners can easily become distracted. Learners are also quick to assume they have been dropped from the network or are experiencing a technical failure if there are long pauses in the audio, the visuals do not change, and animations loop endlessly.

Use a Variety of Strategies.   Real-time audio with visuals can become passive if no interaction is scripted into programs. If you must lecture, keep it short. Lectures are better delivered via text streaming audio, or sent via audiocassette before class. Table 8.2 shows a sample scripting worksheet with time segments. Take advantage of having the class online together to provide interactions that draw from learners' experiences, develop critical thinking, and enable people to direct their own learning. Vary the strategies within a program to keep the lesson interesting (see Table 8.3).

Have Visuals Support the Audio.   The audio portion of the program drives interactions in real time. Because audio interactions are not predictable, try to anticipate the topics, questions, and even side remarks. Prepare a series of visuals to support a number of possible directions in which the class might move. Visuals can include text, pictures, maps, animation sequences, illustrations, and scanned images that can be viewed in a browser. How visuals are created and stored will depend on the software used to develop the program.

Create a Respectful Environment.   Learners must feel free to share their experiences, ask questions, or present differing opinions.

Draw on Audience Experience.   Encourage learners to talk about their experiences. Welcome learner questions and be open to hearing about both positive and negative experiences they have had.

Table 8.2.	Sample Script			
Elapsed Time	**Time**	**Event**	**Audio**	**Visual**
5	2:55–3:00 p.m.	Pre-class	Music	Title graphics with agenda
5	3:00–3:05 p.m.	Introduction	Instructor introduction and review objectives of class	Photo of instructor with text with objectives
7	3:05–3:12 p.m.	Check in	Ask participants to introduce themselves	Map of U.S., highlighting where each person is located
5	3:12–3:17 p.m.	Review of product features and installation requirements (guest speakers/product manager)	Product manager delivers lecture	Presentation (text and graphics)
13	3:17–3:30 p.m.	Question and answer	Product manager fields questions	Picture of new products Whiteboard for product manager

Limit the Length of Programs. Experienced practitioners suggest that programs be limited to sixty to ninety minutes in length. Learners become fatigued due to poor quality audio and the need to concentrate on a busy screen. Live Web-based training screens can involve the learner in participating in chat, annotating slides on a whiteboard, and sending feedback and questions to the instructor simultaneously. This is a demanding delivery medium for learners.

Bring the Program to a Clear Close. Web-based training programs that use real-time audio take place at specified times. Be aware of starting and ending the program on time. Bring the program to a clear end by saying something like,

Table 8.3.	Strategies for Real-Time Audio
Strategy	**Description**
Interview	Interview subject-matter experts for their perspective or accounts of their experiences.
Role Play	Create a controlled environment in which learners develop skills such as interviewing or overcoming objections. Others can practice listening and analysis skills.
Debate	Use debate to provide a forum for opposing views.
Panel Discussion	Bring experts together and provide a moderator to ask questions.
Class Discussion	Invite learners to talk about a given subject in an open format.
Question and Answer	Invite learners to ask questions after a panel discussion, interviews, and presentations.
Games	Create games to engage learners in competitive problem-solving situations or require learners to work in teams to find answers.

A trainer explains the importance of adhering to the announced schedule

We advertised a live WBT class to be delivered by a nationally recognized consultant. The promotional materials stated the class would begin at 10:30 a.m. and end at noon. Much to the consultant's disappointment, we started the class as scheduled with only three of the nineteen registered students logged on. At 10:45 most of the pre-registered students were logged in. At noon the consultant was only two-thirds of the way through his talk, and he was unhappy to see the students logging off.

After debriefing the instructor and reviewing the student evaluation forms, we learned a few things! First, students make appointments, schedule conference calls, and build their calendars around advertised times. Second, consultants and presenters must understand that on the Web you can't exceed your time. I'd say watch your time.

"Before we close, are there any more questions?" or "I'd like to take the last few minutes to talk about the assignment for next week." If you are unable to address all the learners' questions during the program, invite them to contact you after class via phone or e-mail.

Application Sharing/Whiteboards

Application sharing is the ability for learners to work collaboratively on a software application such as a spreadsheet, a PowerPoint® presentation, or a whiteboard. Like real-time audio, application sharing is frequently done in combination with other synchronous interactions such as text-chat and real-time audio. Figure 8.5 illustrates a spreadsheet that can be shared by a group of learners working together. Each learner can add information to the appropriate cell, which automatically changes the bar chart and total.

Figure 8.5. Example of Shared Application

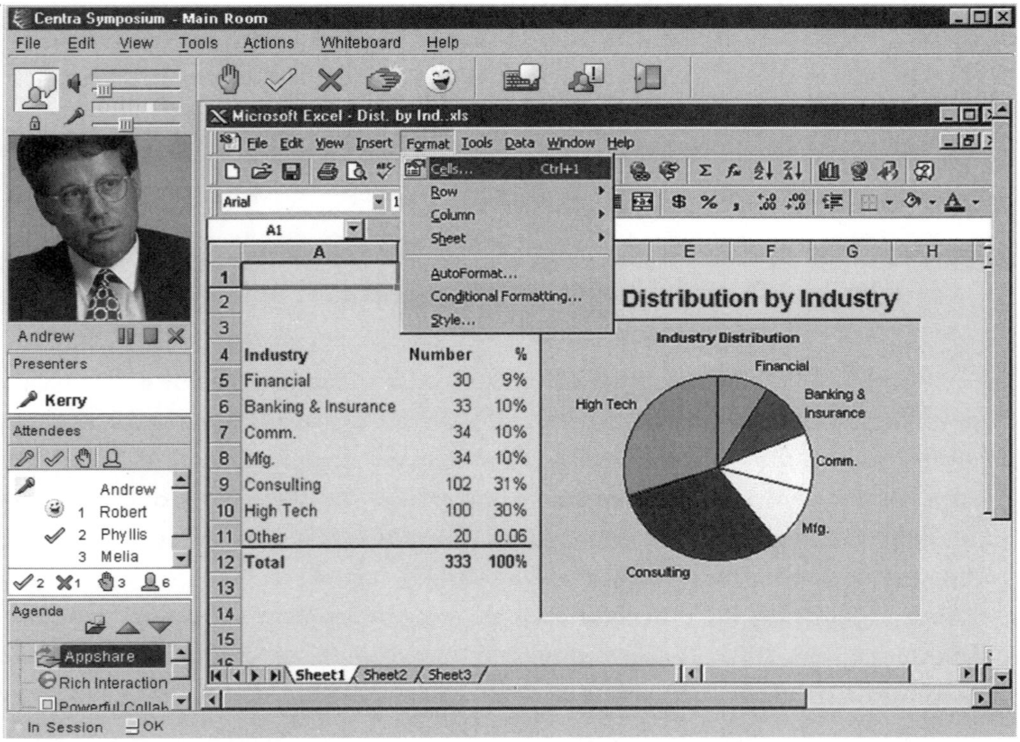

Source: Centra Software
www.centra.com

There are two ways to use shared applications in Web-based training. The most straightforward is as a means of teaching how to use an application. For example, sharing a database program like Access®, an instructor can teach a new salesperson how to set up a customer database, sort records, and create fields. The second way to use application sharing is to teach concepts and skills. For example, a shared database application like Access could be used to demonstrate how customers can be segmented by industry codes and targeted for specific marketing campaigns. In this case, the database is used to illustrate points, but students are not learning how to use the database.

A more generic shared application is the shared whiteboard, which resembles a regular whiteboard. On the Web, learners can write, annotate, draw, and paste items onto the whiteboard. It can be saved, posted to a threaded discussion, or e-mailed to the instructor (see Figure 8.6).

Figure 8.6.   Example of Shared Whiteboard

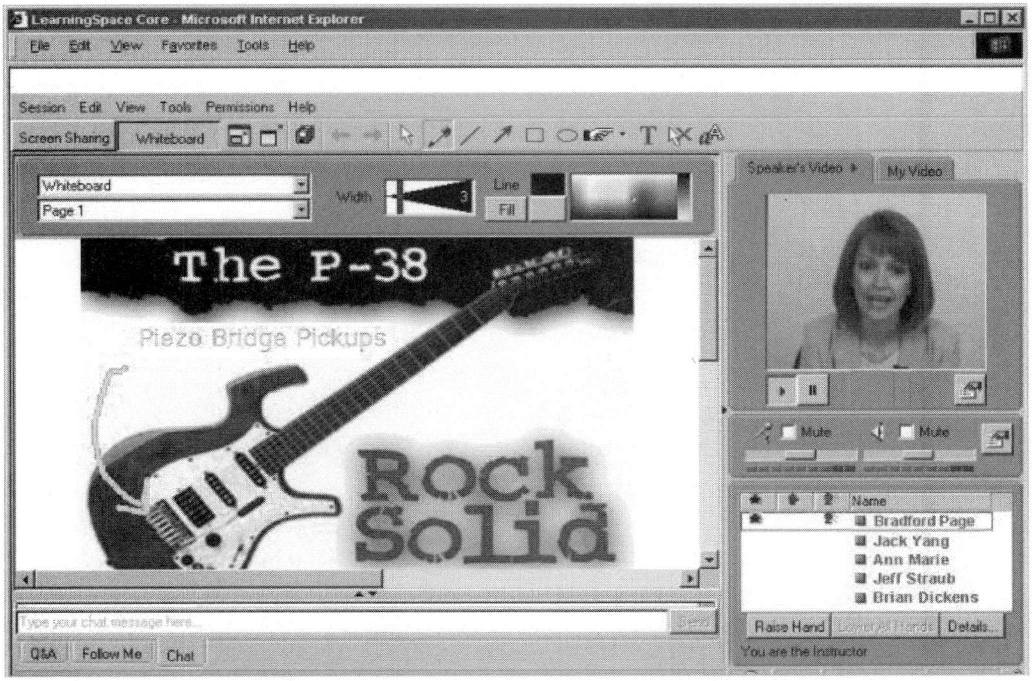

Source: Screen captures or other materials © 2001 Lotus Development Corporation. Copyright IBM Corporation. Used with permission of Lotus and IBM Corporation. LearningSpace is a trademark or registered trademark of Lotus Development Corporation and/or IBM Corporation, in the United States, other countries, or both.

Advantages and Disadvantages

Shared applications are powerful tools that offer collaborative learning opportunities for a range of training needs. As with the other interactions, there are advantages and disadvantages of using this form of interaction.

Working on shared applications enables the learner to practice skills similar to those required on the job. For example, learners can practice searching the company's database or receive coaching while using new software. Software skills can be taught in the context in which they will be used. The ability to provide an authentic experience is a big benefit of application sharing. Another benefit is the opportunity for collaborative learning. Learners can share what they have learned with peers.

The shared whiteboard is also an excellent tool for collaborative activities such as brainstorming, diagramming solutions, and outlining recommendations. Learners can work together to document their work, expand on themes, and summarize the outcomes of their working sessions. The ability to "pass the markers" and engage the entire group in drawing, annotating, and modifying an idea makes it an excellent tool for joint inquiry and problem solving.

Shared applications and whiteboards do have certain limitations and drawbacks. The most significant limitation is the necessary prerequisite knowledge. Learners must understand how the application works. The tools required for writing, erasing, and "passing markers" are unique to each vendor's software package. Learners must become familiar with the icons for the whiteboard tools (e.g., line, circle, bold, erase) and the rules related to taking turns. This presents a complex layering that can be confusing for some learners.

If the application is being used to teach concepts and skills, learners need a significant level of mastery. They must be fluent with the application before they can focus on the concepts and skills being taught.

The second major limitation of application sharing is the need to combine it with other technologies such as the telephone, real-time audio, and text-based chat. Layering these applications requires additional technical and logistical ability.

Guidelines for Using Application Sharing

Application sharing can be used for two main purposes: to teach learners to use a software package and to give learners access to a tool to help them learn another subject. Figure 8.7 provides a checklist for using shared applications to teach software skills.

Figure 8.7. Checklist for Using Shared Applications to Teach Software Skills

- ☑ Teach problem-solving skills.
- ☑ Supplement the shared application.
- ☑ Ask learners to work in teams.
- ☑ Provide problem sets and solutions.
- ☑ Limit class size.

Teach Problem-Solving Skills. Application sharing is best suited for teaching learners to use advanced features of a software application that require problem-solving, assessment, or evaluation skills. For example, application sharing is appropriate for teaching learners to design word-processing templates or to create customized table wizards for a database. Reserve application sharing for problems that involve judgment, experience, and reflection. Avoid the use of synchronous interactions to teach basic cognitive skills (knowledge, comprehension, and application) such as the basics of word processing or spreadsheets. These are better delivered with W/CBT, computer-based training, traditional classroom training, or paper-based instruction. Basic application skills require the use of individual intellectual abilities. They require drill and practice, recall of information, memorization of processes, and the application of rules. There is no benefit from group learning or live interaction with an instructor or peers.

Supplement the Shared Application. Select a communication method to supplement application sharing—one that enables the instructor to explain what is happening. Depending on the tools chosen, the instructor can communicate with the learner via text-chat, telephone, or real-time Internet audio. Assess the impact that typing back and forth or holding a telephone receiver while typing will have on the quality of the learning experience. If you are using the telephone in combination with the Web, make conference call arrangements to bring learners together simultaneously.

Ask Learners to Work in Teams. Design exercises that take advantage of peer learning. Ask learners to work in pairs or small teams so they can share their experiences and help one another. This is a good way to build problem-solving skills and to develop skills of critical reflection, and it reduces the need for the instructor to provide all the answers. In the process, the learners answer one another's questions and learn other skills.

Provide Problem Sets and Solutions.   As you would for traditional classroom programs, you will need to create problem sets or exercises to provide a consistent and structured learning experience. Teaching software skills requires attention to detail and intense preparation. Develop problem sets that work flawlessly to illustrate concepts. It is also important to provide solution sets that enable learners to review the exercise after the live class ends.

Limit Class Size.   Application sharing should be done with small groups to ensure adequate guidance and feedback. The exact size of the group depends on the complexity of the software and experience level of the learners. If all of the learners are new users of the application, the instructor must have a small group and a high level of interaction to provide adequate direction and coaching. On the other hand, programs that teach simple applications or provide an overview of new features in a familiar application can be taught to larger groups because they require fewer interactions.

Guidelines for Using Application Sharing as a Teaching Tool

Figure 8.8 gives some guidelines for using application sharing and whiteboards as teaching tools.

Assess Learners' Knowledge of the Application.   Application sharing and whiteboards can be used to help learners understand concepts, analyze information, and develop models. First, however, learners must be familiar with the application itself. Before building application-sharing exercises, determine if learners know how to use the application.

Figure 8.8.   Checklist for Using Application Sharing as a Teaching Tool

- ☑ Assess learners' knowledge of the application.
- ☑ Explain how it will be used and time limits.
- ☑ Provide a practice exercise.
- ☑ Allow adequate time.
- ☑ Make applications available outside of class time.

Explain How It Will Be Used and Time Limits. Be clear about how the application or whiteboard will be used, when work will be accessed, how long will be given to work on it, and what the expected outcomes are. For example, explain that the class will use application sharing to manipulate existing data, that learners will be expected to turn in their work, and that they will capture whiteboards and post them to threaded discussions.

Provide a Practice Exercise. Plan a brief initial exercise to give learners practice. For example, ask learners to use the whiteboard to brainstorm five problems facing managers who travel and must access their voice mail and e-mail accounts from the road. This type of simple exercise gives learners experience and confidence using the whiteboard before they attempt more complicated tasks.

Allow Adequate Time. Allow adequate time for teams to work on shared applications and the whiteboard. Be sure to pilot the exercises and ask for feedback on the time allotted to shared applications. The time needed to complete an exercise will depend on factors such as network speed, the communication method used to supplement the application sharing, and learners' familiarity with the application.

Make Applications Available Outside of Class Time. If the tool you chose allows learners to work together at times other than during the synchronous class meeting, be sure to make this known to learners. Encourage them to meet synchronously outside of class to work on assignments or projects using application sharing or whiteboards.

Web-Based Videoconferencing

Web-based videoconferencing is the ability to transmit audio and video images to multiple learners via the Internet or intranet. Like real-time audio, Web-based video offers more than one environment. Figure 8.9 illustrates the two ways that Web-based videoconferencing can be delivered. The first diagram shows the instructor's video being broadcast one way to learners. The instructor cannot see the learners nor can they see one another, although they can hear one another. The second diagram illustrates how the instructor and learners are able to see and hear one another in an environment similar to traditional videoconferencing. There are vendor-specific technical limits to how many learners can be connected at one time and how many sites can be viewed simultaneously.

Each Web-based videoconferencing software package provides slightly different features. The technology underlying these packages affects how the programs look,

Figure 8.9. Two Ways to Deliver Web-Based Video Conferencing

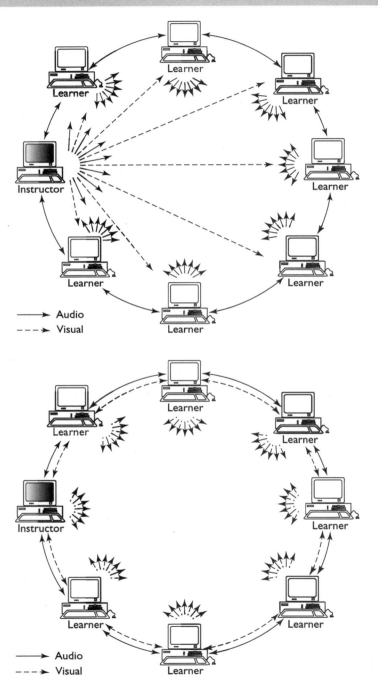

Designing and Running a Live W/VSC Worksheet

Directions: This exercise is designed to give you hands-on experience designing and running a live virtual classroom program. Use the links below to locate a vendor who offers a free trail of their live collaborative program. These vendors have traditionally offered demo sites, trial use, or limited time access to their application to run your own program. Each site provides the details on how to access and use their application. This is an opportunity to use the Real-Time Audio with Visuals Scripting Template on the CD-ROM to design your own program and facilitate it.

Astound, Conference Center (www.astound.com)

Centra, CentraNow eMeeting (www.centra.com)

Microsoft, NetMeeting (www.microsoft.com/)

PlaceWare (www.placeware.com)

RainDance, Collaboration (www.raindance.com/)

WebEx (www.webex.com)
Web-Ex is not designed specifically for training, but many organizations that use it for meetings and collaborative group work also use it for training.

REFLECTION QUESTIONS

- As the facilitator, did you miss nonverbal feedback?

- What tools and techniques were most helpful when determining the learners' degree of interest and understanding?

- What worked and what did not work in your script? What would you change next time?

- What feedback did you receive from learners regarding your directions?

- What kind of questions worked best? Calling on people by name? Open-ended questions? Yes/no polling questions?

- Which live virtual classroom tools were most effective? Whiteboards? Application sharing?

sound, and operate. Additional tools, such as quizzing, sharing documents, and using prerecorded material, are available. Figure 8.10 shows an example of a Web-based videoconferencing product being used for training classes, mentoring, meetings, broadcasts, and seminars.

Advantages and Disadvantages

Like live classroom instruction, Web-based videoconferencing allows participants to see and hear one another. Learners communicate simply by talking, without text-chat or threaded discussion. Learners not only can hear others' voices, but they can see facial expressions and body language as well. In addition, a live videoconference can be supplemented with digital media such as HTML pages, images, video clips, and animations and with actual 3D objects such as paper-based graphics and artifacts using a document camera to digitize pictures, objects, and hardcopy text. Digital cameras eliminate the need for scanning, creating, or preparing files in advance.

Figure 8.10. Example of Web-Based Videoconferencing Options

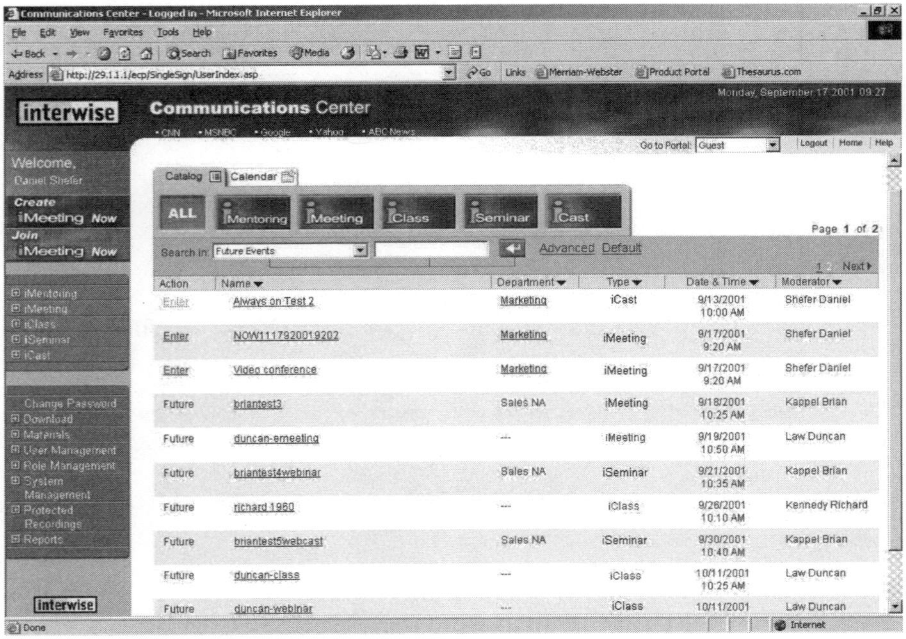

Source: Interwise
www.interwise.com

A limitation of Web-based videoconferencing is the poor quality of the image. It suffers in comparison with the quality of television or traditional videoconferencing programs. Because large amounts of information cross the Internet, the performance may not be as good as telephone or satellite-based solutions. As the technology improves, quality will be less of an issue.

Web-based videoconferencing requires that learners add a microphone, camera, and software to their computers. It is important to identify the resources needed to prepare the learners' computers because these devices add to the complexity of implementing a program. After the microphones, cameras, and software are installed, learners must take responsibility for focusing the camera and positioning the microphones correctly. Plan to spend a few minutes at the start of each program conducting a sound check and adjusting cameras.

Videoconferencing also presents a unique nontechnical dilemma: Many adult learners do not like to see themselves on screen and may be inhibited from talking. Start programs with an exercise that focuses on the content and not the learners. For example, ask learners to introduce themselves and to talk about the challenges that downsizing has created in their division.

Guidelines for Web-Based Videoconferencing

Figure 8.11 provides a checklist for creating a sound Web-based training program using videoconferencing.

Figure 8.11. Checklist for Creating Web-Based Videoconferencing

☑ Test system prior to program date.

☑ Prepare graphics in advance.

☑ Start on time.

☑ Familiarize learners with controls.

☑ Use a variety of interactions.

☑ Call on people by name and allow time for response.

☑ Limit the number of sites.

☑ Summarize key points.

☑ Conclude on time.

Test System Prior to Program Date.   Before running a Web-based videoconferencing program, conduct a test of the system. Ask the learners from each site to log in and check the functionality and quality of the audio and video. Be prepared to provide technical assistance if learners are unable to connect successfully. Also, check the quality of the images that result from using the document camera and the quality of the microphones used by the instructor and learners.

Prepare Graphics in Advance.   Before the videoconference, prepare graphics, text, video clips, and animations and gather props to be shown during the program. The preparation required depends on the kind of software used to scan, digitize, compress, or render these items. Allow adequate time to develop and test digital media. Use a document camera to include paper-based graphics (i.e., hard-copy printouts of PowerPoint slides, hand-lettered signs, pages of books), photographs, and maps. Test the legibility of these pieces before the class. One of the benefits of Web videoconferencing is the ability to use a wide range of images and objects to support a lesson.

Start on Time.   Respect those participants who are on time by starting on time. Establish a process for providing participants who join in late the information they missed. You may want to provide them with copies of the graphics, a set of the instructor's notes, and an opportunity to stay logged in after class to talk to the instructor.

Familiarize Learners with Controls.   Before using all the buttons and tools found on the interface, conduct an icebreaker activity to give learners experience using the controls. For example, ask participants to use the microphone to introduce themselves or ask them to raise their hands if they completed the pre-reading. Introduce the features slowly to allow learners time to learn how the buttons and tools operate. If the interface has features such as the ability to signal a raised hand, send the instructor a message, participate in a breakout room, and take a quiz, introduce the tools one at a time. Give learners adequate time and allow them to master one tool before introducing another.

Use a Variety of Interactions.   As you did with multipoint real-time audio, combine a variety of instructional techniques in Web videoconferencing. Avoid the talking head syndrome; seeing the instructor's face adds little value to a program. Limit segments to five to seven minutes. Keep in mind that watching Web videoconferencing can be a passive experience. Use instructional strategies that engage the learner. All of the techniques presented in Table 8.3 for real-time audio also work for videoconferencing. Table 8.4 shows strategies unique to this mode of synchronous interaction.

Call on People by Name and Allow Time for Response. Depending on the system used, the display of learner names may not indicate which ones want to be called. During roll call or an icebreaker activity, find out how learners want to be addressed. Allow time for your message to reach the learners' computers and time for the learners with the slowest connections to respond. Traffic on the Internet/intranet will cause lags in response time, so do not be quick to admonish participants for not answering.

Limit the Number of Sites. The number of sites able to participate in a program depends on the interaction level, technological limitations, and facilitation skills of the instructor. As the number of sites increases, interaction decreases. Highly interactive programs require adequate time for everyone to talk or respond. In other cases, the number of sites will be limited by the technology. Some videoconferencing programs allow a large number of sites to be connected if the program is one-way. Others allow a small number of sites for multipoint videoconferencing. The last factor limiting the number of sites participating is the skill of the instructor. As instructors become skilled at managing multiple sites, the number can be increased.

Table 8.4. Strategies for Multipoint Web-Based Video Conferencing

Strategy	Description
Demonstration	Use full-motion video to show participants steps in a process such as connecting cabling, replacing a computer board, or using a scanning wand.
Analysis	Perform a task and ask class members to critique it, such as counting back cash to a customer. Ask learners to watch the demonstration and to explain what was done well and what could have been done better.
Monitor	Monitor learner performance, such as having them hold up parts of an engine as the parts are called out.

Summarize Key Points.   As the program progresses, be sure to summarize key points. This is a good way to segue from one part of the program to another.

Conclude on Time.   Be respectful of the learners' time and conclude the program as scheduled. If the program has not accomplished all of the stated goals, check with participants before extending the program. Consider scheduling another Web-based videoconference.

Record and Playback of Live Virtual Classroom Programs

In the last three years, software for the live virtual classroom has come a long way. Leading software programs now have the ability to record and playback. This is an excellent solution for addressing problems that arise when learners miss a class or when time zones make it difficult for everyone to participate. Using this record and playback feature, an expert's presentation can be recorded and archived for use in the asynchronous mode, or it can be edited and a segment used in future programs.

An interesting trend to monitor is the unintended use of the record and playback feature as an authoring application. Some organizations are using record and playback to create programs that are never delivered live. Subject-matter experts simply create a set of PowerPoint slides and lecture to them or use application sharing to demonstrate a new product while talking about it. These sessions are quick and easy to create because there is little or no instructional design used to create the materials. The programs are often recorded without an audience or with a "studio" audience to ensure quality questions. This use of live Web-based training software may be cost-effective, but organizations need to follow up to determine whether lectures delivered via the Web are providing information or training.

Technical and Logistical Considerations

The logistical issues related to planning synchronous interactions are not the focus here, but do address those issues before designing the interactions described in this chapter. First, assess the feasibility of synchronous programs for learners located around the world and across the country. Consider local holidays, religious holidays, and time-zone differences. If the time-zone differences are irreconcilable, plan to run the program more than once. Next, consider the environment in which people will be learning (see Chapter 5). Think about the effect that microphones and cameras will have in the learners' workspaces. Determine how comfortable learners are talking to their computers and how supportive their managers are.

Technical issues are a major consideration when planning synchronous Web-based training programs. Software applications that enable real-time interactions vary in complexity and system requirements. Determine what kind of real-time interaction is needed, then work with the system manager to determine which applications best meet your needs. Avoid adopting technology that is not fully supported. Select tools that are easy for learners to use and will not require dozens of calls to the helpdesk for support. Explore the amount and kind of network and system-management resources required. Keep in mind bandwidth limitations, server resources, and end-user requirements. These technology requirements should not interfere with the organization's abilities to conduct business.

Summary

Web/virtual synchronous classroom programs are not appropriate for every situation, but they are the only solution when live interaction is essential. These tools foster synergy among learners, enable immediate feedback, and allow just-in-time development and delivery. Synchronous tools also enable instructional strategies not possible in other types of Web-based training, such as demonstrations, live debates, role plays, and discussions.

Four broad categories of synchronous tools are used to deliver live interactive programs: Internet relay chat, real-time audio with visuals, application sharing/whiteboards, and videoconferencing. These tools can be found as individual software applications or as bundled packages that bring together several synchronous and asynchronous tools. The descriptions presented in this chapter are general; each vendor's application varies slightly.

Synchronous and asynchronous interactions are the building blocks for developing Web-based training programs. Once you have your design strategies in place, you are then ready to develop and communicate your Web-based program to the rest of the organization via a document blueprint, which is the topic of the next chapter.

Suggested Readings

Barron, T. (2000). *Online learning goes synchronous.* [Online] Available: www.learningcircuits.org/jan2000/trends.html

Bradshaw, T. (1990). *Audiographics distance learning.* London: Wested.

Collis, B. (1996). *Tele-learning in a digital world: The future of distance learning.* New York: International Thomson.

Emery, M., & Schubert, M. (1993). A trainer's guide to videoconferencing. *Training, 30*(6), 59–63.

Gunawardena, C.N. (1992). Changing faculty roles for audiographics and online teaching. *American Journal of Distance Education, 6*(3), 58–71.

Hoffman, J. (2001). *The synchronous trainer's survival guide.* Unionville, CT: InSync Training Synergy.

Robinson, B., & Lockwood, F. (1996). *Achieving quality in open and flexible learning.* New York: Nichols Publishing.

Schieman, E., & Jones, T. (1992). Learning at a distance: Issues for the instructional designer. *Journal of Adult Education, 21*(2), 3–13.

√ Real-Time Audio with Visuals
√ Scripting Template

Directions: Review the sample script outline in Table 8.2. Then develop your own script for a real-time audio with visuals Web-based training program.

Elapsed Time	Time	Event	Audio	Visual

Chapter 9

Developing Blueprints

The last two chapters provided an overview of strategies for designing online instruction for asynchronous and synchronous interactions in three distinct modes. This chapter provides a high-level overview of what it takes to communicate the project's design to others. This chapter is well worth reading, even if you are going to outsource the job. Understanding the kinds of documents required and the purpose of each document will ensure that you know why you are reviewing them. Understanding at which points changes can be made without adding significant costs to the project or affecting the timeline is invaluable.

If you had an opportunity to visit the sites recommended as exemplars throughout the book, then you understand the complexity of Web-based training and the need for clear blueprints or directions for building online courses and blended solutions. This chapter address the second D for "develop" in the ADDIE model, shown in Figure 9.1.

What You Will Learn in This Chapter

After completing this chapter, you will be able to

- Develop a design document;
- Draft a detailed program flow chart; and
- Create a script and storyboard.

Figure 9.1.　The ADDIE Model

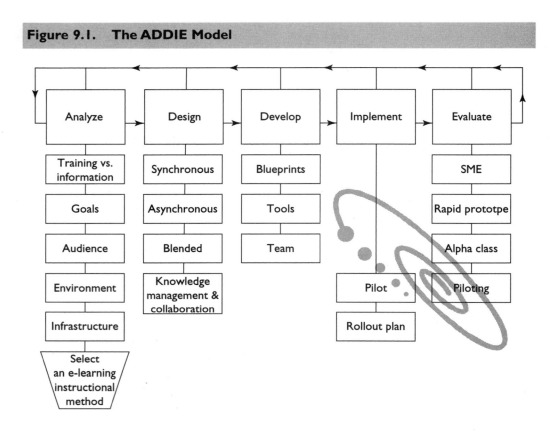

The creation of a Web-based training program is guided by planning documents that detail how the program is to be built. These documents are like blueprints that detail how a home will be constructed. Four kinds of planning documents are required to communicate the design of a Web-based training program. Table 9.1. lists the documents.

All forms of Web-based training need a design document; nonlinear forms (W/CBT, W/EPS, W/VAC) need a flow chart. Live linear programs (W/VSC) need a script. All forms benefit from storyboards. If you have chosen to outsource the creation of your Web-based program, these are documents that your vendor should provide. Drafting these documents is a significant cost, but the money is well-spent. It is far easier to make corrections during the planning phase than after the program is up and running.

	W/CBT	W/EPSS	W/VAC	W/VSC
Table 9.1. Required Documents for Development				
Design Document	X	X	X	X
Flow Chart	X	X	X	
Script				X
Storyboard				X

Design Documents

Design documents are detailed plans that provide the development team and client with a vision of the final product. Clients should review and agree to the specifications outlined in the design document before the development team invests time in creating storyboards or scripts and creating media.

Design documents should be jargon-free, detailed, and easy to understand. Design documents will differ, depending on the client organization, program content, project size, length, and production quality. Table 9.2 shows recommended sections for a design document and the types of content found in each section.

Let's now look at each section of the design document.

Introduction

Background. The introduction should set the context for the WBT program. Provide background information on the organization for which you are developing the program. Inform the reader about why a distance-education solution is appropriate (i.e., geographically dispersed learners, just-in-time demand for knowledge).

Opportunity Statement. Draft an opportunity statement. Explain how this program will enable an organization to improve productivity, reduce costs, limit legal liability, or increase profits. If possible, quantify the benefits of filling a skill or knowledge gap.

Audience. Describe the intended audience or learners. When possible, define learners based on job title and provide details regarding the expected entry-level skills and learner characteristics. It is important to document such assumptions before developing the program.

Goals/Objectives. Explain the goals of the program in easy-to-understand language. Create a goal statement that is clear and easy for a nontechnical person to

Table 9.2.	Outline of Design Document	
Section	**Content**
Introduction	Background
	Opportunity statement
	Audience
	Goals/objectives
Instructional Strategy	Presentation of information
	Learner participation
	Evaluation strategy
Navigation Map/Treatment & Web-Based Training Outline	High-level graphic map/treatment statement
	Lesson outline for each unit
	• Title
	• Goal/objectives
	• Length
	• Content
	• Learning activities
	• Assessment
Resources	Development resources
	Delivery resources
	Maintenance resources
Program Management	Timeline
	Roles and responsibilities
	Risks and dependencies
Budget	Skilled labor
	Production value
	E-learning software
	Hardware
	Stock images and media
Deliverables	Files
	Documents

understand. Include the objectives so the reader can understand what skills and knowledge the learner must master in order to achieve the program goal. Figure 9.2 shows an example of a goal statement for a technical, Web-based training program.

It is up to the developer to decide how much detail to provide regarding objectives. High-level objectives, called *terminal* objectives, may be adequate. In other cases, detailed, low-level objectives, called *enabling* objectives, may be required to fully explain the skills and knowledge required to achieve the goal. Terminal objectives are the significant measurable outcomes that support the achievement of a program goal. Enabling objectives are smaller and more granular objectives that must be achieved in order to master a terminal objective. When you are working in content areas that are complex or unfamiliar, it is useful to outline the goal, terminal objectives, and enabling objectives. The better the designer understands the skills and competencies required to reach the goal, the more accurate the pricing and scoping and the better the pedagogical design. Figure 9.3 provides an example of an outline for teaching salespeople how to use a new expense account program.

Instructional Strategy

Presentation of Information.   Provide an overview of the look and feel of the program. Explain how you plan to present the course content (i.e., text-based, lecture, video, audio with graphics). If the presentation style is not one with which your clients or project sponsors are familiar, be sure to explain it. For example, if you are streaming video, describe what that means.

Learner Participation.   Provide details about how learners will participate in the lesson (i.e., self-paced reading, online dialogue with instructor, text-chat, Web-based videoconference with peers). If the lesson involves practice exercises or activities that enable the learner to apply what they have learned, describe these elements.

Evaluation Strategy.   Discuss how you will assess learners' mastery of the content. If you plan to use asynchronous assessments such as tests and quizzes, consider the tools available such as true/false, multiple choice, fill in the blank, short answer, and essay. In live e-learning programs, the testing tools will vary with

---

Figure 9.2.   Sample Jargon-Free Goal

Field Service Engineers in Europe, North America, and Asia will be able to install, customize, and troubleshoot the Office King 9000 laser printer.

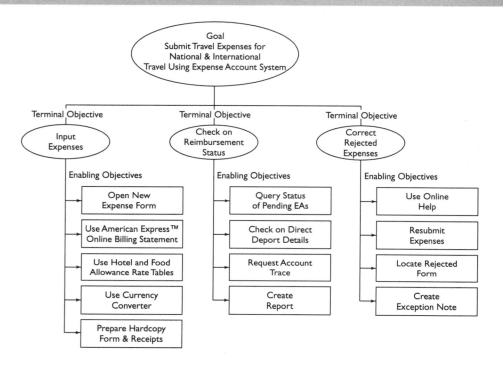

Figure 9.3.   Terminal and Enabling Objectives

the software application. However, in most Web/virtual synchronous class (W/VSC) environments, the previously listed tools are available as well as the ability to ask students to demonstrate their mastery in a live format, for example by verbally delivering an answer or by using application sharing to demonstrate mastery of software. Also consider using a whiteboard to diagram a solution while describing it.

Navigation Map/Treatment and WBT Outline

High-Level Graphic Map.   Navigation maps provide an overview of how the program is structured. They give visual pictures of the Web-based training outline, as seen in Figure 9.4. They are effective for nonlinear programs in which learners can select unique paths. They are appropriate for W/CBT, W/EPS, and W/VAC.

Treatment Statement.   Web/virtual synchronous classroom programs take place in real-time and therefore have a linear structure. For such a program, it is more informative to provide a treatment statement, i.e., a brief description of the program, such as the one shown in Figure 9.5.

Figure 9.4.   Sample Navigation Map

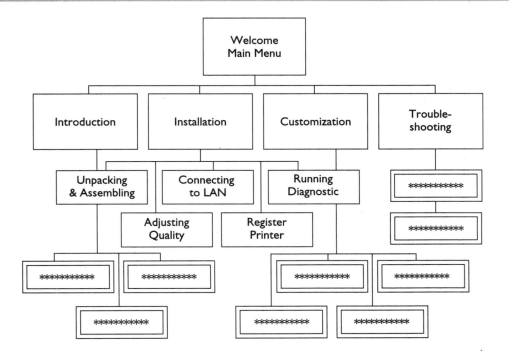

Figure 9.5.   Sample Treatment Statement

This is a one-hour customer-service refresher training program. Bob Smith, VP of Customer Service, and Kathy Albright, a recognized expert in customer service, host the program. It is a talk-show format with Bob Smith as the moderator and Kathy Albright as the guest. Learners are invited to send in questions via Internet text-chat while the program is being broadcast.

Lesson Outline for Each Unit.   The more details provided in the outline section, the easier it will be to estimate the developmental requirements. In addition, clients benefit from a detailed outline because they understand what will and will not be included in each lesson.

Figure 9.6 depicts the hierarchy of the elements in a course. Each course has a number of lessons, and each lesson has a goal and objectives. Plan to spend time analyzing and synthesizing the course content to develop the outline. Each lesson should have a title, a goal statement, and three to five objectives. Estimate the

Figure 9.6.   Hierarchy of Course Structure

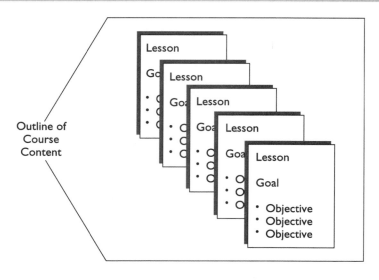

length of the lesson—how long it will take the average learner to complete the lesson. Outline the content that will be covered and, when possible, identify the source. Possible sources are user documentation, system specifications, and subject-matter experts.

In addition, include the learning strategies that are compatible with the modes of Web-based training delivery. For example, since W/CBT is most effective for teaching highly structured and measurable skills and knowledge, the most appropriate learning strategy would be drill and practice, quizzes, question and answer, and reading. Table 9.3 shows the types of learning strategies that are best suited to each mode of Web-based training delivery.

Last, provide a brief description of how you plan to measure how much the learners have learned. Assessment or testing does not have to be in a traditional form; see Chapter 7, Designing Asynchronous Interactions, for more details on testing, quizzing, and nontraditional assessment options. If you choose not to test, inform the client and the learners, and explain why. Figure 9.7 is a sample outline for a simple lesson in a Web-based training program.

Resources

The resource section of the document is intended to clearly communicate the staffing and hardware and software resources required in each step of the process.

	W/CBT	**W/EPS Systems**	**W/VAC**	**W/VSC**
Instructional Strategies	Drill and practice, simulations, reading, questioning, and answering	Problem solving, scientific method, experiential method, project method	Experiential tasks, group discussions, team projects, self-directed learning, discovery method	Dialogue and discussions, problem solving, and maximum interaction
Instructional Technology Elements	Multimedia, hypertext, hypermedia, simulations, application exercises, e-mail, listserv, and bulletin boards, communication with instructor	Multimedia, hypertext, hypermedia, bulletin boards, notes conferences, modules of Web-CBT, and e-mail access to facilitator and peers	Multimedia, hypertext, hypermedia, bulletin boards, notes conferences, modules of Web-CBT, and e-mail access to facilitator and peers	Synchronous audio- and videoconferencing, shared whiteboards, shared applications

Table 9.3. Matching Instructional Strategies to Delivery Systems

Developing a Web-based training program requires a team of professionals, potentially drawn from many sources. In addition, special hardware and software may need to be ordered.

Design, Development, and Delivery Resources. Make separate lists for the resources needed to design, develop, and deliver phases of the project. Remember, many of the team members, such as the system manager, webmaster, and subject-matter experts, are drawn from other departments (see Chapter 2). Making separate lists for each phase of the project helps departments plan schedules and anticipate their level of involvement. Include a list of resources required to maintain the program; this will ensure that clients are not surprised in a few months when the program needs to be updated. Table 9.4 shows the three phases of a project and identifies the resources needed in each.

Figure 9.7.   Sample of Web-Based Training Outline

Office King 9000 Laser Printer Web-Based Training

Lesson Title	Time		
1:OK 9000 Installation	8 min	Goal:	Field service engineers will be able to install the Office King 9000 (OK9000).
		Objectives:	After completing this lesson, field service engineers will be able to • Unpack and assemble the OK 9000 • Make network connections to LAN • Run a diagnostic test pattern • Adjust quality of output • Register the printer with customer service
		Content:	• Unpacking and assembling directions • Network connections diagrams • Steps for running diagnostic test pattern • Quality matrix (problem/recommended fix) • Directions to send registration via Internet to customer service group at HQ
		Learning activities:	• Reading • Internet chat room • Responding to questions • Problem solving using EPS systems
		Assessment:	Multiple choice test, 10 items

Program Management

Timeline.   Include a section in the design document that deals with project-management issues. Provide a timeline that lists the start and end dates for milestones, like the example in Table 9.5. Break the tasks into manageable activities with clear beginning and end points. Activities that are too large may discourage members of the development team, because they take a long time to complete. Shorter activities give team members a sense of satisfaction and provide frequent opportunities to check progress.

Table 9.4. WBT Process and List of Resources

| Phase | List of Potential Resources | |
	People	Equipment (hardware, software)
Design	Instructional designers	Computers
	Subject-matter experts	Software to develop prototype
	Project manager	
Develop	Instructional designers	Computers
	Course developers	Servers
	Pilot subjects	Network access
	Graphic artists	Software to create
	Editors	• Audio
	Programmers	• Animation
	Facilitators	• Text
	Administrators	• Graphics
		• Video
Deliver	Facilitator	Computers
	System manager	Servers
	Local installation support	Network
	Helpdesk staff	Software
	Webmaster	
	Programmers	
	Course developers	

One of the most difficult things to explain to clients and members of the team is the pace of the project. The expectation is that after the first few meetings they should be able to see tangible results such as prototype modules or media elements. The reality is, the majority of the time and budget are spent in the first phase of the project doing instructional design and content creation. Figure 9.8 shows what experienced developers and project managers believe to be the breakdown by percentage of time for instructional design/development, production, and quality assurance.

Table 9.5.   Example of Project Timeline

Timeline for WBT Project

Activity	Start Date	End Date	Comments
Project kickoff meeting	January 12	January 12	Bob from Texas office will participate via teleconference
Draft Lesson 1 content	January 13	January 23	
Draft questions for IRC	January 13	January 23	
SME reviews & signoff Lesson 1	January 24	January 30	
Revisions to Lesson 1	February 2	February 6	
Graphics for Lesson 1	February 12	February 16	Icons developed for Lesson 1 will be used for all lessons
Interactions developed	January 23	February 4	

Figure 9.8.   Percentage Allocation of Project Hours

38 percent of hours go toward instructional design and content creation

42 percent go toward production—the graphic artist, the technicians, and the authors

20 percent are quality assurance—testing, tweaking, and cleaning up

Roles and Responsibilities.   List the roles and responsibilities of team members internal and external to the organization. Make it clear who is responsible for tasks such as reviewing content, maintaining hardware, installing software, negotiating access to resources, and communicating with learners.

Risks and Dependencies.   Create a section that discusses risks and dependencies. Let clients and team members know about risks—potential problems beyond your control. Risks can include failure to upgrade the end-user systems, last-minute changes in content, and lack of knowledgeable reviewers. Take time to identify when a success depends on things you do not control. Dependencies can include standardization on the latest version of Netscape Navigator or employee access to the Internet on a 28.8 modem or higher.

The Budget

Before looking at the nuts and bolts of creating a budget for the project plan, it is helpful to grasp some of the factors that impact budget. It is also helpful to have a rough idea of what you can expect to pay.

Forecasting E-Learning Costs

One of the most frequently asked questions is how much does e-learning cost. Brandon Hall (1998) provided an outstanding analysis of costs. He focused on the little understood fact that the cost of e-learning is primarily driven by the costs associated with labor.

Skilled Labor.   Whether your program is developed in-house, outsourced, or created with the help of contractors, the first thing you need to do is determine your labor costs. Figure 9.9 provides a list of the going rates for e-learning professionals. An informal survey of firms supplying e-learning professionals reveals that the rates have generally stayed the same since 1998. Survey participants suggested that there has been no sharp increase in rates because there has been an increase in the availability of skilled practitioners. A note of caution: The rates vary widely across the United States and they do not reflect the costs of similar professionals in Europe, the Middle East, or Asia.

Figure 9.9.   The Going Rates

- Instructional technologist, $65 to $100/hour
- Instructional designer, $75 to $100/hour
- Writer/editor, $40 to $65/hour
- Graphic artist, $35 to $65/hour
- Programmer/authoring specialist, $30 to $65/hour
- Java/CGI programmer, $85 to $120/hour
- Media expert, $65 to $120/hour

Review the expenses related to staffing the project at each phase. Look at three sources of staff: outside consultants, internal resources from other departments, and staff from the training or HR organization. Determining the costs for contractors and consultants may be the easiest part of budgeting. Don't make assumptions about access to internal resources. Ask questions such as: Will internal organizations assess a charge-back fee to the project for services rendered? Will I have to pay for access to subject-matter experts? If I need a dedicated person in IT to support the application, will I have to fund a full or partial head count?

Production Value. Because the cost of e-learning is dependent on the labor costs, it is more useful to derive costs based on the number of hours required to develop programs than to state an outright dollar figure. Work done by Katherine Golas (1993) to estimate costs for interactive courseware (ICW) provides an excellent framework for organizing ballpark time estimates for the development of one hour of e-learning. Table 9.6 shows the results of an informal survey of twelve training professionals who estimated development times based on Golas' three production levels. Their estimates were within the range of estimates Golas found for

Table 9.6.   Estimate of Hours Needed to Develop One Hour of Web-Based Training

Golas' Estimate of Hours Needed to Develop One Hour of ICW	Production Quality	Estimates from WBT Practitioners in 2001	
		Soft Skills	**Technical Skills**
30–200	Basic I Basic linear presentation, limited interaction, and simple media	90	100
75–250	Medium II Moderate levels of interaction, rich media, and moderate nonlinear branching	170	190
200–600	High III Highly interactive program using rich media and complex nonlinear branching	490	480

developing interactive courseware. The hour ranges vary widely because variables such as subject-matter expertise, stability of the content, familiarity with the development tools, and experience of the development team differ greatly.

Developer talks about the challenge of estimating time and the exponential relationship to quality

Estimating the time required to develop online content is a challenge. There are many variables that need to be considered. Past experience is often the best indicator. Most developers will agree that ten hours of development per hour of instruction is the starting point for the development of online courseware (basic quality). Our experience is that development time does not increase in proportion to quality. It is better described as an exponential relationship. In other words, doubling the quality of production will take four times the development effort (i.e., it increases as the square).

E-Learning Software.   A quick review of Chapter 4, Tools of the Trade, can help you identify the software applications you will need to author and manage your program. Depending on the kind of tool(s) you select, you may need to consider the following related expenses:

- *Training.* If the tool is complex, you may want to attend a training program to learn how to use the application. Depending on where the training is held, you will need to budget for travel and travel-related expenses as well as tuition. Skipping this step can be costly if the learning curve is steep and your timeline is short.

- *License.* Be sure to ask questions about the license. The cost of the license should spell out things such as how many developers the license supports, whether the developers are unique users (every developer has his or her own account) or concurrent users (there are ten seats and even if you have one hundred developers they can use all of the systems as long as there are never more than ten developers using the tool at the same time).

- *Support.* Does the application require that you buy a service contract? Is there a minimum level of service and are there a minimum number of years for which you must contract?

- *Updates.* Are you obligated to upgrade each time the vendor issues a new version or new release? Is there a cost associated with new releases?

- *Integration.* Will the e-learning software need to be integrated with other software applications such as an employee database, employee development plans in the human resources information system, or enterprise resource planning (ERP) systems such as SAP or PeopleSoft?

Hardware.   Hardware tends to be a minor cost, but due to the process for acquiring hardware this can be one of the more difficult aspects. In some organizations hardware purchases are planned for a year in advance, so start early. Determine the hardware needs for the development team, such as computers with additional memory or graphics capabilities, servers, and modems. Next, determine what kind of hardware will be needed to run and maintain the program. Ask questions about the items that may not be as obvious, such as: Who will pay for the server, network connections, and dial-in modem pool if needed? When budgeting, don't forget the learners and don't assume that because you have designed it for high-end PCs the learners' departments will purchase these machines. Decide who is budgeting for the hardware needs of learners, who may require sound cards, speakers, microphones, and high-color monitors. This expense may be the responsibility of the field organization or it may have to be on the WBT program budget.

Stock Images and Media.   If you need images, video, graphics, animation, or other media and do not have a graphic artist on staff, consider using stock images. Using stock images not only saves a great deal of cost associated with hiring an artist, but these images add a great deal of polish to a program. Figure 9.10 provides a list of sites that offer photos, video clips, audio clips, and animation. Many of these sites let you download thumbnail sketches free of charge. These thumbnails are reduced resolution images with watermarks that can be inserted in your

---

Figure 9.10.   Sources for Stock Images

- *Corbis Collection* (www.corbis.com/)
- *EyeWire* (www.eyewire.com)
- *Getty Images* (www.gettyworks.com)
- *PhotoDisc* (www.photodisc.com/)

---

program to give it the look and feel you want. When you and the client agree on the look and feel you can go back to the stock image site and purchase rights to use the images and download an image free of the watermark and having the appropriate resolution.

Deliverables

Files and Documents.　The final section of the design document lists the deliverables, that is, the items that will be given to the client at the end of the project. Deliverables can include files, documents, disks, CD-ROMs, digitized video clips, and film negatives. List and explain what they are to help the client understand the work required to develop a Web-based training program.

A consultant talks about the value of design documents

I charge my clients for writing a detailed design document because they [design documents] take several weeks of work. I do content analysis, learners analysis, assess the infrastructure, recommend software, and I spend time getting the details and the timeline nailed down so I can bring in a realistic budget. Another reason I charge is that I've had a company take a design document and do the work themselves and not pay me. A good design document is a road map, and it contains some of the hardest and most important work—consulting, planning, and documenting of the solution.

Program Flow Charts

Flow charts are highly detailed maps that illustrate how programs are organized. They are important tools for communicating the design of nonlinear programs. Use flow charts as maps to guide the development of W/CBT, W/EPS, and W/VAC.

Because flow charts require a great deal of analysis of learning objectives, content, and detailed instructional design, they are developed after the specifications in the design document are approved. Creating a detailed flow chart prior to approval invites the risk of having to make major revisions. The benefits of creating flow charts are that they provide more detail than the navigation map or design document, create a shared vision for cross-functional teams, and establish an independent measure of accomplishments. Let's look at each one.

✓ Design Document Worksheet

Directions: Use this worksheet to reflect on design questions. When you have completed the worksheet, review it with the development team.

Introduction

Describe the organization for which the training is being developed. What gap in skills and knowledge will this program fill?

Who are the learners?

What is the goal of the program?

List five to seven objectives.

1.

2.

3.

4.

5.

6.

7.

Instructional Strategy

How will the information be presented (text, lecture, CBT)?

How will learners participate (answer questions, role play, discussion)?

How will you determine whether the learners have mastered the content of the course (test, quiz, performance-based assessment)?

Navigation Map/Outline

On a separate sheet of graph paper, sketch a navigation map.
On a separate sheet of paper, create an outline for each lesson in your course. Be sure to include: title, goal/objectives, length, content, learning activities, and assessment of this lesson.

Resources

Before answering the following questions, see page 27 for a list of possible team members.

DESIGN PHASE

Who is needed to help you design the program?

What software, hardware, or equipment do you need?

DEVELOPMENT PHASE

Who is needed to help you develop and create the program?

What software, hardware, or equipment do you need?

DELIVERY PHASE

Who is needed to help you deliver and maintain the program?

What software, hardware, or equipment do you need?

Project Management

Create a timeline and list the major milestones for this project.

Activity	Start Date	End Date	Comments

What are the roles and responsibilities of each team member? (*List what you expect of each person identified in the Resources section.*)

Create a line-item budget. List all expenses related to this project: software, stock images, music libraries, consultants, and internal cross-charges.

Description of Item	Cost
_____	_____
_____	_____
_____	_____
_____	_____
_____	_____
_____	_____
_____	_____
_____	_____
_____	_____

TOTAL $

List the risks and dependencies (things that are beyond your control) so that others are aware of anything that may affect development dates, product functionality, and performance of the course.

Deliverables

What tangible items will be given to the client during the project (e.g., storyboards, pilot lessons, weekly reports)? Describe the items.

What are the final deliverables or items that will be given to the client at the end of the project (e.g., HTML files, images, master CD-ROM, Java or X-Active code)? Describe the items.

> The CD-ROM at the back of the book has a template to help you create your own design document. Use the information from the design document worksheet to fill in the template. The template is a Microsoft Word file that you can copy to your desktop and modify. A copy of the design document template can be found at the end of this chapter.

Provide More Detail.   Flow charts are highly detailed versions of the navigation maps included in the design document. Figure 9.11 shows how a piece of the navigation map shown in Figure 9.4 was expanded to create a flow chart.

Create Shared Vision.   Flow charts offer the cross-functional team a shared vision of the final product. The visual representation of lessons provides a tool to analyze content overlap, variations in instructional strategies, and omissions. In addition, the flow chart helps identify potential problems.

Establish Measures.   The flow chart is a yardstick against which to measure your work. Provide those who test your program with a copy of the flow chart and ask them to compare the functionality, navigation, and flow of the program to the flow-chart specifications.

Figure 9.11.   Sample Flow Chart from Navigation Map

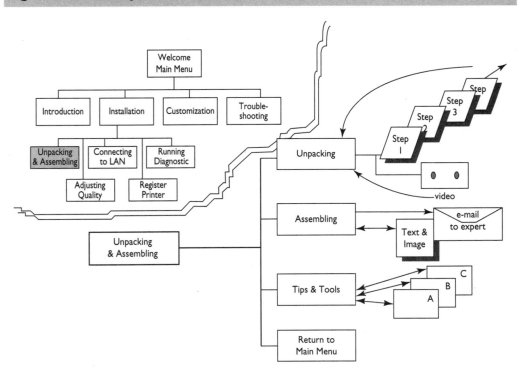

✓ Flow Chart Worksheet

Directions: This exercise is designed to give you practice flow charting and an opportunity to analyze the design of an existing Web-based training program. Using the links provided below, create a flow chart of the navigation, lesson flow, and content hierarchy on a sheet of flip-chart paper. Use the questions below to reflect on your experience.

Digital Think (www.digitalthink.com)
e-Learning Center (www.e-learningcenter.com/)
MindLeaders (www.mindleaders.com)
SmartForce (www.smartforce.com)

REFLECTION QUESTIONS

- After creating the flow chart, did you see relationships among sections that you did not see before?

- What were the easiest relationships to depict? What were the most difficult? Why were they easy or hard to depict?

- Look at the flow chart you created and think back to one of the W/CBT programs you experienced in previous exercises. Is there a relationship between the sections of the W/CBT you liked best and the flow chart? Were there places in the W/CBT in which you felt disoriented? Does the flow chart provide any clues about why you felt this way?

Program Script

A program script is a plan or set of directions for the live Web/virtual synchronous classroom. This text-based document outlines what will take place section by section. Nonlinear programs such as W/CBT, W/EPS, and W/VAC allow learners to take a number of paths and require graphic depiction to communicate the flow. A distinguishing feature of W/VSC is that learners and the instructor participate in a live, real-time linear experience. The benefits of creating program scripts are that they break instructions into clear sections, provide appropriate levels of detail, list supporting media, and match objectives to instructions.

Break Instructions into Clear Sections. The program script should have clear sections, such as an opening, information presentation, exercises, interaction, and closing. Distinctive sections give learners a sense of pacing and completion. Estimate the time needed for each section; this will help you plan and execute the program. When you pilot the program, track the actual times and make adjustments.

Provide Appropriate Level of Detail. When scripting the audio portion, do not provide word-for-word text. Scripting the program too tightly reduces spontaneity. Work with the facilitator to develop audio scripting or directions that provide adequate guidance while allowing for innovation and responsiveness.

List Supporting Media. Record a description of the visuals you plan to use and the source file names. Tracking the media files in the program script makes it easy to assemble the program, swap out images, and identify missing media.

Match Objectives to Instruction. Compare the script to the objectives stated in the design document, making sure they agree. This is a good double-check for the entire design. Table 9.7 shows a sample script.

Storyboards

Storyboards have their origins in the production of movies and cartoons. Storyboarding is a technique used to illustrate how a program will unfold. Each scene is drawn on a sheet of paper and posted on a wall so that the development team and client can follow it. In Web-based training, this technique helps show how the pages of a lesson relate. Teams find storyboards helpful because the storyboards provide visualization, sequencing, and gap identification.

Table 9.7. Sample W/VSC Script			
Time	**Audio Directions**	**Visual**	**Media/Files**
Pre-start time −5 to 0	Music	Title screen showing course name and start time (this is what learners see who log in before class starts)	Title Screen; Intro.music—intro.wav
0–2	Instructor welcomes class to New Product Introduction Training. *Ask if everyone was able to locate and read the BBS postings on new products.*	Photo of instructor	b_smith.jpg
	Review objectives and ask for questions from learners.	List of objectives	objective.ppt
2–5	*Review the features and benefits of the CyberTop family of computers.*	Pictures of the models 300, 500, 700 List of features and benefits	Cyber300.gif; Cyber500.gif; Cyber700.gif
5–9	*Ask students to brainstorm the products that will compete with CyberTops*	Online electronic whiteboard	Draw freehand
9–14	*Introduce Tom Dowling, product manager, and invite students to ask questions.*	Picture of product manager; *Give Tom whiteboard to supplement his talk.*	t_dowling.html; Draw freehand

 The CD-ROM at the back of the book has a template for scripting a live W/VSC program. Copy the template from the CD-ROM to your desktop and create your own scripts.

Comparing and Contrasting Two Modes of Web-Based Training Worksheet

Directions: This exercise is designed to help you think about ways to enhance the adult learning experience in W/CBT and W/VSC programs. Think about how the blueprints for a class to teach job skills would differ from a self-paced W/CBT program to a live W/VSC program. Use this worksheet to list the differences.

	W/CBT	W/VSC
How might the goals and objectives differ? Are some cognitive objectives better suited for one type of Web-based training than another?		
Describe the role of the instructor. Describe the activities in which the instructor would be involved.		
Describe the role of the learner. What is expected of the learner?		
List three to five interactions, exercises, or instructional strategies you would use to help adults develop job-search skills.		
How would you test or quiz learners?		

	W/CBT	**W/VSC**
List the resources required to design, develop, and deliver each kind of program. How similar or different are the resources? How similar or different are the resources?		
List the deliverables, the items to be given to the client at the close of the project. How similar or different are they?		
Describe the benefits and limitations of a nonlinear program (W/CBT).		
Describe the benefits and limitations of a linear program (W/VSC).		

Provides Visual of Program Flow.   Storyboards are used for linear and nonlinear programs. The same information presented in the script or flow chart is used in the storyboards but presented visually. Storyboards help a client understand the path through the main menu, sub-menu, content presentation, interactive exercise, summary, and review. The path may be clear in the flow chart, but still hard for clients to envision.

Enables Content to Be Resequenced.   While the program is being put into storyboards is a good time to make revisions to flow and content. Resequencing, deleting, or adding sections is easier before time and money are invested in developing the final media elements.

Highlights Gaps in Content or Dead-End Paths.   Storyboards also provide an opportunity for the entire development team to view the program at once, highlighting gaps in content, assumptions about how things will flow, and paths that are dead ends.

The level of detail in storyboards depends on how they are to be used. If they are being used to provide an overview of the flow of the program and a sense of the level of interactivity, rough hand-drawn pieces of paper may work well. If they are being used to communicate details to graphic artists and communicate the look and feel of the program to clients, a detailed drawing created with a sophisticated graphics program may be required.

A simple storyboard created with PowerPoint software allows the designer to print 8½-by-11-inch visuals and to print multiple visuals on a single page with annotation. These options allow many ways to communicate the design of the program.

The 8½-by-11-inch visuals are large enough for the entire team to see at one time. This makes it easy to walk through with the instructional designer as he or she explains the program, points to elements on the visuals, and clarifies the interactions. Yet another option is to send team members a document that contains the visuals and a brief explanation of what is taking place in each. Figure 9.12 is an example of a simple storyboard created in PowerPoint that combines visuals and annotation.

Summary

The design document, flow chart, script, and storyboard are blueprints that guide the development team. There is a direct relationship between the time and effort put into developing these documents and the quality of the program that is

Figure 9.12. Sample Storyboard

Visual	Explanation
	Program title
	Screen that displays as Bob Smith introduces himself and explains how to reach him after this class.
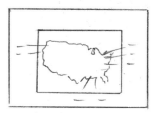	Outline map of the United States. Participants are asked to introduce themselves and to indicate where they are from.
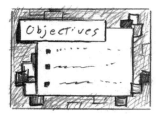	The instructor reviews the objectives and asks the learners if they would like to add any other objectives

A developer recommends using PowerPoint and clip art to create storyboards

I am a terrible artist and don't like to draw, so I use the clip art in PowerPoint® to make my storyboards. It is faster than hand-drawn boards and easier to update.

produced. Designers who document the program's goals, objectives, and audience are developing a solid foundation. Clear descriptions of the information presented, learner participation, and the evaluation strategy set client expectations. Detailed navigation and treatment maps guide graphic artists, programmers, and members of the IS staff.

Web-based training programs are resource intensive. Successful programs require cross-functional cooperation among members of the training department, information-systems staff, line managers, field managers, learners, and subject-matter experts. Complex and expensive hardware, software, and infrastructure are required to support Web-based training. It is essential to understand what is required during the design, development, and delivery phases. Test your assumptions regarding the functionality of software and hardware and partner with members of your information-systems group to explore options.

Use these documents as a yardstick against which the development team and client can measure success. After the program has been developed, decide whether it achieves what the blueprints specify. Chapter 10 presents techniques and strategies for evaluating programs.

Suggested Readings

Hall, B. (1998, July). The cost of custom WBT: Are you getting your money's worth, or paying the price for poor planning. *Inside Technology Training Magazine.*

Greer, M. (2000). *Manager's pocket guide to project management.* New York: HRD Press.

Golas, K. (1993). Estimating time to develop interactive courseware in the 1990s. *Proceedings of the 15th Interservice/Industry Training Systems and Education Conference*, Orlando, Florida, November 29–December 2, 1993. [Online] Available: www.coedu.usf.edu/inst_tech/resources/estimating.html.

Whalen, T., & Wright, D. (2000). *The business case for web-based training.* Boston, MA: Artech House.

McNally, K., & Levine, A. (1998). *Studio 1151 guidebook: Storyboard production.* From Maricopa Center for Learning and Instruction (MCLI), Maricopa Community Colleges. [Online] Available: www.mcli.dist.maricopa.edu/authoring/studio/guidebook/storyboard.html

Scripting Template for Live W/VSC

Time	Audio Directions	Visual	Medial/Files
Pre-Start 0—			

Chapter 10

Implementing and Evaluating WBT Programs

The last two phases of the ADDIE model are the most challenging to execute because they come at the end of the process when the enthusiasm for the project is waning and the deadline is looming. The analysis, design, and development phases often take more time than anticipated and program managers are tempted to take shortcuts in the implementation and evaluation phases. This is particularly true for the first program because it is hard to estimate how long it will take to learn new tools, work with subject-matter experts, author the content, and create graphics. Also, teams become impatient to see the program published to the Web; the steps required to evaluate the program are sometimes viewed as unnecessary and providing little tangible benefit. In reality, careful execution of the implementation and evaluation phases can significantly improve a program.

A word of caution! The ADDIE model is excellent for working with cross-functional teams who don't care about the details of the instructional design process, but the downside of the model is that it tends to oversimplify the process. The oversimplification is most acute in the last two steps, implementation and evaluation. If you are the project manager or if you are planning to outsource the work, it is important to understand the complexity of the last two steps.

The model is complex because it is iterative, that is, it involves repeating a sequence of steps in order to achieve the desired results. The "I" in the ADDIE model refers to the implementation of the pilot and, eventually, when the pilot has resolved the problems with the course, the "I" then refers to implementing a full-scale rollout of the course. Likewise the "E" in the ADDIE process means evaluate, and this is not one step but rather a series of steps that take place throughout the process (see Figure 10.1).

Take a close look at the model and refer to it as you read this chapter. The implementing and evaluating phases are shown as linear steps; in reality the process moves back and forth between implementation and evaluation and there are checks back to earlier steps in the process. This chapter explains the iterative and complicated steps required to implement and evaluate a Web-based training course.

What You Will Learn in This Chapter

After completing this chapter, you will be able to

- Explain the iterative processes for implementation and evaluation;

- Summarize the steps required to evaluate a Web-based training program;

Figure 10.1.   The ADDIE Model

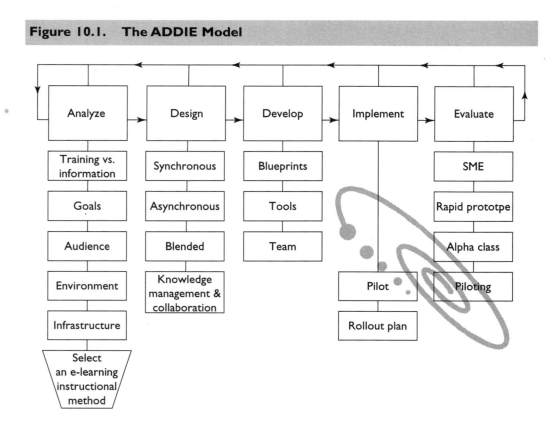

- Implement a pilot; and
- Implement an enterprise rollout.

Implementing and Evaluating

The steps in this process are interwoven. Although the model shows the implementing as coming before evaluation, this is not how you want to do it. The dotted line circling through the five steps denotes the iterative nature of the process. There is evaluation at each step of the process. Let's look at four kinds of evaluation and where they take place. Table 10.1 provides an overview of the evaluation phase and when each type of evaluation is conducted.

The following sections explain how to conduct each of the four kinds of evaluations in the order in which you will want to conduct them.

Subject-Matter Expert Evaluation

First assess the accuracy of the content by asking a subject-matter expert (SME) to examine it for factual integrity and completeness. Involvement of a subject-matter expert can start as early as the analysis phase. During analysis it is helpful to have an SME review the goals statement to ensure that the outcome of the program is well-focused and on target. The SME can also suggest sources for building the content outline and will act as a resource for evaluating the content outline. During the development phase, provide the SME with detailed storyboards, hand-drawn examples of interactions, full-length scripts, content for text screens, and quizzes (provide the correct and incorrect answers). Wait for the SME review of content before spending time and money designing HTML pages and complex interactions. Giving the SME clear directions regarding the kind of feedback you want and the dates by which the material must be reviewed can accelerate the process.

If possible, target sections of the program to be reviewed by different SMEs. Ask those most familiar with a specific topic to review the sections related to that topic. Shorten the evaluation process by having several sections reviewed at the same time by more than one SME. If the recommended changes are substantial, ask the SMEs to review their sections again after responding to their comments.

There are two other kinds of subject-matter experts: people who know a good deal about the intended audience and people who have expertise in developing computer-based training. If you are designing a program for an audience for which you have never designed training, it can be beneficial to check with someone who knows the learners. This is particularly true if you are working on developing

Table 10.1. Steps in the Evaluation Phase

Type	Why Conduct This Evaluation	When to Conduct This Evaluation	Hints
Subject-Matter Expert (SME)	Use SME evaluations to find errors and inaccuracies in the content and to identify technical and educational problems.	Conduct this as soon as the storyboards, blueprints, scripts, and navigation maps are ready.	The better your documents and the more clearly your thinking is laid out, the easier it is to get accurate feedback.
Rapid Prototype	Use rapid prototyping to identify issues related to user interface, navigation, and flow of paths, instructional strategies, and client satisfaction.	Conduct this after developing the first module or a significant portion of the first module.	Be sure to use a representative audience to provide feedback and not a convenient sample.
Alpha-Class	Use the alpha test to determine whether instructor-led materials can be used as intended.	Conduct this as soon as there is a significant body of work to be taught and a pilot audience is ready.	The instructor should be a member of the development team who is familiar with the course and technology.
Pilot	Use the pilot to evaluate the complete program for educational effectiveness and to identify and correct tactical implementation issues such as network bandwidth, Internet connectivity, and platform problems.	Conduct this as soon as the program and audience are ready.	If the pilot involved instruction that is essential to the bottom line, have a fall-back plan for teaching the content should the pilot fail.

 **A trainer at a start-up software company recommends that WBT developers tell SMEs what they are and are not expected to review**

A Web-based training developer for a software company recently received feedback from an SME that was of little value and cost the company a great deal of money. The SME was a senior network system engineer who was given insufficient directions. He spent a great deal of time critiquing the website's design, page layout, and the technical optimization of interactions. Better direction would have focused the SME's attention on the network content; the resulting feedback would have been more valuable.

programs for international audiences. People who are SMEs on working with learners in Asia, Latin America, or Eastern Europe are quickly able to identify potential problems with strategies such as instructional games based on American TV shows, analogies that do not translate easily, or the use of examples that are not relevant.

The third kind of SME is someone who has experience developing WBT programs and who can identify potential technical and educational problems. It may be an excellent investment to ask someone with expertise to review your plans before the first line lesson is authored. Experts in designing programs can point out technical issues related to using collaboration tools, building tests, and creating remediation paths.

Rapid-Prototype Evaluation

The concept of rapid prototyping comes from the manufacturing sector, where it is used to build physical models and archetypes. In manufacturing it is faster and more cost-effective to evaluate a model than to wait for the full system to be built. The advantage of using rapid prototypes in e-learning is similar. Rapid prototypes allow developers to test designs and concepts at an early stage when the changes can be made easily because the costs are low.

Developers use prototypes to address a number of issues, such as assessing the interface, testing branching logic, gauging the effectiveness of the format, and gaining client approval. Assessing the user interface is one of the most important functions of prototyping because a confusing interface and poor navigation undermine a program. A difficult and valuable test during the prototype evaluation is assessing the instructional paths and branches. Do learners become lost? Are there logical transitions along the paths? Will each path cover the complete set of objectives? This is also an opportunity to gauge the appeal of the program and to check whether the instructional strategies meet with learner approval. Do learners like the game format? Is the strategy of using case studies appealing? The prototype pays dividends when working with clients because it provides them with a concrete sense of the program's look and feel.

Evaluating a rapid prototype of a lesson requires a number of steps and many decisions along the way. Figure 10.2 lists the steps.

Make a Rapid Prototype for One Lesson.   The amount of detail in a rapid prototype depends on the tools, audience, budget, and time available for the project. Figure 10.3 illustrates the range of prototypes, from abstract, paper-based lessons to fully functioning Internet lessons.

Figure 10.2.   Steps for Conducting a Rapid Prototype Evaluation

1. Make a rapid prototype for one lesson.
2. Identify learners.
3. Develop a plan to gather feedback.
4. Use one-on-one sessions.
5. Explain the purpose.
6. Create a comfortable environment.
7. Take notes.

Figure 10.3.   Range of Rapid Prototypes

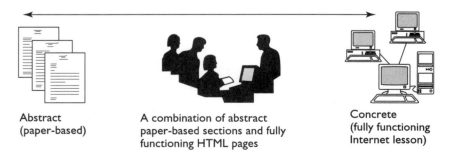

Abstract
(paper-based)

A combination of abstract
paper-based sections and fully
functioning HTML pages

Concrete
(fully functioning
Internet lesson)

The most abstract kinds of prototypes are paper-based lessons, pictures of screens on paper described to the learner. Abstract prototypes are easy to build using simple tools such as word processors, PowerPoint slides, and hand-drawn pictures. Concrete prototypes that look and act exactly like the final training program are more time-consuming and costly to produce.

Although prototypes range from the abstract to the concrete, most are somewhere in between. For example, in a simple W/CBT program that uses only hypertext and images, the prototype may be concrete. In this case it is possible to develop a concrete prototype of the lesson that looks and functions like the final program. In contrast, a complex W/CBT program that uses sophisticated Java applets and sections of compressed video may be evaluated using a more abstract prototype. In this case, the developer would create a series of paper-based drawings to indicate where video or Java applications belonged in the program. During the evaluation, the developer would explain these sections to reviewers.

The complexity and cost of the tools used to build the prototype influence where the prototype falls along the continuum. If the final training program requires the development of Java applets, CGI scripts, compressed video, simulations, and Macromedia Shocked™ images, it may be too costly to develop a prototype with fully functioning interactions. In their place, developers can create paper-based screens or simulate the interactions using PowerPoint slides.

The pilot audience for a rapid prototype will also influence how abstract or concrete it is for review purposes. People familiar with the Web and e-learning will be more capable of understanding how a paper-based version of the program will work on the Web. Learners who have spent limited time using a browser, the Internet, or CBT programs may have difficulty understanding how a paper-based prototype will work on the Web. Feedback on the clarity of directions, level of interest, and effectiveness of instruction can only be assessed if those reviewing the program understand how the program will operate.

The project's budget and timeline influence the prototype. Developing a concrete prototype may be disproportionately expensive and time-consuming relative to the balance of the project. A fully functioning prototype requires that the graphic style be defined and that interactions, quizzes, and images be created. These are time-consuming to design and develop, but if the prototype elements are determined to be effective, these initial items become templates—reusable elements for the final program.

It is difficult for clients to understand that, although the prototype appears to be expensive, it is actually a way to save money. It is less expensive to learn that an icon is confusing or that certain types of interactions are too "cutesy" during the prototype than after the program has been fully developed. The steps in the rapid prototype are described below.

A developer creating a class for nontechnical managers shares her insights regarding the different degrees of detail needed in a rapid prototype

I have developed many programs for technical people. Quick-and-dirty prototype screens worded well. I was able to use simple graphics as placeholders for detailed diagrams that had not been created and a box with the phrase "photo goes here" to represent an image or a photo. When my learners are technical people familiar with the Web, HTML, and CBT, they understand what my shorthand means. Dealing with less technically sophisticated learners, I found that they were not able to understand my shorthand. These kinds of learners require a more fully developed prototype that uses the real images, icons, working interactions, and functioning navigation.

Identify Learners.   Work with your client or the organization sponsoring the program to identify learners who are representative of the audience. Find learners who represent the full spectrum of skills and experiences: those who are experienced and inexperienced in the content area and those who are skilled using the Internet and those who are not.

Use a grid like the one shown in Figure 10.4 to select a representative sample. Six to nine users will provide sufficient feedback on the content and the issues related to using a browser.

Your sample audience may not be as diverse as the one shown in Figure 10.4. If you are training in an environment in which Web-based training is new, you may not have any experienced browser users in your audience.

 The CD-ROM at the back of the book has a template for helping you identify prototype learners.

Figure 10.4.   Identify Prototype Learners

Familiarity with Browser	Familiarity with Content		
	Novice	**Practitioner**	**Expert**
Beginner User	Tom	Gene	Scott
Intermediate User	Sue	Tim	Terry
Experienced User	Karen	Nora	Jose

Develop a Plan to Gather Feedback.   Develop a plan to collect data from pilot learners. Focus on collecting information regarding the clarity of content and level of difficulty in using the browser. Create checklists or questions that will guide the evaluation sessions, such as the one in Figure 10.5.

 The CD-ROM at the back of the book has forms for gathering feedback.

Use One-on-One Sessions.   After you have prepared the evaluation guidelines, invite the pilot learners to evaluate the prototype during one-on-one sessions in which it will be easier to collect information. Also, if the prototype is abstract, you will be able to explain how interactions, hypertext links, or icons work.

Explain the Purpose.   Explain the purpose of the evaluation to the learners. Stress that learners' experiences and feedback are valued. Explain that the program is not perfect or error free and that they are being asked for their opinions. Remember that they are the best qualified people to guide the development of the program.

Create a Comfortable Environment.   Create a comfortable environment for conducting an evaluation. As with one-on-one evaluations for conventional training materials, the role of an evaluator in Web-based training is to be critical of the material being presented. In the context of Web-based training, this role is more complex because the learner must be critical not only of the content and design, but also of the computer interface. Help the learners feel comfortable with the role of evaluator. Do not be impatient with novice browser users. Separate the criticism of the

Figure 10.5.   Sample Questions for Rapid-Prototype Session

Content

☑ Are the directions clear?

☑ Does the content meet the objectives?

☑ Is the vocabulary appropriate?

☑ Do the examples add clarity to the lesson?

☑ Is there adequate practice?

Browser or Software Running in Browser

☑ Are the icons clear?

☑ Is the navigation intuitive?

☑ Are the screen "hot spots" clear?

☑ Are pop-up windows confusing?

☑ After using a hypertext link, is it easy to return to the program?

content, design, and interactions from the learners' frustrations with network speed and browser interface.

Take Notes.   Keep track of feedback. If you are using a fully developed Web-based training program, print out the screens and take notes directly on the screen prints. This will make it easy to keep track of feedback in nonlinear programs. Use a copy of the navigation map to note navigation problems or interactions that create confusion.

After the rapid-prototype evaluation, make the recommended changes, and develop all of the lessons.

Evaluation Paths

After the rapid prototype, the evaluation paths differ somewhat among the four kinds of Web-based training. At this point Web/CBT or W/EPS programs are ready to pilot if the content has been checked for accuracy and completeness and the rapid prototype completed. These programs do not require an alpha-class evaluation because they do not involve an instructor. However, when an online learning program requires an instructor to facilitate, teach, or monitor the program, an alpha class is beneficial. Table 10.2 provides a summary of the evaluations that are best suited for each kind of Web-based training.

Table 10.2. Evaluation and Implementation				
	W/CBT	**W/EPS**	**W/VAC**	**W/VSC**
Subject-Matter Expert	X	X	X	X
Rapid Prototype	X	X	X	X
Alpha Class			X	X
Pilot	X	X	X	X

If the materials you have created do not require the intervention of an instructor, go to the section on evaluating the pilot. Web-based training programs that involve any kind of facilitation should conduct an alpha class evaluation.

Alpha-Class Evaluation

The purpose of an alpha class is to assess the effectiveness of the changes made as a result of the rapid-prototype evaluation and to determine whether the materials can be used by the instructor as intended. In this phase, the learners are using fully developed materials, including graphics, page layout, interactions, tests, and links to other sites.

The alpha class is the first time the materials are used over the Web as intended. In the case of W/VSC and W/VAC, the developer acts as the instructor. Based on the developer's experience as an instructor, changes are made to the instructor's notes or instructor's guide. These notes can be useful for conducting a train-the-trainer session. Figure 10.6 lists the steps required to evaluate Web-based training programs that are self-paced or instructor-led.

Identify Learners.   The learners should be representative of the population for whom the training is being developed. This is the first evaluation of the training program by remote learners of instruction delivered via the browsers. Use a representative sample of learners to provide broad feedback on technical difficulties and instructional issues.

Plan How to Gather Feedback.   Identify the data to be collected from the alpha class and create a plan to collect it. Make a list of questions about relevance of content, clarity of instructions, effectiveness of instructional design, and the ease of use of the interface and computer interactions. Because the audience is often scattered and the data is important, consider a range of data-collection tools (see Table 10.3).

Figure 10.6. Steps to Evaluate an Alpha Class

1. Identify learners.
2. Plan how to gather feedback.
3. Explain the purpose of the alpha-class evaluation.
4. Help learners feel comfortable and collect data.
5. Compile the data and make necessary changes.

Table 10.3. Considerations for Collecting Data

Planning Data Collection	Sample Data Collection Methods
How will data be collected?	• E-mail
	• Telephone
	• Text-chat
	• Survey sent via postal service
What methods for collecting data will be used?	• Individual interviews
	• Focus groups
What areas will be assessed?	• Design
	• Content
	• Technical functionality
	• Interactions
	• Timing

Determine how feedback will be collected (phone, e-mail, text-chat, or survey). Use methods that are familiar to the learners. If they are not familiar with a method, their feedback may be limited. Think about the methods of collecting data. In some cases you may want to have a focus group, and in others you may want to invite people to contact you by phone or e-mail. In addition, attempt to find a learner and ask whether you may observe him or her using the program. Observing learners helps you to see the environment in which the program will be used. Observation also helps identify frustrations caused by unclear navigation, delays in downloading files, the level of engagement, and other issues that may not be voiced in feedback sessions.

Explain Purpose of Alpha-Class Evaluation. Explain the purpose of the alpha-class evaluation to learners. Inform them that the class is being piloted and that their feedback is important. Before the class begins, explain what kind of information you will be collecting so that learners can take notes. Set learners' expectations regarding frequent stops for feedback and the need to complete exercises, to take quizzes, and to participate in text-chat sessions and threaded discussions.

Help Learners Feel Comfortable and Collect Data. Help learners feel comfortable delivering feedback, as well as acknowledging their technical limitations. Much of the data will be collected at a distance via telephone, e-mail, and surveys, which makes it difficult to sort the technical obstacles from the instructional problems. Learners must feel comfortable and be encouraged to provide honest feedback. In some cases, the designer will need to ask follow-up questions to determine which problems are technical and which are educational. If learners are unfamiliar with the browser or if tools such as text-chat and threaded discussions frustrate them, the developer needs honest feedback. Effective feedback from learners regarding unclear directions will lead the developer to improve the directions rather than eliminate the exercise.

Compile Data and Make Necessary Changes. Compile the data and make changes as indicated by the alpha class. Additional changes are still possible, of course. One of the benefits of Web-based training is that minor modifications and changes can be made quickly and cost effectively. Changes to complex elements such as Java applets, compressed video segments, and other multimedia elements can be expensive because they require more effort and access to resources such as programmers, hardware, and software.

Web/virtual synchronous classes and Web/virtual asynchronous classes are now ready for a piloting. Pilots test the effectiveness of directions to the instructor and how well the class runs when delivered by someone other than the developer.

Implementing and Evaluating the Pilot

Yes, you must implement the pilot before you can evaluate it, but let's stay with the theme of evaluation. There are two distinct areas that must be evaluated during the pilot. The first area is the program effectiveness and the second is the technical execution.

Program Effectiveness

Like traditional classroom programs, a Web-based training program can be evaluated using Kirkpatrick's four levels. See Table 10.4 for an overview of the Kirkpatrick model as it applies to e-learning. The number of levels you choose to evaluate will depend on what your client or funder demands, what your budget allows, and what your timeline permits. Most people choose to evaluate at the reaction and learning levels.

Table 10.4.	**Kirkpatrick's Four Levels of Evaluation**	
Level	**Measures**	**Web-Based Examples**
Level I	Reaction—measures learner's satisfaction with course.	Survey at end of WBT program asking eight to twelve questions about what learners liked and did not like about the program.
Level II	Learning—measures how much of the content a learner has mastered based on the course objectives.	Multiple choice quiz, fill-in-the blank, or short answer questions requiring students to demonstrate they can do what the objectives state they should be able to do.
Level III	Transfer—measures the amount of skills and knowledge learners are able to apply on the job several weeks or months after the course.	A checklist is sent to the learners' manager asking him or her to evaluate the learners' ability to demonstrate mastery or what they learned in the WBT program.
Level IV	Business Results—measures the financial improvement to the organization's bottom line several months or a year after the course.	A sales team is randomly selected to participate in a WBT program using course tracking data. This group is compared to a control group. The comparison is used to determine how much the group that was given a WBT generated additional sales. Based on the additional sales resulting from a WBT intervention, the organization can calculate the return on investment in training.[1]

[1]Level IV calculations are difficult to make because it is impossible to isolate the entire variable contributing to improved performance. Most organizations lack the resources and motivation to conduct the kind of controlled study needed to deliver valid and reliable data.

Technical Execution

Tactical problems, such as poor Internet access, slow modem speeds, and the inability of learners to adjust settings, are problems that must be resolved before the enterprise-wide rollout of the program. The pilot presents all the tactical challenges of a full implementation, but on a scale that allows easy corrections.

There are five areas in which to look for technical problems. The first area is connectivity; this refers to a program or device's ability to link to other programs or devices. When conducting a technical evaluation, the connectivity considerations include any obstacles that keep the learners from gaining access to your program. Other technical problems are found at the desktop level. There are some technical difficulties, which are not hardware or software related but caused by the learners' inability to make the needed adjustments to their computers. In some cases there are technical problems associated with hardware or software that are beyond the learners' control. In larger organizations in which the e-learning program must link to other software applications such as a learning management system or human resource information system, there may be integration problems. Table 10.5 provides an overview of the potential problem areas.

Implementing the Pilot

Understanding the four kinds of evaluation and the sequence in which they take place is important. Three of the phases, the SME review, the rapid prototype, and if necessary, the alpha class should be completed and the changes made before implementing a pilot. Figure 10.7 provides a summary of the steps required to implement a pilot.

Build a Team.   One of the keys to successfully implementing a pilot and later an enterprise-wide rollout is a strong team with the skills needed to address technical, political, and educational problems. Members of this team should be involved in the assessment, design, and development phases so they have accountability for the specifications to which the program was developed, buy-in regarding the goals, and a sense of ownership. If possible, the team members should remain consistent and not be swapped in and out. A consistent team will have a better understanding of the decisions and tradeoffs that were made and will be more willing to live with the consequences than team members who walk in unaware of how and why decisions were made.

Acquire an Audience.   Once the pilot/implementation team is in place, select the audience. This should be an extension of the needs assessment phase in which

Table 10.5. Technical Evaluation Issues

Potential Problem Areas	Things to Look For
Connectivity: Why is the learner not able to access the program?	Firewall problems Lack of access to the network System configuration problems
Learners' Technical Abilities: What end-user activities are learners having difficulty doing?	Installing plug-ins Adjusting system settings such as sound, screen resolution Managing Windows
Hardware: What hardware problems are being encountered?	Are systems meeting the specifications for sound cards, monitors, and modems? Are desktop computers "locked down," that is, end users cannot make any adjustments?
Software: What software problems are being encountered?	Are there problems associated with different versions of browser software? Are applications required to open pre-course documents available, such as Microsoft Office Word and Excel?
Integration: Is the e-learning program integrated with other back-end programs so that data is sent and received properly?	Is the e-learning program integrated so as to track learner data to your learning management system (LMS)? Are you able to use an existing employee database to automatically complete registration fields?

the target audience members were identified. During the pilot phase, the learners move from being defined in general as executives, new hires, and engineers to a specifically identified group of "sales" executives, new hire "customer service reps," or "sales support" engineers.

One of most important aspects of a piloting is to start small. Choose a group of twelve to twenty-five participants. Starting small allows you to collect data in great

Figure 10.7. Steps for Implementing a Pilot

1. Build a team.

2. Acquire an audience.

3. Confirm learner skill level.

4. Qualify hardware.

5. Test software and plug-ins.

6. Check network connectivity.

7. Set dates.

8. Ask the right questions.

9. Deliver the pilot program.

10. Gather and analyze data.

11. Summarize the pilot data and make changes.

detail and to make corrections before launching a massive program. If the program is a live synchronous program, consider numbers as small as six to eight to allow the instructor time to become used to interacting in virtual space and to allow your technical staff the time needed to address the technical challenges associated with Internet protocol (IP) audio.

One of the key tasks during audience acquisition is to contact the managers who are responsible for your audience. These managers are key to the success of the program because they will set the tone for it. If managers see the program as a distraction or as little more than an educational "Game Boy," the pilot is doomed. During the acquisition phase, work with middle managers to communicate the purpose of the program, the benefits to their organization, and the level of commitment required for participation.

Confirm Learner Skill Level. The most successful pilots are conducted with learners who have adequate computer skills. Confirm that learners have keyboarding, mousing, and Windows management skills. Ask about the learners' level of comfort using a browser and interpreting Internet conventions such as underlined works for links, and navigation using forward and back arrows.

Like a traditional classroom, it is important to determine whether the learners have appropriate prerequisite knowledge of the topic. A program that is too advanced will frustrate learners, while a program that is too simple will bore learners.

Dealing with global audiences provides a unique set of rollout challenges related to language. Do all the participants speak and read English well enough to learn from the program? Don't assume that because the company's official language is English that students comprehended well enough to learn from your program.

Qualify Hardware.   It is essential that the pilot audience have access to computers that support the WBT program. Document the computer platforms that support the program, that is, make a list of the specifications such as operating system(s), chip speed, modem speed, audio cards, color monitors, and other important information. Don't assume everyone has a PC. Check for Mac and Unix workstations.

Test Software and Plug-Ins.   Determine that the audience has the right version of the browser. If your program is optimized to run on Internet Explorer (IE) and the audience has Netscape, make plans for installing the IE. Take the time to test systems for any plug-ins you may need, such as Macromedia's Flash or Real.com's player. In addition, many WBT systems require what is called a "thin-client," a small piece of software installed on students' computers allowing the students' computers to interact with the training program on the server.

Don't assume that the audience has plug-ins or that they can install plug-ins. Plug-ins and thin-client issues can take significant time to resolve. If students are not comfortable installing plug-ins and thin-clients, then make plans to have someone else install these items. Another potential issue is getting permission to install software. Organizations frequently have a standard configuration for PCs. In these cases the computer is locked down, which disables users from installing software. These locking measures help MIS groups limit the number of problems that arise due to users installing software that conflicts with existing programs and limits the potential for introducing viruses. Getting new software installed or getting permission for plug-ins may take a significant amount of time if the software must be approved by committee, tested for conflicts, and then rolled out from MIS.

Check Network Connectivity.   Implementation plans should include time to assess the learners' access, impact on network performance, and the reliability of connections. Start your check of network connectivity with some questions about where the learners will be connecting from. Will it be from their desktops, the road, or home? The speed of the connection is an important factor to consider when rolling out the program. If the learners are using 28.8 modems from home, the program may not be as smooth and engaging as using the program at work or on a local area network with good bandwidth.

Work with MIS to determine whether there are times of day at which the network is at full capacity and at which times it would not be appropriate to run synchronous training. Understanding the impact that training can have on the network will help you choose the right times to run a live synchronous program or to stream rich media.

If the program is being used worldwide, ask questions about the cost of connectivity and telephone charges. Telephone charges are frequently metered perminute in countries outside North America, making it very expensive to take programs that require learners to be connected for several hours.

Set Dates.   It takes time to roll out a WBT program, so be sure to communicate the dates for preparing systems, installing software, and the actual pilot start and end dates.

When implementing a program, work with the local offices and audiences to identify dates that are problematic. Speak with managers regarding end-of-quarter dates, regional events, and other dates that would create a conflict. When working on worldwide implementations of synchronous programs, be sure to avoid dates that conflict with international holidays and religious holidays.

Planning a pilot is complicated and it is easy to lose sight of all the details. Figure 10.8 provides a checklist to help. This checklist can be expanded to include more items and to list who is responsible for action items. There is a template on the CD-ROM that can be used as a starting point for creating your own checklist.

Ask the Right Questions.   During the program evaluation, we asked questions about the educational effectiveness of the program and the students' reaction to the material. During the pilot there are many other audiences who need to be consulted. The technical evaluation is the time to determine whether the program is technically acceptable to field managers, information systems managers, and the managers in training and development. It is possible for a program to be well-regarded by the learners but consume an unacceptable amount of bandwidth, conflict with the field office scheduling, and fail to demonstrate transfer of learning.

The right questions when doing a technical evaluation do not have to do with the content or the educational issues; they have to do with technical performance. These are benchmarks that must be established by asking each member of the

Figure 10.8. Pilot Implementation Checklist

Audience Acquisition

- ☑ Recruit the audience.
- ☑ Contact managers in field offices.
- ☑ Confirm the learners are the appropriate audience.

Learner Skill Level

- ☑ Confirm that learners have adequate computer skills.
- ☑ Verify learners have prerequisite knowledge of topic.
- ☑ Validate learners have adequate browser and Internet skills.

Hardware

- ☑ Document computer platforms (i.e., PC, Mac, UNIX) will support WBT software.
- ☑ Confirm that learners have modems and/or network connections.
- ☑ Verify technical requirements are met (i.e., color monitor, resolution, audio capabilities).

Software

- ☑ Specify and verify learners have correct version of browser (Microsoft/Netscape).
- ☑ Test that learners have downloaded plug-ins.

Network Connection

- ☑ Verify learners can connect to the network.
- ☑ Document learners' connection speed and set performance expectations.
- ☑ Assess reliability of connection.

Dates

- ☑ Check calendar to avoid end-of-quarter rush and holidays.
- ☑ Identify and avoid dates that conflict with international holidays and religious holidays if the pilot is evaluating synchronous WBT tools.

 The CD-ROM at the back of the book has a template for a Pilot Implementation Checklist.

implementation team to create a list of items that will indicate the project has gone well. The list below provides examples of measures from a variety of constituencies.

Training

- 85 percent of learners complete the program.
- The level II evaluations show 95 percent of students who complete the program achieve mastery.
- 60 percent of line managers report improved productivity among employees who participated in the WBT pilot.
- Courses can be developed as quickly as they are developed for stand-up training.

Management Information Systems

- Less than 7 percent of students call helpdesk for support.
- Bandwidth tests reveal no adverse impact on the network.
- Must run on Mac, PC, and UNIX platforms.
- WBT software conforms to corporate software standards.

Field Managers

- Reduces the number of days sales reps are out of the field by .5 days per month.
- Increased flexibility of scheduling because customer service representatives can take training at more convenient times.
- No new hardware or software required.
- New hires can be brought on when hired instead of waiting for scheduled new hire orientation program.

Work with the team to create measurable benchmarks. Turn soft benchmarks such as "like," "understand," "appreciate," and "improve" into concrete gauges. Make these items observable and measurable.

The final step is to weight each item. Not all measures are of equal importance. Some of the benchmarks are more important than others, for example, should technical considerations outweigh education considerations? It is the team's responsibility to reach consensus on which benchmarks to use and how to weight each one.

Deliver the Pilot Program.   Establish start and stop dates for the pilot. Ask your e-learning champion to communicate the importance of the program. A pilot should not drag on indefinitely. Start by communicating with the learners'

Figure 10.9.   Hints for Piloting Instructor-Led Classes on the Web

Conduct a rehearsal run for instructor-led W/VSC and W/VAC classes. Allowing the instructor time for rehearsals enables him or her to become familiar with the interface and the content. Use this as an opportunity to make last-minute adjustments before the pilot runs. Remember the alpha class was taught by one of the developers. The formal instructor is faced with a new interface as well as a new course.

managers to warn them of the pilot dates. Let learners know when the pilot begins and ends, and encourage them to complete the program. Send students e-mail at the two-week, one-week, and two-day marks to warn them that the pilot is coming to an end. As you did during alpha class, respond to requests for assistance promptly to avoid creating frustration. Resolve technical issues quickly because student frustration with access and reliability can spell disaster. See the hints in Figure 10.9 above.

Gather and Analyze Data.   Collect data while the pilot is taking place; take note of subtle changes in students' attitudes toward the program as they become more familiar with it or capture data related to students' initial responses to the interface. Be sure to include Kirkpatrick Level I and II assessment of the program itself. Make use of telephone surveys, e-mail questionnaires, and online forums to gather other data. Consider enlisting nontrainers as data gathers, who simply observe learners taking Web-based training programs. These data gathers don't need to understand the content; they are watching for general human behavior, such as attentiveness, the level of engagement, restlessness, and note taking.

As a team, return to the weighted metrics created before the pilot and analyze the outcome. Interpret the data by asking: What does the data reveal? Are there contradictions? How did the pilot measure up against the established benchmarks? Did employees learn? Did employees like WBT as a delivery methodology? What were their frustrations? Were there any surprises? How did managers in field offices like WBT? Were there technical problems? What computer issues were most bothersome to learners? Are there questions that the team wished they had asked? Can the team follow up on those questions?

Summarize the Pilot Data and Make Changes.   Keep in mind the purpose of a pilot is to discover facts about implementing Web-based training and to learn how well the technology works in your environment. Your analysis of the data and report should summarize the facts and make recommendations regarding how best to implement WBT. Use the data to make changes to the program and to correct technical problems. A successful enterprise-wide implementation depends on resolving the problems identified in the pilot.

Back-Up Plans

If things don't go according to schedule, be prepared to scale back the size of the pilot audience, reduce the technical requirement to participate, or reschedule the pilot to allow for the installation of new PCs or renting a server. Even though the needs assessment may have indicated that everything should work, leave room for glitches. If the pilot program is designed to teach mission critical skills such as the launch of a new product or the rollout of a systems upgrade, be prepared to have alterative plans for self-paced materials or instructor-led classes.

Implementing an Enterprise Wide Rollout

One would like to say implementing the pilot is the final step, but in online learning that is not accurate. Once the educational and technical issues are resolved, it is time to make the program available to a wider audience.

Enterprise-wide implementation requires more than simply posting the program on the server and forgetting it. A full-scale implementation requires that you communicate the availability of the program and that you monitor the activity. A pilot program often benefits from the halo effect and attention paid the learners and their suggestions. Once a program is available enterprise-wide on a regular basis, the tracking data should be monitored over time. Tracking data will provide information about how often the program is used, how learners see the program's value, where learners encounter difficulty, where they drop out, and what parts of the program, if any, they return to at a later point. This kind of data should be used to suggest changes to the program when it is next updated, and the data should inform design considerations for future programs.

Updating and maintaining programs presents unique challenges in Web-based training. This is an activity that people often fail to leave time or budget for doing. Maintenance is an issue that should be well-thought-through for projects developed in-house, as well as for those that are outsourced. Part of the enterprise-wide implementation plan should be a maintenance plan that provides a scheduled check to ensure links are still working, the program's content is current and accurate, and the changes suggested by the tracking data are made.

If a vendor has developed a program, there are two choices: The vendor can be contracted to maintain the course for a set number of updates or you can take ownership for updating the course. The best time to contract for updates is during the initial contract negotiations. If you choose to update the course yourself, be sure to contract for the source files so that you can modify them. For example, if the graphics were created in PhotoShop™ and saved as GIF files, get the source files so you can return to PhotoShop and edit the photos.

Updating a course in-house using your own resources demands good planning. Planning for updates starts during development when proper naming conventions are used for files, directories are created, and a read-me file is established. The read-me file describes what software applications were used to create media, the version, the naming conventions, and any information that will be helpful to the update team. The second challenge to assuming responsibility for the update is access to the resources. After the enterprise-wide implementation, the team is usually assigned to new projects. The fastest way to do the update is to bring back the original developers, who know how things work and understand the history of the project. If the original team is not available, updates may take longer because new team members must come up to speed.

No matter who does the update, there is expense involved. A quick estimate for update costs is shown in Figure 10.10. An implementation plan may also set a date for obsolescence and removal from the server.

Piloting Third-Party Content

If you are buying off-the-shelf programs, it is also a good idea to implement a pilot before you implement the program enterprise-wide. The pilot may identify issues with the quality of the program and learner satisfaction or technical problems, such as bandwidth demands, firewall difficulties, and incompatibility with your learning management system. You will not need to conduct the other forms of evaluation because changes cannot be made to off-the-shelf programs.

Figure 10.10. Simple Formulas for Maintenance

Cost of Program × Percent of Content Change = Maintenance Cost Per Year

Program cost		10 percent change	
50K	×	10%	= 5K to maintain

Summary

Because WBT is a technology involving many parts of the organization, it is essential to have a well-structured plan to pilot, evaluate, and implement it. Although implementation and evaluation are the final steps in the process, they are important. Corrections are easier and less costly to make before a program is implemented enterprise-wide. The use of SME evaluations, rapid prototypes, alpha classes, and pilots are part of the iterative process that little by little perfects the program.

Piloting, evaluating, and implementing an online learning program is a full-time job. The project manager is the link who directs developers, communicates with field end users, keeps the champion updated, and works political and organizational issues. The guidelines provided here are a starting point for training professionals who wish to lead a pilot.

The next chapter looks at the road ahead and what training managers can expect. Web-based training is forecast to be a $23 billion dollar business by 2004. This kind of exponential growth forecast has serious implications for anyone involved in online learning.

Suggested Readings

ASTD Learning Circuits. (2001). *E-learning evaluation method gains support in Canada.* [Online] Available: www.learningcircuits.org/jul2000/jul2000_newsbytes.html#july4

Barksdale, S.B., & Lund, T.B. (1997). Setting standards for evaluating Internet-based training. *Multimedia & Internet Training Newsletter, 4*(11), 4–5, 10.

Clark, R.E. (1994). Assessment of distance learning technology. In E.L. Baker & H.F. O'Neil, Jr. (Eds.), *Technology assessment in education and training.* Hillsdale, NJ: Lawrence Erlbaum Associates.

Flagg, B.N. (1990). *Formative evaluation for educational technologies.* Hillsdale, NJ: Lawrence Erlbaum Associates.

Kirkpatrick, D. (1994). *Evaluating training programs: The four levels.* San Francisco: Berrett-Koehler.

Wetzel, M. (2001, February). Stuck in the middle. *Online Learning Magazine,* p. 30.

Wilson, B.G., Jonassen, D.H., & Cole, P. (1993). Cognitive approaches to instructional design. In G.M. Piskurich (Ed.), *The ASTD handbook of instructional technology* (pp. 21.1–21.22). New York: McGraw-Hill.

Template to Identify Prototype Learners

Familiarity with Browser	Familiarity with Content of Lesson		
	Novice	Practitioner	Expert
Beginning User			
Intermediate User			
Experienced User			

Template Questions for Rapid-Prototype Sessions

Developer/Instructional Designer:
Prototype Learner:
Date:

	Questions	Observations/Recommended Changes
Content	Are the directions clear? (e.g., What does the learner have questions about? What frustrates him or her?)	
	Does the content meet the objectives? (e.g., Can the student complete the exercises? Can the student pass the assessments? Which objectives are problematic?)	
	Is the vocabulary appropriate? (e.g., Are there words that are too difficult? Do you need a glossary? Should acronyms be eliminated?)	
	Is there adequate practice? (e.g., Did the student have too much/too little practice at the simple, moderate, and complex levels before assessment?)	
	Do the examples add clarity to the lesson? (Add your own questions here.)	

	Questions	Observations/Recommended Changes
Navigation	Are the icons clear?	
	Is the navigation intuitive? (e.g., If learners elected not to read the getting started module, could they navigate the chapter?)	
	Are the screen "hot spots" clear? (e.g., Do students click on the right places? Are things like underlined text or icons causing confusion?)	
	Are pop-up windows confusing? (e.g., Does the program pop up new windows of take the learner "out" of the program?)	
	After using a hypertext link, is it easy to return to the program? If so, which hyper-text links are creating problems?	

Template for Pilot Implementation Checklist

Owner	Due Date	Action Item	Status
		Audience Acquisition Recruit the audience. Contact managers in field offices. Confirm the learners are the appropriate audience.	
		Learner Skill Level Confirm learners have adequate computer skills. Verify learners have prerequisite knowledge of topic. Validate learners have adequate browser and Internet skills.	
		Hardware Document computer platforms (i.e., PC, Mac, UNIX) will support WBT software. Confirm that learners have modems and/or network connections. Verify technical requirements are met (i.e., color monitor, resolutions, audio capabilities).	
		Software Specify and verify learners have correct version of browser (Microsoft/Netscape). Test that learners have downloaded plug-ins.	

Owner	Due Date	Action Item	Status
		Network Connection Verify learners can connect to the network. Document learners' connection speed and set performance expectations. Assess reliability of connection.	
		Dates Check calendar to avoid end-of-quarter rush and holidays. Identify and avoid dates that conflict with international holidays and religious holidays if the pilot is evaluating synchronous WBT tools.	

Chapter 11

Looking Ahead

When we started the book, we looked at some of the reasons for implementing Web-based training: a global workforce, shorter production cycles, diverse needs of employees, a contingent workforce, and the current challenge in retaining valued workers. We discussed the organizational requirements needed to establish Web-based training, including technical infrastructure, an ability to embrace new ways of thinking, and a significant investment in time and money. And we explored the expected return on investment for the organization, namely to help it better meet business objectives and also reduce costs of training employees.

Chapter 2, Best Practices for WBT Implementation, delved more deeply into these and other guidelines for ensuring success of a company's venture into this new learning environment. Chapter 3, Principles of Adult Education and Instructional Design, provided an overview of the phases of learning and details on facilitating adult learning and motivating adult learners. Chapter 4, Tools of the Trade, examined the range of instructional technologies available and provided a framework for sorting out the options. The remaining chapters then focused on how to understand the process of developing and implementing a Web-based training program that is grounded in sound principles of adult learning and instructional design, using the ADDIE model of development. Woven throughout the book were additional guidelines on how to communicate with senior management throughout the process of incorporating WBT in an organization;

how to establish the need for such a training delivery method; how to establish an implementation team and communicate the project's status to others; and how to draw up blueprints for the Web-based training design so that others could easily understand the goals and design of the training.

The book has given training managers the information and how-to tools to manage and build a Web-based program. Business managers learned the basics of how to evaluate WBT options and how to champion the selected project to a successful end. And instructional designers and systems professionals gained a richer understanding of how to enhance their involvement on a WBT implementation team.

In order to round out the discussion of Web-based training, this chapter places WBT into a larger context and discusses the future trends and challenges managers face as they make decisions regarding e-learning delivery methods. It also discusses the infrastructure managers will put in place to manage course development and implementation and to track employee participation via learning management systems and the use of learning content management systems. It presents ideas for making WBT part of a larger strategic plan for training and development, and describes the roles and environments that leaders of learning will be facing in the near future. Finally, within the context of new training trends and roles—and with consideration for the kinds of skills that training professionals currently need for successful implementation of Web-based training—the chapter closes with a discussion of career development opportunities for the e-learning professional.

What You Will Learn in This Chapter

After completing this chapter you will be able to

- Identify key trends of business environments, time factors, and technology and their implications on training organizations;

- Understand the components to a strategic plan for training and development; and

- Plan e-learning career development activities in your role as either a business manager, training manager, or instructional designer/course developer.

Macro and Micro Trends

There are two trend lines to watch: macro trends related to the general economic environment and micro trends related to training and development. The ability to recognize and synthesize these trends in light of your organization is a key to success. These trends can be grouped into three areas: the business environment, time, and technology. We have briefly discussed these trends in Chapter 1, Tactical and Strategic Advantages. However, it is important to emphasize that anyone responsible for setting direction for training and development in an organization should be aware of these trends. Monitoring trends is essential not only when making a business case for investment in learning, but also when putting WBT into the broader strategic training plan.

The Business Environment

In a recent Conference Board (2001) report, managers from North America, Asia, and Europe were asked what their major concerns were relative to business. The ranking of their concerns varied, but the leading concerns were consistent: increased competition, the Internet, industry consolidation, the war for talent, and downward pressure on prices.

These trends are all related to the rise of the knowledge economy, in which information and knowledge are the key factors in creating wealth. In the past wealth was produced by labor and capital, and before that by land and labor. With the increased mobility of information and the global workforce, knowledge and expertise can be transported instantaneously around the world. Globalization means that any advantage gained by one company can be eliminated by competitive improvements overnight. The only comparative advantage companies will enjoy will be their process of innovation. The ability to combine market and technology know-how with the creative talents of knowledge workers to solve a constant stream of competitive problems will provide a competitive advantage.

So What? Impact on Training Organizations

Training organizations are directly feeling the impact of the knowledge economy. They are taking a greater role in developing knowledge workers. The strategy for developing workers in the new economy may be formal courses delivered both in the classroom and online and a host of informal solutions. Informal solutions include: a growing reliance on knowledge management tools, communities of practice, electronic performance support systems, and instructional strategies such as collaborative learning and action learning.

Time

There is one commodity that is in short supply at every level of every corporation—time. The scarcity of time and the demands on time are macro and micro trends. At the enterprise level, managers are dealing with shorter product lifecycles, worldwide competition and innovation, and increasing customer demands for 7/24 response. At the micro level, time pressure is being felt by employee and training organizations.

Shorter Product Lifecycles.   Increased global competition, and the constant need to innovate are driving faster product development and shorter product lifecycles. In the new economy, products are created, distributed, and retired faster than ever before. Reduced cycles require marketing, development, manufacturing, sales, and customer support to quickly learn about the new product or service. This has a direct impact on the training organization, which must quickly develop training for salespeople, customer service representatives, customers, and others. The challenge for training organizations is to have training ready before the product ships, even if the product is still being finalized and changes are being made up to the last minute.

Customer Demands.   Pressure from customers who expect organizations to respond seven days a week and twenty-four hours a day is another time trend. The relentless focus on time is most acute for organizations that sell or deliver service over the Internet because this channel is always on. Organizations that sell product and services around the world can no longer afford to operate in a single time zone. Customers in Europe, Asia, Latin America, and Africa expect to be able to access the company during their working hours. This means that organizations must extend their hours of operations.

Pressure on Employees.   Employees are feeling pressures of being asked to do more with less during economic downturns. Technologies such as the Internet, mobile devices, and notebook computers are extending the time people work and shifting work time to home time. One of the items being shifted to after hours and home is the time required to learn new skills and knowledge. A recent report by IDC Canada (2001) asked managers about their beliefs regarding the benefits of e-learning today and in the future. Of those surveyed, "40 percent [thought] that students will be learning on their own time." When asked about what they think the future holds, managers reported "that [learning on their own time] will increase to about 88 percent by the time [they] implement" an e-learning solution.

Employees may feel the need to take greater responsibility for learning given the half-life of information, even if that means learning on their own time. Research has shown that 50 percent of an employee's skills become outdated in three to five years. This phenomenon is known as the half-life of information (Moe, 2000). The effect of the half-life of information was driven home in a presentation given to a group of engineering students by Louis Ross, Ford Motor Company's chief technology officer. He told the students, "In your career, knowledge is like milk. It has a shelf life stamped right on the carton. The shelf life of a degree in engineering is about three years. If you're not replacing everything you know by then, your career is going to turn sour fast."

So What? Impact on Training Organizations

At the micro level, training organizations are witnessing trends associated with time. They are being asked to produce training programs faster and to reduce the amount of time learners need to spend in training.

Produce Training Faster. Two factors are driving the demand for training organizations to produce programs faster: shorter product life cycles and increased program development costs. The impact of a short product life cycle is less time to create programs and a reduced time for payback. When courses have a short period of marketability, they then have a short period in which to earn revenue to pay back the costs of development. The second time factor is related to the cost of developing programs. The ratios for hours of development to hours of instruction can range anywhere from 10:1 to 600:1, depending on the factors discussed in Chapter 9, Developing Blueprints. Organizations are seeking software applications and new processes to reduce development time. Later in this chapter, we will explore some of these alternatives.

Reduce Training Time. The early impetus for implementing e-learning programs was to reduce the number of days employees spent away from their jobs. E-learning was seen as a way to eliminate the opportunity costs associated with traditional classroom training. The mantra of reducing training time has reached a fevered pitch, and there are efforts underway to reduce the time learners spend studying e-learning programs. One trend discussed earlier is the idea of shifting the learning from work to home. A second trend is the use of learning objects and other technologies that enable just-in-time, just-for-me, and just-enough learning. The latest trend is to provide very personalized learning that wastes no time. The learner studies the skills and knowledge needed at the moment, rather than taking training in anticipation of needing the skills and knowledge in the future. The training programs are tailored to the learner's preferences to speed up the learning, and these programs maximize teaching time by focusing on must-know skills and eliminating nice-to-know.

Technology

Technology trends at the organizational level are important because they have both a direct and an indirect impact on training and development. Examples of technology trends are the use of intranets and the Internet, e-business, mobile computing, and knowledge management. This section closes with an examination of three e-learning technologies that are shaping up to have a major influence on how training is designed, developed, and delivered. These technologies have a direct relationship to the trends identified in the business environment, time, and enterprise technology.

The Internet

The growing number or Internet users is an important trend for training managers because it means the infrastructure for delivering e-learning is in place for an increasing number of employees, customers, and business partners. The worldwide growth of the Internet also has implications for the delivery of services and products in multiple languages.

Table 11.1 is an estimate of how many people are online throughout the world. This data from NUA.com provides an "educated guess" as to how many are online worldwide as of November 2000. And the number is 407.1 million.

Having worldwide Internet access has major implication for online learning because the delivery of training requires more than the technical ability to deliver courses. Research shows that people learn best in their primary language. It is forecast that by 2005, 60 percent of Internet users will speak a language other than

Table 11.1. People Online Worldwide as of November 2000	
Area	**Number (in millions)**
World Total	407.1
Africa	3.11
Asia/Pacific	104.88
Europe	113.14
Middle East	2.40
Canada & U.S.	167.12
Latin America	16.45

English. This means that to efficiently reach worldwide audiences, training materials will need to be translated and internationalized. Table 11.2 provides a snapshot of the languages on the Web and the number of speakers in millions as reported in 1999 by Global Research.

The Internet does a great deal more than allow businesses to communicate and complete transactions via computers. As companies become more connected via the Web, the possibilities for educating the entire supply chain emerge. Using the Internet, companies can educate their supplier, employees, resellers, partners, and customers. One of the first links in the supply chain to be addressed is the customer link using *educommerce*.

Educommerce is an example of how companies doing business on the Internet are directly impacting training. Educommerce (Connell, 2001) is the "convergence of online learning and e-commerce to promote a company's online sales and marketing strategy." Companies are using online education to preserve and expand their customer base. Barnes and Nobles's Online University offers customers free courses as a way to build customer loyalty and to create a reason for customers to return to their site. Another example of the Internet being used to educate a link in the supply chain is Herman Miller's online learning program for their office

Table 11.2. Languages on the Web

Language	Speakers (in millions)
English	128.0
Japanese	19.7
German	14.0
Spanish	9.4
French	9.3
Chinese	7.0
Dutch	4.4
Korean	4.3
Swedish	3.6
Italian	3.4
Portuguese	2.9

furniture resellers. Using online learning programs, resellers learn about new products and sales promotions. In this example, a second link in the supply chain is "connect, reseller." To gain first-hand experience of the educommerce for customers, complete the exercise on the facing page.

Mobile Computing

Mobile computing refers to the use of mobile devices such as palm size PCs, mobile phones, and personal digital assistants (PDAs) to access information through wired or wireless connections anywhere. This technology is changing how work is performed, because workers now have access to applications and data once limited to their workstations and offices. The ability to access information and collaborate with others enables faster problem solving.

Clark Quinn (2000) defines mLearning as "the intersection of mobile computing and e-learning: accessible resources wherever you are, strong search capabilities, rich interaction, powerful support for effective learning, and performance-based assessment." There are examples of mlearning today: some are delivered entirely using wireless devices and other solutions are blended solutions. While there is still room for debate over the effectiveness of mlearning, the availability of mlearning technology and examples of mlearning are here today. Review the links in the exercise given on page 272.

Knowledge Management

Knowledge management (KM) is the systematic process of finding, selecting, organizing, distilling, and presenting information in a way that improves an employee's comprehension in a specific area of interest. These things can be done with technology or without technology, but technology-based knowledge management systems present one of the more interesting trends. This technology is being embedded in processes such as sales, customer service, project management, and e-mail.

Training professionals must think about e-learning as a form of knowledge management that enables learners to work together, to collaboratively learn, and to expedite the exchange of knowledge. Some of the technologies included in KM are instant messaging, virtual meetings, discussion groups, project spaces, knowledge bases, portals, and expertise locators. The challenge is to figure out how to commandeer existing KM tools to extend the reach of training. There are a number of examples of KM tools being used as part of e-learning initiatives today.

Instant Messaging.   Consider the learning possibilities for instant messaging. It enables a user to be aware of the presence of others online and to communicate

✓ Educommerce Worksheet

Directions: This exercise will allow you to experience educommerce at some popular Internet retail sites. The exercise also includes a set of questions to help you reflect on educommerce at these sites or at your favorite retail sites.

Use the following links to find examples of educommerce. Log on to at least two sites and consider the reflection questions.

Barnes and Noble (www.barnesandnoble.com/index.asp)
Barnes and Noble University offers more than fifty courses every month on a wide variety of subjects—from poetry to finance to programming.

Code Warrior (www.codewarrioru.com/CodeWarriorU)
Courses on software development from the makers of Code Warrior.

REI (www.rei.com)
Learn about sports equipment from a leading sports equipment vendor.

Link Finder: If these links don't work, search for authoring tools using the following terms: e-learning, educommerce, education-based marketing, education-based marketing solutions, online learning, marketing solutions, customer acquisition, customer retention, online marketing strategies, online customer training, educommerce, online courses, and Internet marketing.

REFLECTION QUESTIONS

- How are educommerce courses similar and dissimilar to other online courses?

- What role does community play in these programs?

- What is different about the content and assessment in educommerce?

- What assumptions have these firms made about their customers?

✓ mLearning Worksheet

Directions: This exercise will allow you to explore the possibilities for mlearning. A set of questions has been developed to help you reflect on the advantages and disadvantages of this technology.

Use the URLs below to explore stories and descriptions of educational solutions for mobile devices. Use the reflection questions to think about mlearning.

PalmPilot (www.palm.com/education/). Scan the educational programs for the PalmPilot.

Advanced Work (www.advancework.com/). Consider the English language courses offered using Web-delivered content on portable devices, including the PocketPC™ and other palm-top computers.

Fast Company (www.fastcompany.com). If you own a wireless device, go to FastCompany.com and download articles to go!

Link Finder: If these links don't work, search for authoring tools using the following terms: m-learning, mlearning, PDAs, e-learning, PalmPilot, and mobile technology.

REFLECTION QUESTIONS

- Is mlearning really learning, or is it information distribution?

- What are the limitations for using mlearning as a standalone learning tool?

- How might mlearning be blended with Web-based training?

- If you experienced the Fast Company wireless articles, what did you like or not like about them?

with them via text, audio, or video. This technology is being used at IBM to enable learners in an online management development class to see when other class members are online and to communicate in real time about assignments, readings, and case studies. Instant messaging facilitates the finding and sharing of information and collaborative problem solving.

Project Spaces.   The use of project spaces or applications that provide a virtual place for teams to share documents, maintain a calendar, and communicate are powerful tools for project-based learning. These spaces enable learners scattered across the country to work together to complete assignments, prepare a case study, or build a presentation. Project spaces are primarily designed to focus on project management, but they offer structure that would also be beneficial to online learning group projects.

Knowledge Portals.   A knowledge portal is analogous to information on a car dashboard that can be customized by the organization or the individual. Imagine a home page that could put relevant information at the user's fingertips, just like the gauges on a car dashboard. This application enables employees to find the most valuable information in the organization with minimum effort. A knowledge portal will search though databases, document management systems, e-mail folders, and selected external websites simultaneously and presents the user with a selection of pertinent information. Organizations can have knowledge portals for each job function, such as a knowledge portal for marketing that puts all the information needed for that function at the fingertips of the user. This could include advertising rates, a calendar of publication deadlines, contact names at advertising agencies and media outlets, databases with competitive information, analysis reports, access to an archive of old press releases, and yellow pages, as well as the capability to locate experts for each of the company's products. It is also possible to create a reminder for learners that it is time for recertification; let learners know they have been moved from a waiting list into a class they want to take; or suggest readings and advertise courses of potential interest.

These examples are a small sample of the potential that knowledge management tools have to extend e-learning. Use the following exercise to gain first-hand experience with a number of KM applications.

E-Learning Technologies

The most dramatic turns in the road ahead may be related to e-learning technologies, including teaching management, content management, and authoring. On the

Knowledge Management Tools Worksheet

Directions: This exercise will allow you to experience a range of knowledge management tools. The questions that accompany these tools will help you reflect on where learning merges with collaboration, communication, and knowledge management.

Use the links below to explore complementary knowledge management technologies. Consider the reflection questions below.

Technology	Links
Instant Messaging. Instant messaging is a convenient way to see when friends and colleagues are online and communicate with them in real time.	*Yahoo Messenger* (http://messenger.yahoo.com/) *AOL Instant Messenger* (www.AOL.com)
Project Spaces. Provides a central online workspace for sharing content, creating a shared milestones and calendars, and sharing a process.	*QuickPlace* (www.lotus.com) *e-Room* (www.eroom.com)
Discussion Groups. Virtual areas that allow you to bring together colleagues, friends, and associates through a website and e-mail group for dialogue.	*Yahoo! Groups* (www.yahoo.com) *WorldCrossing* (http://worldcrossing.com/)
Document Management. These applications enable groups to share documents/Web pages and provide features such as revision control, routing, and annotating.	*netXtract* (www.netxtract.com/) *Docushare* (http://docushare.xerox.com/)
Expertise Locators. These applications help organizations find experts who can give answers and and share knowledge. Using a website, organizations provide a central point for submitting a question or business problem.	*AskMe* (www.askme.com) *Ask an Expert* (www.askanexpert.com/)
KM-Based Portals. These give employees, partners, and customers a page that can be personalized to display information that is relevant to them, such as company databases, shared documents, calendars, and other software applications that can be distributed over the Web.	*K-Station* (www.lotus.com) *Plumtree* (www.plumtree.com/)

Link Finder: If these links don't work, search for authoring tools using the following terms: knowledge management, knowledge enterprise, knowledge portal, information technology, knowledge sharing, organization strategy, organizational learning, knowledge strategy, business innovation, competitive intelligence, intellectual capital, best practices, chief knowledge officer, and document management.

REFLECTION QUESTIONS

- How might these technologies be used as part of an online course?

- Which of these technologies might be best for pre-course or post-course support?

- What objections, if any, might your learners have about using these tools?

- Which of these are collaboration, communication, knowledge management versus instructional technologies? Should there be a hard and fast line among these categories?

surface, these applications offer improved productivity and increased ability to manage the design, development, and delivery of training. What may not be so clear are the assumptions that underlie these applications and the business process redesign needed to optimize their effectiveness. Chapter 4, Tools of the Trade, provided an overview of the functionality of these applications. This chapter looks at the implications for business and training organizations.

Learning Management Systems. In the last two years, the biggest technical news has been the arrival of learning management systems (LMS). According to Brandon Hall, there are over one hundred LMS vendors. And 48 percent of the LMS systems in his report, *Learning Management Systems: How to Choose the Right System for Your Organization,* are new to the market since 1998. These systems allow organizations to plan, organize, implement, and control all aspects of the learning process.

These systems are attractive because they provide an enterprise resource planning module for training and development. As a mater of fact, LMS systems can be specialized modules of an enterprise resource planning (ERP) system such as PeopleSoft™ and SAP™ or a dedicated standalone application such as Docent™, SABA™, or TEDS™.

So What? Implications for Training Organizations

On the road ahead, LMS systems will influence the structure and the visibility of training and development organizations. Like any ERP system, an LMS system is an enterprise-wide application and a major investment of time and money. Early statistics compiled by Bryan Chapman indicate that a five-year implementation for eight thousand employees averages $280,000. This investment historically has happened two ways. The system is either purchased by someone senior in the organization, or the system is purchased by combining resources from fragmented training organizations throughout the company. In either case, purchasing a system results in the centralization of training at least from the tracking and reporting stance. This may mean that fragmented training organizations must centralize processes and give up some degree of autonomy.

Like any ERP system, an LMS system requires the training organization to document and create processes in order to build the systems. For example, if your LMS system is going to provide the ability to create a wait list of students, there are a number of decisions that you will need to make in order to optimize the functions. The first decision is to decide the basis of wait listing: Will it happen first-come-first-serve, based on job code, or based on employee seniority? Do you want learners to be able to see where they are on the wait list? Who, if anyone, should be able to move learners up on a wait list? If the class is one in which both employees and customers are enrolled, do you want two wait lists or one? These may seem like fussy details, but this is the level of control that these systems provide for managing. In my experience there are two challenges when implementing LMS systems: namely, defining the processes that don't exist and reaching consensus when there are competing processes.

LMS systems make training organizations more visible because of the robust reporting capability and strong integration with back-end systems. Accountability and return on investment are hot buttons for training organizations seeking to justify their existence. On the road ahead, reports will be available to account for number of student days delivered, average scores for a given class, instructor rating, and a summary of the number of employees with a critical set of competencies. The challenge will be making a case for bottom-line results based on Level I (student reaction) and Level II (learning) assessments. One way to assess Level III (skill transfer) and Level IV (business results) results will be to integrate LMS systems with human resource information systems, customer relations management software, call center applications, sales automation software, and other systems that can track performance.

Learning Content Management Systems. Learning content management systems (LCMS) are software applications enabling training organizations to manage their learning-related content. Early statistics compiled by Bryan Chapman for the upcoming LCMS report on this fledgling industry indicate that a five-year implementation of an LCMS for 8,000 employees averages about $585,000. These systems are very important because they enable organizations to produce training materials quickly and promise to make the production faster and more cost-effective than traditional processes. Today these systems can be purchased as standalone solutions or they can be purchased as a module within an LMS.

The value of these systems is based on the idea that all learning can be broken down into learning objects and that learning objects can be mixed and matched to create new courses. The concept of learning objects has been around for several years, and there is still no agreed-on definition. Each organization defines learning objects differently. This presents a challenge if you hope to purchase objects from third-party vendors of if you plan to swap objects with other organizations. The key to making these systems work is to define what constitutes a learning object. Once there is an agreed-on definition, organizations must enforce the use of the definition internally and externally in order to create objects that can be mixed and matched. The last challenge is to develop a large enough library to make mixing and matching possible. Organizations will need to assess whether they will be producing enough learning objects to make a mix and match scheme viable.

So What? Implications for Training Organizations

These systems offer a way to potentially reduce the development to delivery ratios that make e-learning expensive and time-consuming to produce. These systems also promise significant productivity gains. Productivity is achieved through the LCMS's workflow and collaboration features that enable teams to develop courses. Using workflow and collaboration tools, learning objects can be checked in and checked out, routed for review, and divided up by a system so that a single object can be worked on by multiple users. Workflow and collaboration assume the development process is team-based, that is, one person working alone does not develop courses. In addition to improving the process, the LCMS can reduce development time through the concept of author/one-use/many. These systems enable learning objects to be created once and then rendered to be delivered in multiple formats and to a wide range of devices such as workstations, personal digital assistants, and wireless devices.

Authoring Tools.   The new authoring tools for SME are software applications that enable experts and other nontraining professionals to create courses, reusable learning objects, and artifacts such as quizzes, job aids, and simulations. These tools are changing the training landscape because they make it possible to expand the number of people who can create training materials. These applications are part of the democratization of publishing, in which people have the tools needed to make their worthy ideas heard. The new authoring applications can potentially speed up development by eliminating a step in the course development process. They will also change the role of course developers and instructional designers. Training professionals will spend less time interviewing SMEs and synthesizing the content to writing models. Instead, course developers and instructional designers will spend their time creating templates for SMEs, acting as editors for SMEs, and managing the publishing of learning materials.

Organizations can respond to these trends using point solutions such as e-learning courses and a performance support application, but these one-off events can be less than optimal solutions. A truly effective response requires an evaluation of options within a strategic plan that looks at the larger context into which these solutions fit. The following section provides an overview of a strategic plan for training and development that places e-learning in the context of a larger solution.

√ Authoring Tools Worksheet

Directions: Use the links below to try course authoring technologies. Use two or more of these tools to create a simple lesson. Some of the tools can be used from within your browser; others will require that you download and execute a file. Use the reflection questions to think about the impact of democratization of authoring.

ReadyGo.com (www.readygo.com). Using ReadyGo, a product or sales manager, vice president, or secretary, or any other subject-matter expert can develop content is a simple, guided format. By eliminating complexity, the cost to develop the site is dramatically reduced.

ViewletBuilder (www.qarbon.com/). ViewletBuilder lets you create animated online demos of software for online marketing, employee training, and customer support program. The primary focus of this tool is animated online software demos and not e-learning, so it does not meet the standards for educational products.

ToolBook II Assistant (www.click2learn.com/). ToolBook Assistant is an e-learning authoring program that is specifically designed for ease of use. Its interface is ideal for those who want to create interactive learning applications quickly without programming. Using the simple drag-and-drop interface in Assistant allows anyone to author effective standards-based courses.

TrainerSoft (www.trainersoft.com). TrainerSoft creates online courses, network, and CD-ROM-based training. This program is based on a book metaphor in which course developers fill in a table of contents and then drag and drop chapters and pages into place. There is also a Course Wizard available for those who would like more guidance.

Dreamweaver (www.macromedia.com/). A free thirty-day trial version of Dreamweaver can be downloaded from the Macromedia site. Dreamweaver is not specifically designed to be a WBT authoring tool, but it is very popular in training organizations that do sophisticated authoring.

Link Finder: If these links don't work, search for authoring tools using the following terms: eLearning tools, authorware, authoring tools, WBT authoring tools, Web-based training, classroom training, ebusiness training, e-commerce training, Internet training, intranet training, assessment, survey, and extranet training.

REFLECTION QUESTIONS

- How do these tools differ?

- How much knowledge about instructional design and course development do these tools assume users have?

- Would subject-matter experts in your organization have the technical skills needed to use these tools?

- Could these tools improve the speed at which programs are developed? What changes in your current course development process might be required?

- Do these tools optimize instruction or information?

A Strategic Plan for Training and Development

Strategic plans are not common in training organizations. Many organizations are too busy responding to internal customer demands and don't believe they can take time out to write such a plan. Writing a strategic plan is worth considering if you are making a request for additional resources to take advantage of e-learning delivery platforms, learning management systems, learning content management systems, or knowledge management applications. Integrating e-learning technologies often means rethinking the budget, the processes for taking on new work, the organization's service levels, staff levels, and hardware and software needs. This requires that you step back and take the broad view of all training and development activities.

Writing a strategic plan has several benefits. It provides a framework for decisions, such as approval of additional funding, support for new headcount, and agreement on goals and non-goals. Even if an organization does not need additional resources, a strategic plan can be helpful in explaining the role of training and development. These kinds of communications serve to inform, motivate, and involve others in training. The strategic plan can also provide a documented benchmark against which performance can be measured.

The following section provides a brief description of the key sections found in a strategic plan. Many readers will already be familiar with the components of such a plan. However, for those who are not, this will provide a useful first step in understanding and writing a strategic plan for training. The hardest part of writing the strategic plan will be reaching consensus on key issues and making sure that the plan provides a closed loop. A good plan requires that the vision be supported by the strategies, which are executed through measurable goals, and that the milestones and budget provide adequate time and funding to accomplish the goals. If there is any inconsistency among the sections of the strategic plan, it is doomed to fail. Most strategic plans have seven sections.

Mission. The mission statement is a jargon-free declaration of why the training organization exists, whom it serves, and how it delivers services. For example:

> VebTech University is a corporate university dedicated to providing professional skills development for VebTech employees and their clients, as well as business and channel partners worldwide. We are committed to delivering timely, high quality, and continuous learning opportunities through a variety of business and technology curricula, enabling individuals and organizations to acquire the skills and knowledge needed to succeed.

Vision. The vision statement is a shared picture of what the organization hopes to become in its ideal future state. This statement does not dwell on tactical issues such as how to achieve the vision or on how to measure it. For example:

> VebTech University will be the first stop and preferred resource for formal and informal training for professional development and skills training for employees at all levels and product knowledge and skills for customers and employees.

Strategy. The strategy section is where the plan becomes tactical. Create five to seven high-level strategies or approaches that outline what you must do to accomplish the vision. For each strategy, there such be a number of goals and key performance indicators. For example:

> VebTech will:
>
> - Make informal learning resources widely available to all employees;
> - Establish kiosks on the shop floor with documentation and self-paced courses;
> - Extend the existing management mentoring program to sales and operations;
> - Provide lunch-and-learn sessions and other informal learning opportunities; and
> - Create a company yellow pages to identify experts in key subject areas.

Milestones. Milestones can either be placed in a separate section or integrated into the performance indicators. The point of creating milestones is to give funders and clients benchmarks to assess the progress of the program. Milestones can include the dates by which things will be accomplished, dollar amounts saved or spent, number of programs initiated, number of learners served, and reduction in time to performance.

Budget. There is no hard-and-fast rule that a strategic plan must include a budget. The links listed in Figure 11.1 provide examples of plans with and without budgets. It is a good idea to include a budget if you need money for headcount, hardware, software, third-party content, and outsourcing. Budgets can also help clarify how money will be reallocated, even if the budget is not going to be increased.

Risks and Dependencies. Even the best strategic plan is subject to forces beyond your control. It is helpful to call out risks associated with the plan, such as the risk of choosing a three-year contract for an LMS application service provider. The contract may have good rates for the current level of users, but a sharp increase in users could make this contract more expensive than owning a system.

Figure 11.1.   Links to Strategic Plans

National Archives and Records Administration (www.nara.gov/nara/vision/naraplan.html). This is an example of a strategic plan that uses a question and answer format and provides a context for the strategic plan.

Redwood City Library (www.redwoodcity.org/library/reference/strategic.html). This plan is rich in clear measurable strategies to reach the goals.

Department of Agriculture and Land Affairs Province of the Eastern Cape, New Zealand (www.ecprov.gov.za/documents/policy/1999/strategicland.htm). This plan is complex, and it provides detailed goals that outline not only what has to be done but by whom and by what date.

Eleanor Roosevelt National Historic Site (www.nps.gov/elro/2001strat_plan.html). This plan has a simple and well-organized budget page.

Link Finder: If these links don't work, try the terms strategic plan, vision, mission, budget, and strategies.

 There is a template in the tools section of the CD-ROM that can be used as a starting point for developing a strategic plan.

Appendices.   There will be many places in the document in which you will need to provide backup information such as organization charts, statistics on how many people were served, the breakdown of services per region, and other detailed information.

The format and presentation of these sections differ from plan to plan. A frequent request from training managers is to see an example. The challenge in finding sample strategic plans is called out in their names. Strategic plans are just that—strategic. Private companies do not post their strategic plans, but often nonprofit and government organizations post theirs. Figure 11.1 provides links to several strategic plans from nonprofit organizations. Although these are not examples from training organizations, the sample plans are helpful because they make it easy to see options for structuring a plan, differing levels of detail, and examples of measurable goals.

Markers on the Road Ahead

Cataloging all the efforts related to learning, knowledge, education, performance improvement, and professional development and putting them into a strategic plan for training and development should be an eye-opening experience. If you are like most training professionals, you will come away from this exercise challenged to write a coherent plan. In many cases you will find hundreds of initiatives, dozens of people formally and informally responsible for training, and thousands of untraceable dollars invested in these programs. To help organizations make the kinds of learning decisions we have discussed in this chapter, many are creating the new position of chief learning officer, discussed in the following section.

Chief Learning Officer

The proliferation of educational staff is another case in which training and development is experiencing a phenomenon much like that of information technology. At one time, information technology initiatives were launched by departments, project groups, and individuals. The result was a proliferation of applications such as e-mail, databases, and word-processing software that were redundant, costly to support, lacked economies of scale, and did not operate together. In response to this problem, the role of chief information officer (CIO) was created. The role of the CIO is designed to provide enterprise-wide directions and business strategies for acquiring, using, and maintaining information technology. Since 1996 there has been an increased focus on creating a similar position for training and development entitled chief learning officer (CLO).

The chief learning officer (CLO) is responsible for an organization's overall learning and knowledge initiatives. A working definition of the role of CLO varies greatly from organization to organization, but three characteristics are consistently cited: people skills, technical knowledge, and the ability to see the big picture.

People Skills.   People skills deserves to be in first place given the CLO's needs to work across departments with competing needs. The CLO is also required to be the intermediary among training departments, the information system group, and business units. Solutions often require these groups to reach consensus in order to create solutions. This requires a CLO with strong people skills.

Technical Knowledge.   Technical knowledge in the case of a CLO is his or her ability to monitor the e-learning marketplace and to monitor his or her industry in terms of rapidly changing applications and technologies. Evaluating new technologies requires a fundamental knowledge of technical issues such as networks, system integration, databases, and security. Technical knowledge also encompasses the ability to understand how training applications will impact training departments, end-users, and customers.

Big Picture. The ability to see the big picture is equally important. The CLO must understand how training as a business function relates to the bottom line. This means leaving one's training hat behind and focusing on all the ways that intellectual capital can be expanded. The CLO is responsible for embedding learning into processes, encouraging knowledge sharing, and fostering invention. Taking a broader view may mean placing an emphasis on learning by experience, focusing on informal learning, sponsoring group projects, or changing reward systems rather than recommending more traditional training.

Anecdotal evidence suggests that the position of chief learning officer comes about in one of two ways: (1) Leading-edge organizations create a CLO position and actively recruit for the position, whereas (2) other organizations are prompted to create the position for someone within the organization who is able to build a case for this post.

Most organizations would benefit from a chief learning officer as either a way to increase profitability or as a means of reducing costs. The emergence of the knowledge economy points to the value of information and knowledge as sources of wealth creation. A CLO could improve the speed at which innovation occurs and increase productivity and profitably. Another line of reasoning that is easier to demonstrate is that a CLO can reduce the costs associated with training. The proliferation of training initiatives found in most companies suggest that there is room for cost savings by streamlining initiatives, eliminating redundancy, and taking advantage of economies of scale.

Career Development

The purpose of the last section of this chapter is to answer a question that readers may have, namely, "Now that I know some of the basics of e-learning, how do I further my knowledge and expertise in this growing field?" From my perspective, each of the three audiences for this book, business managers, training managers, and instructional designers/course developers have different needs and interests. The appendices at the end of this book provide resources for locating additional information for each group. The resources have been chosen to provide opportunities for learning that range in cost, content, and time commitment. Accessing these resources has been made easier because the appendices are also on the CD-ROM, so that you can simply click on the links to access these resources.

Resource Sites.   Some of the best things in life are free! The place to finding content and resources related to business, technology, and training is in Appendix C, Resource Sites and Conferences. Explore these sites and bookmark those you wish to monitor. There are sites related to educational theory, distance education, business, knowledge management, and technology.

Conferences.   One of the best places to see the latest technology and to meet people who are using e-learning platforms, learning management systems, learning content management systems, and authoring tools is at conferences. Appendix C provides a list of the leading conferences in the United States, Asia, and North America. The dates of the conferences and locations change from year to year, but the focus is online learning. Conferences can be expensive, but there are alternatives to paying for a full conference registration. Many conferences offer reduced fees for limited access to the tradeshow floor and access to vendor demos.

Professional Organizations.   An alternative to conferences, which offer once a year opportunities to network with peers and learn from others, is professional organizations. Appendix B, Training Organizations, provides a list of organizations that provide websites, journals, local chapter meetings, and online newsletters.

E-learning is a challenging and interesting field to monitor because it touches so many facets of an organization's processes. It is sometimes difficult to grasp just how important it is and how much it is going to impact the way in which traditional training is delivered. IDC predicts that, in the United States, e-learning content, tools, and services alone will grow from $4.2 billion in 2001 to $18 billion by 2005. This kind of spending and the rapid changes in business and technology make it essential that professionals have multiple outlets for following e-learning.

Summary

According to *Training* magazine's 2001 Industry Training Report, American organizations spent $56.8 billion on training. This figure includes spending on both traditional training and e-learning. The e-learning segment is large and becoming more important each year. Gartner forecasts the worldwide e-learning market to account for $33 billion by 2005. The increase in spending on training and development can be linked to changes brought about by the new economy. In the new economy, the key factors for creating wealth are information and knowledge. The ability to solve problems and innovate is a competitive difference, and it is based on the knowledge worker. Training has taken on a more central role because of its part in teaching skills to knowledge workers.

This book has provided an overview of Web-based training from the educational, technical, and organizational perspective. In closing, it is essential to put Web-based training in context. Web-based training is simply a delivery methodology that supports a number of instructional strategies from the literal metaphor of a physical classroom being put online to a collaborative learning environment that fosters organizational learning.

After a successful pilot, the challenge is to integrate this instructional technology into a larger strategic plan. Because e-learning is resources intensive, highly visible, and enterprise-wide in scope, it can act as the catalyst for organizations to rethink their training strategies. This chapter considered writing a strategic plan that answers three questions: Where do we want to be? How do we get there? and How will we know we made it? It has also stressed the importance of monitoring trends in the business environment and e-learning. Finally, it has presented resources on identifying key skills for a chief learning officer (if that is your aspiration) and directed you to additional resources that you can pursue in the dynamic e-learning world. Good luck!

Suggested Readings

Chapman, B. (2000). *Brandon-Hall dispatch.* [Online] Available: www.Brandon-hall.com

Conference Board. (2001). *The CEO challenge: Top marketplace and management issues—2001.* New York: The Conference Board.

Dixon, N.M. (2000). *Common knowledge: How companies thrive by sharing what they know.* Boston, MA: Harvard Business School Press.

Hall, B. (2000). *Learning management systems: How to choose the right system for your organization.* Sunnyvale, CA: www. Brandon-hall.com publishing, p. 10.

Kaufman, J. (2001). *Gaining a learning edge.* IDC presentation at Toronto, Ontario.

Moe, M. (2000). *The knowledge web.* Princeton, NJ: Merrill Lynch Global Securities Research and Economics Group, p. 229.

Napier, R., Sanaghan, P., Sidle, C., & Saraghan, P. (1998). *High impact tools and activities for strategic planning: Creative techniques for facilitating your organization's planning process.* New York: McGraw-Hill.

Nilson, C. (1999). *How to start a training program: Training is a strategic business tool in any organization.* Washington, DC: ASTD Press.

NUA. (2001). *How many are online?* [Online] Available: www.nua.ie/surveys/how_many_online/index.html

Pastore, M. (1999). *The language of the web.* [Online] Available: http://cyberatlas.internet.com/big_picture/demographics/article/0%2C1323%2C5901_150171%2C00.html

Prusak, L., & Davenport, T. (2000). *Working knowledge.* Boston, MA: Harvard Business School Press.

Quinn, C. (2000, Fall). *mLearning, mobile, wireless, learning in your pocket.* [Online] Available: www.linezine.com/2.1/features/cqmmwiyp.htm

Sveiby, K.E. (2000, April). *What is knowledge management?* [Online] Available: www.sveiby.com.au/KnowledgeManagement.html

Svenson, R.A., Rinderer, M.J., Svenson, R., & Rinderer, N. (1992). *The training and development strategic plan workbook.* Upper Saddle River, NJ: Prentice Hall.

Wagner, E.D. (2000, Fall). Emerging technology trends in e-learning. *LineZine.* [Online] Available: www.linezine.com/2.1/features/ewette.htm

A strategic planning template is on the CD-ROM at the back of this book. The template is a Microsoft Word™ file that you can copy to your hard drive and edit. The following pages show what the template contains.

Strategic Plan for _____

[Your Organization's Name]

Edit Recommendations for Cover Page
- Replace the image with your logo.
- Increase or decrease the number of signature lines and the titles to reflect your organization.
- Edit the footer to include your organization's name and the right level of restricted distribution.

_____
[Training Director/Name   Date]

_____
[Human Resource Director/Name   Date]

_____
[VP of Lines of Business/Name   Date]

_____
[VP of Lines of Business/Name   Date]

_____
[Information Technology Manager/Name   Date]

_____
[Geographic Location One/Name   Date]

_____
[Geographic Location Two/Name   Date]

Issues by: _____

Phone: _____

Fax: _____

E-mail: _____

Address: _____

_____

_____

Table of Contents

Executive Summary
[Describe the overall strategy and the benefits to the organization.]

Edit Recommendation
- Use bullets and lists to make it easy for the reader to scan the benefits in the executive summary.
- End the executive summary by asking for the reader to do something such as fund, approve, or support something.

Introduction
[Explain the purpose of this document.]

Mission
The mission statement is a jargon-free declaration of why the training organization exists, whom it serves, and how it delivers services.

Vision
The vision statement is a shared picture of what the organization hopes to become in its ideal future state. This statement does not dwell on tactical issues such as how to achieve the vision or how to measure it.

Strategy
The strategy section is where the plan becomes tactical. Create five to seven high-level strategies or approaches that outline what you must do to accomplish the vision. For each strategy, there should be a number of goals and key performance indicators.

Strategy One
- Goal and key indicators
- Goal and key indicators
- Goal and key indicators

Strategy Two
- Goal and key indicators
- Goal and key indicators
- Goal and key indicators

Strategy Three

- Goal and key indicators
- Goal and key indicators
- Goal and key indicators

Strategy Four

- Goal and key indicators
- Goal and key indicators
- Goal and key indicators

Strategy Five

- Goal and key indicators
- Goal and key indicators
- Goal and key indicators

Strategy Six

- Goal and key indicators
- Goal and key indicators
- Goal and key indicators

Strategy Seven

- Goal and key indicators
- Goal and key indicators
- Goal and key indicators

Milestones

Milestones can either be placed in a separate section or integrated into the performance indicators. The point of creating milestones is to give funders and clients benchmarks to assess the progress of the program. Milestones can include the dates by which things will be accomplished, dollar amounts saved or spent, number of programs initiated, number of learners served, and reduction in time to performance.

Activity/Milestones	Description	Start Date	End Date

Budget

There is no hard-and-fast rule that a strategic plan must include a budget. It is a good idea to include a budget if you need money for headcount, hardware, software, third-party content, and outsourcing. Budgets can also help clarify how money will be reallocated even if the budget is not going to be increased.

Risk and Dependencies

Even the best strategic plan is subject to forces beyond your control. It is helpful to call out risks associated with the plan, such as the risk of choosing a three-year contract for an LMS application service provider. The contract may have good rates for the current level of users, but a sharp increase in users could make this contract more expensive than owning a system.

Appendices

Audience Grids

Show whom training serves using grids. The grids can be organized by division, by content area, by region, or by division. How these tables are organized depends on what and how best to communicate who is served and who is not served.

Example of Audience Grid Organized by Region		
Region	**Audience**	**Course**
North America	Sales	Intro to Sales
		Sales Tools and Technology
		Product Training
		New Product Training
		Advanced Sales
	Operations	Reporting, Tracking, and Operations Basics
		CAE System Basics
		Microsoft Excel™ Basic/Intermediate/Advanced
	Customer Service	
	Marketing	

Example of Audience Grid Organized by Topic or Subject Area							
Topic	**Audience**	**Courses**					
		SF101	SF102	SF200	SF202	SF900	SF950
Safety Training	Shipping	x	x			x	
	Manufacturing	x		x	x	x	
		SS101	SS220	SS300			
Supervisory Skills							

Curriculum Maps
Provide graphical representation of how courses in a curriculum are related.

Organizational Charts
Provide a snapshot of how the training organization is structured and where it reports in the hierarchy; include any dotted-line relationships.

Curriculum Inventory Forms
Provide a catalog of the current courses that are offered. This can be organized by audience, by how it is developed and delivered (i.e., in-house, outsourced), by region, or by topic.

Training Design, Development, and Delivery Process
Describe how training will be designed, developed, and delivered.

Appendix A

Software Applications for E-Learning

This section provides a list of software applications for designing, developing, delivering and managing e-learning. The list is organized by the four types of Web-based training each applications is best suited for creating, tools for authoring, and tools for managing learning and managing content. Products often fall into multiple categories but for the purpose of this appendix, applications are placed in a category that reflects that application's primary focus.

Descriptions and comparisons are not included because the technology changes too quickly to provide a meaningful analysis. The list in this appendix is not exhaustive but rather it is representative of the better known and better established products. The e-learning marketplace is experiencing an extreme shake out, so many of these links may be gone by June of 2002. Use this list as a starting point in your search for software applications to create programs.

Web/Computer-Based Training

Brainshark
7 New England Executive Park
Burlington, MA 01803
 Tel: (781) 313–3000
 Fax: (781) 273–2682
 www.brainshark.com/

Connected Learning Network Inc. (CLNI)
The Brown Suite 400
323 West Broadway
Louisville, KY 40202
 Tel: (800) 569–6505
 Fax: (502) 583–0092
 www.connectedlearning.net/

Course Info

Blackboard Inc.

1899 L Street N.W., 5th Floor

Washington, DC 20036

　Tel: (202) 463–4860

　www.blackboard.com

eSocrates

eSocrates.com

905 Harrison Street, Suite 120

Allentown, PA 18103

　Tel: (800) 469–0684

　Fax: (610) 770–1043

　www.esocrates.com/

IntraLearn/IntraLearn Software Corporation

155B Otis Street

Northboro, MA, 01532

　Tel: (508) 393–2277

　Fax: (508) 393–6841

　www.intralearn.com

MentorWare

4701 Patrick Henry Drive, Suite 1101

Santa Clara, CA 95054–1863

　Tel: (408) 566–8800

　Fax: (408) 566–8808

　www.mentorware.com

Merlin

Merlin Development Unit

Institute for Learning

The University of Hull

Hull HU6 7RX

United Kingdom

　Fax: +44 (0)1482 341334

　www.hull.ac.uk/merlin/

Serf

Seftsoft Corporation

11 Amaranth Drive

Newark, DE 19711

　Tel: (302) 368–7025

　Fax: (302) 368–7025

　http://serfsoft.com/

SyberWorks

SyberNet, Inc.

9 Court Street

Arlington, MA 02476

　Tel: (781) 646–3826

　www.syberworks.com

Webmentor

Avilar Technologies, Inc.

8750–9 Cherry Lane

Laurel, MD 20707–6208

　Tel: (888) 873–7014

　Fax: (301) 725–0980

　http://avilar.adasoft.com

Web Electronic Performance Support Systems

Web/EPSS applications range from simple Web pages that provide steps and procedures to highly sophisticated tools such as agents and knowbots that look for information on behalf of the learner.

　The following are examples of software applications for creating HTML help pages.

RoboHTML

Ehelp Corporation

7777 Fay Avenue

La Jolla, CA 92037

　Tel: (800) 793–0364

　Fax: (858) 551–2485

　www.ehelp.com

Sophisticated W/EPSS Application Development Tools

Assistware®

Baydon Solutions

28 State Street, Suite 1100

Boston, MA 02109

　Tel: (617) 573–5009

　Fax: (617) 573–5090

　www.baydon-solutions.com

CoachWare
Sterling Resources, Inc.
6 Forest Avenue
Paramus, NJ 07652
Tel: (201) 843–6444
Fax: (201) 843–3934
www.sterlingnet.com/

HyperKnowledge
Sheraton House
Castle Park
Cambridge, England CB3 0AX
Tel: +44 1223 846655
www.hyperknowledge.com/

MMhelper
E.S.M.M.I., Ltd.
Ein-Semer Man Machine Interface
Kibbutz Ein-Semer D.N. Hefer
37845, Israel
Tel: (972) 6–6374343
Fax: (972) 6–6231786
www.esmmi.com/

ProCarta
Domain Knowledge
500 Queen's Quay W., Suite 6W
Toronto, Ontario M5V 3K8
Canada
Tel: (877) 885–6288
www.domainknowledge.com/

Vuepoint Learning System (VLS)
Vuepoint
4 Expressway Plaza, Suite 200
Roslyn Heights, NY 11577
Tel: (888) 883–7646
Fax: (888) 883–3291
www.vuepoint.com

X.HLP
X.HLP Technologies ASA
Havnelageret
Langkaia 1
0150 Oslo, Norway
Tel: +47 22 34 03 00

Fax: +47 22 34 03 01
www.xhlp.com/

Xstream Software
2280 St. Laurent Boulevard, Suite 200
Ottawa, Ontario K1G 4K1
Canada
Tel: (613) 731–9443
Fax: (613) 731–9615
www.xstreamsoftware.com

Web Virtual Asynchronous Classroom Applications

Anlon
Anlon Systems Inc.
115 East Hickory, Suite 400
Mankato, MN 56001
Tel: (507) 388–7933
Fax: (507) 388–2646
www.anlon.com/

Athenium
Athenium, LLC
16 Sutton Place
P.O. Box 76
Weston, MA 02493
Tel: (781) 893–9448
Fax:(781) 899–2308
www.athenuim.com

CampusPipeline
Campus Pipeline Inc.
155 North 400 West, Suite 500
Salt Lake City, UT 84103
Tel: (888) 682–7473
Fax: (801) 485–6606
www.campuspipeline.com/

ClassNet
Iowa State University
209 Durham
Ames, IA 50011
Dr. Pete Boysen
Tel: (515) 294–6663
Fax: (515) 294–1717
http://classnet.cc.iastate.edu

FirstClass
Centrinity Limited
Centrinity House
Shannon Business Park
Shannon, County Clare, Ireland
  Tel: +353.61.472.877
  Fax: +353.61.472.388
  www.centrinity.com/

Learning Space
IBM/Lotus Software
One Roger Street
Cambridge, MA 02142
  Tel: (617) 577–8500
  www.lotus.com

QuickCourse
Collaborative Learning Network Inc.
129 Advanced Technology Centre
Edmonton Research Park
9650—20 Avenue N.W.
Edmonton, Alberta T6N 1G1
Canada
  Tel: (780) 438–9282
  Fax: (780) 439–9282
  www.Co-Learn.Net

Theorix
e-com inc
236 Saint George Street, Suite 210
Moncton, New Brunswick E1C 1W1
Canada
  Tel: (506) 867–3266
  Fax: (506) 382–3799
  www.theorix.com

TopClass
WBT Systems
Reservoir Place, Block C
1601 Trapelo Road
Waltham, MA 02451
  Tel: (781) 839–2800
  Fax: (781) 290–5021
  www.wbtsystems.com

VLEI
Virtual Learning Environments Inc.
515 West Hastings Street, Suite 7300
Vancouver, British Columbia V6B 5K3
Canada
  Tel: (604) 268–7982;
  Fax: (604) 268–7977
  www.vlei.com

WebCT
WebCT Canada
#200–2389 Health Sciences Mall
University of British Columbia
Vancouver, British Columbia V6T 1Z4
Canada
  Tel: (604) 225–2225
  www.webct.com/company/

WebTeach
Chris Hughes
Professional Development Centre
UNSW
Sydney 2052
Australia
  Tel: 61–2–9385–4940
  Fax: 61–2–9385–5970
  E-mail: c.hughes@unsw.edu.au
  www.pdc.unsw.edu.au/webteachdemo/welcome.html

Web Virtual Synchronous Classroom Applications

Astound Conference Center
Astound Inc. Genesys SA
304 The East Mall, Suite 800
Toronto, Ontario M9B 6E2
Canada
  Tel: (416) 207–0605
  Fax: (416) 207–9744
  www.astound.com

HorizonLive
HorizonLive Inc.
520 8th Avenue
23rd Floor

New York, NY 10018

Tel: (212) 533–1775

Fax: (212) 533–6041

www.horizonlive.com/

InterWise

InterWise Inc.

2334 Walsh Avenue

Santa Clara, CA 95051

Tel: (408) 748–7800

Fax: (408) 748–7801

www.interwise.com

LearningSpace

IBM Lotus Software

One Rogers Street

Cambridge, MA 02142

Tel: (617) 577–8500

www.lotus.com

MeetingPlace

Latitude

2121 Tasman Drive

Santa Clara, CA 95054

Tel: (408) 988–7200

Fax: (408) 988–6520

www.latitude.com

Mentergy

LearnLinc

2000 River Edge Parkway, Suite 850

Atlanta, GA 30328

Tel: (770) 612–9129

Fax: (770) 859–9110

www.mentergy.com/

NetMeeting

Microsoft Corporation

One Microsoft Way

Redmond, WA 98052–6399

www.microsoft.com/netmeeting

PlaceWare Auditorium

PlaceWare, Inc.

296 North Bernardo Avenue

Mountain View, CA 94043

Tel: (888) 256–6170

Fax: (650) 526–6199

www.placeware.com

Raindance

Raindance Communications, Inc.

1157 Century Drive

Louisville, CO 80027

Tel: (800) 878–7326

Fax: (303) 928–2832

www.raindance.com/

Symposium

Centra Software, Inc.

430 Bedford Street

Lexington, MA 02173

Tel: (781) 861–7000

Fax: (781) 863–7288

www.centra.com

Web-4M™

JDH Technologies LLC

11834 Canon Boulevard, Suite J3

Newport News, VA 23606

Tel: (757) 873–4747

Fax: (757) 873–8484

www.jdhtech.com

WebSeminar

Pixion, Inc.

4234 Hacienda Drive, Suite 200

Pleasanton, CA 94588

Tel: (925) 467–5300

Fax: (925) 467–5310

www.pixion.com

Learning Management Systems

Docent Enterprise

Docent Inc.

2444 Charleston Road

Mountain View, CA 94043

Tel: (650) 934–9500

Fax: (650) 962–9411

www.docent.com

Isopia
Sun
200 University Avenue, 4th Floor
Toronto, Ontario M5H 3C6
Canada
Tel: (416) 964–2001
Fax: (416) 964–3700
www.isopia.com

Geo Learning
4600 Westown Parkway, Suite 301
West Des Moines, IA 50266–1000
Tel: (800) 970–9903
Fax: (515) 222–5920
www.geolearning.com

Gen21
Generation 21 Learning Systems
1536 Cole Boulevard, Suite 250
Golden, CO 80401
Tel: (303) 233–2100
Fax: (303) 233–1404
www.gen21.com

KP Learning
Knowledge Planet
11490 Commerce Park Drive, Suite 400
Reston, VA 20191
Tel: (800) 646–3008
Fax: (703) 716–0237
www.knowledgeplanet.com

NEBO
LearnFrame
12637 South 265 W
Draper, UT 84020
Tel: (800) 970–9903
Fax: (515) 222–5920
www.learnframe.com

Pathlore Learning Management System
Pathlore
7965 North High Street, Suite 300
Columbus, OH 43235
Tel: (888) 728–4567
Fax: (614) 781–7200
www.pathlore.com

Plateau
Plateau Systems Ltd.
4041 University Drive, Suite 400
Fairfax, VA 22030
Tel: (703) 934–0100
Fax: (703) 934–1362
www.plateausystems.com

Saba
Saba Inc.
2400 Bridge Parkway
Redwood Shores, CA 94065–1166
Tel: (630) 696–2500
www.saba.com

TEDS
CBM Company
P.O. Box 700
235 Mountain Empire Road
Atkins, VA 24311
Tel: (540) 783–6991
www.teds.com

YNotLearn.COM
875 Sabre Street, Suite 200
Virginia Beach, VA 23452
Tel: (757) 431–9787
Fax: (757) 368–4644
www.ynotlearn.com

Test and Assessment Applications

CQuest
Cogent Computing Corporation
1742 Regal Ridge
Las Cruces, NM 88011
Tel: (888) 876–0044
Fax: (909) 257–7661
www.cogentcorp.com/

Perception

Question Mark Corporation

5 Hillandale Avenue

Stamford, CT 06902

Tel: (800) 863–3950

Fax: (800) 339–3944

www.questionmark.com

Riva

Riva Technologies Inc.

2310 Gravel Drive

Fort Worth, TX 76118

Tel: (817) 595–8877

Fax: (817) 595–8878

www.riva.com/

TestEngine

Testengine.com

204 Ridge Street

Charlottesville, VA 22902

Tel: (804) 296–3060

www.testengine.com

TestGenerator

FAIN & Company

660 Elkmont Drive

Atlanta, GA 30306

Tel: (404) 876–4668

Fax: (404) 876–4085

www.testshop.com/

TestPilot

ClearLearning

6900 Indian Bluff Road

Battle Ground, IN 47920

Tel: (765) 567–2220

Fax: (309) 213–9670

www.clearlearning.com/

Utest

Microburst Technologies, Inc.

1707 Elm Street, Suite F

Rockledge, FL 32955

Tel: (321) 639–7377

Fax: (321) 639–3739

www.uburst.com/uTest/

Content Libraries

Business Training Library

745 Craig Road, Suite 210

St. Louis, MO 63141

Tel: (314) 432–3077

Fax: (314) 567–4783

www.bizlibrary.com

ElementK

500 Canal View Road

Rochester, NY 14623

Tel: (716) 240–7500

Fax: (716) 240–7760

www.elementk.com

Learn2.Com

1311 Mamaroneck Avenue, Suite 210

White Plains, NY 10605

Tel: (914) 682–4300

Fax: (914) 682–4440

www.learn2.com

NETg

1751 West Diehl Road, Suite 200

Naperville, IL 60563–9099

Tel: (630) 369–3000

www.netg.com

Opera Multimedia SPA

Strada 4 Palazzo A10

Assago Milanofiori, MI 20090

Italy

Tel: 02 5778951

Fax: 02 577895620

www.operamultimedia.com

SkillSoft

20 Industrial Park Drive

Nashua, NH 03062

Tel: (603) 324–3000

Fax: (603) 327–6960

www.skillsoft.com

SmartForce
900 Chesapeake Drive
Redwood City, CA 94063
  Tel: (888) 714–5900
  Fax: (068) 384–7623
  www.smartforce.com

Authoring Applications

DazzlerMax
MaxIT Corporation
2771–29 Monument Road MS-355
Jacksonville, FL 32225
  Tel: (904) 998–9520
  Fax: (904) 998–0221
  www.maxit.com

Director/Authorware
Macromedia, Inc.
600 Townsend Street
San Francisco, CA 94103
  Tel: (415) 252–2000
  Fax: (415) 626–0554
  www.macromedia.com

Digital Trainer
MicroMedium Inc.
1434 Farrington Road
Apex, NC 27502
  Tel: (919) 303–6022
  Fax: (919) 303–6011
  www.micromedium.com

EasyProf
ITACA: Interactive Training Advanced Computer
Applications, S.A.
Brazil
  Tel: +34 93 3221757
  www.easyprof.com/Homeenglish.htm

iAuthor
NYUonline, Inc.
594 Broadway, Suite 400
New York, NY 10012
  Tel: (212) 226–2788 x2750

  Fax: (212) 226–4588
  www.nyuonline.com/vn_6/development/development.html

NewMediaMentor
IDON East
230 Metcalfe Street, Suite 301
Ottawa, Ontario K2P 1R7
Canada
  Tel: (613) 230–3040
  Fax: (613) 233–7088
  www.idoneast.com

Qarbon
84 West Santa Clara Street, Suite 790
San Jose, CA 95113
  Tel: (408) 792–3800
  Fax: (408) 792–3808
  www.qarbon.com

ReadyGo.com
ReadyGo Inc.
918 N. Rengstorff Avenue, Suite B
Mountain View, CA 94043
  Tel: (888) ReadyGo; (650) 969–4902
  Fax: (650) 960–2958
  www.readygo.com

SWIFT Author
Gemini Learning Systems Inc.
736 8th Avenue S.W., Suite 1100
Calgary, Alberta T2P 1HA
Canada
  Tel: (403) 263–8649
  Fax: (403) 261–4688
  www.gemini.com

TenCORE
Computer Teaching Corporation
1713 South State Street
Champaign, IL 61820
  Tel: (217) 352–6363
  Fax: (217) 352–3104
  www.tencore.com

ToolBookII
Click2Learn
110–110th Avenue N.E., Suite 700
Bellevue, WA 98004
  Tel: (425) 462–0501
  Fax: (425) 637–1504
  www.click2learn.com

Learning Content Management Systems (LCMS) Applications

Avaltus
14 Ridgedale Avenue, Suite 205
Cedar Knolls, NJ 07927
  Tel: (973) 326–8989
  Fax: (973) 326–8997
  www.paybacktraining.com/

Global Knowledge
475 Allendale Road
King of Prussia, PA 19406
  Tel: (800) 387–8878
  http://kp.globalknowledge.com/

Knowledge Mechanics
60 Monroe Center N.W., Suite 300
Grand Rapids, MI 49503
  Tel: (616) 233–1301
  Fax: (616) 456–5250
  www.knowledgemechanics.com/

LeadingWay Knowledge Systems
One Technology Drive, Suite B-123
Irvine, CA 92618
  Tel: (949) 453–1112
  Fax: (949) 453–8115
  www.leadingway.com/

Mind Leaders
851 West 3rd Avenue, Building 3
Columbus, OH 43212
  Tel: (800) 223–3732
  Fax: (614) 781–6510
  www.mindleaders.com

WBT Systems
Reservoir Place
1601 Trapelo Road
Waltham, MA 02451
  Tel: (781) 839–2800
  Fax: (781) 290–5021
  www.wbtsystems.com/

Appendix B

Professional Organizations

Developing e-learning brings together the skill and knowledge of many different kinds of professional. Because of the cross-disciplinary nature of the field, many organizations provide resources to developers. The major ones are listed below:

American Association for Higher Education (AAHE)
1 Dupont Circle, Suite 360
Washington, DC 20036
    Tel: (202) 293–6440
    Fax: (202) 293–0073
    www.aahe.org

AAHE's conferences and publications highlight a broad range of issues. They have developed many in-depth, long-term commitments to specific programmatic areas, such as quality, service-learning, teaching/peer review, and technology. AAHE's Technology Projects seek to mainstream the effective use of technology for instructional purposes.

American Society for Training and Development (ASTD)
1640 King Street
Box 1443
Alexandria, VA 22313–2043
    Tel: (703) 683–8100
    Fax: (703) 683–8103
    www.astd.org

ASTD's mission is to provide leadership to individuals, organizations, and society to achieve work-related competence, performance, and fulfillment.

Association for Educational Communications and Technology (AECT)
1800 North Stonelake Drive, Suite 2
Bloomington, IN 47407
www.aect.org

The mission of AECT is to provide leadership in educational communications and technology by linking professionals with a common interest in the use of educational technology and its application to the learning process.

Association for Information and Image Management International/AIIM International
1100 Wayne Avenue, Suite 1100
Silver Spring, MD 20910
Tel: (301) 587–8202
Fax: (301) 587–2711
www.aiim.org

AIIM International is the leading industry association and trade show for IT professionals in document-intensive businesses. Its mission is to help institutional users understand document technologies and how they can be applied to improve critical business and exploding enterprise and Web-based processes. AIIM's focus is information and process management, including Web-enabled document management, workflow, and industry-specific solutions.

Computer Education Management Association (CEdMA)
Nancy Lewis
Association Manager
P.O. Box 749
Scotch Plains, NJ 07076
www.cedma.org

CEdMA's goal is to provide formal and informal forums for education managers to discuss critical training and business issues encountered in high-tech companies. CEdMA also provides opportunities for members to participate in initiatives to shape excellence in education and training.

Computer Education Management Association Europe (CEdMAE)
www.cedma-europe.org

CEdMAE is a European-based association dedicated to raising the profile of online training and developing standards for the information technology training industry.

Educause
4772 Walnut Street, Suite 206
Boulder, CO 80301–2538
Tel: (303) 449–4430
Fax: (303) 440–0461
www.educause.edu

The consolidation of the training organizations CAUSE & Educom, Educause's mission is to help shape and enable transformational change in higher education through the introduction, use, and management of information resources and technology in teaching, learning, scholarship, research, and institutional management.

Education Online
Street Loyes House, Suite 1000
20 St. Loyes Street
Bedford MK40 12L
United Kingdom
www.edon.org.uk

The mission of Education Online is to promote multimedia access to education and training in European society and establish by consensus a standard for online learning.

The Human Resource Planning Society
317 Madison Avenue, Suite 1509
New York, NY 10017
Tel: (212) 490–6387
Fax: (212) 682–6851
www.hrps.org

The Human Resource Planning Society's mission is to improve organizational performance by creating a global network of individuals who function as business partners in the application of strategic human resource management practices.

Information Technology Training Association, Inc. (ITTA)
4210 Spicewood Springs Road, Suite 103
Austin, TX 78759
Tel: (512) 502–9300
Fax: (512) 502–9308
www.itta.org

ITTA's mission is to provide vision, leadership, and opportunity for those involved in learning to enable the effective use of information technology.

International Society for Performance Improvement (ISPI)
1400 Spring Street, Suite 260
Silver Spring, MD 20910
Tel: (202) 408–7969
Fax: (202) 408–7972
www.ispi.org

ISPI is the leading association dedicated to increasing productivity in the workplace through the application of performance and instructional technologies.

Institute of Educational Technology
Walton Hall
Milton Keynes MK7 6AA
United Kingdom
www.iet.open.ac.uk

The Institute is the largest center for educational technology in the world and has top rankings for its contributions to teaching and for its research. In addition to its work on courses across the Open University, the Institute is engaged in many collaborative projects in all parts of the world, as part of its mission and objectives.

Knowledge Management Consortium International (KMCI)
P.O. Box 41
Vernon, CT 06066
www.kmci.org

Knowledge Management Consortium International is an organization and individuals coming together to develop a shared vision, common understanding, and aligned action about knowledge and knowledge management.

Knowledge Management Professionals Association (KMPA)
www.kmpa.org/

KMPA offers a forum for customer service and support professionals to exchange, leverage, and promote the best practices of knowledge management.

Society for Applied Learning Technology (SALT)
50 Culpepper Street
Warrenton, VA 20186
Tel: (540) 347–0055
www.salt.org

The society is oriented to professionals whose work requires knowledge and communication in the field of instructional technology. SALT provides a means to enhance the knowledge and job performance of an individual by participating in society-sponsored meetings and through receiving society-sponsored publications. It enables one to achieve knowledge in the field of applied learning technology by association with other professionals in conferences sponsored by the society.

Society for Human Resource Management (SHRM)
1800 Duke Street
Alexandria, VA 22314
Tel: (703) 548–3440
Fax: (703) 535–6490
www.shrm.org

The mission of SHRM is to lead, encourage, and financially support research and educational activities that further the growth and development of the HR profession.

Society for Technical Communication (STC)
901 North Stuart Street, Suite 904
Arlington, VA 2203–1822
www.stc-va.org

The mission of STC is to advance the arts and sciences of technical communication by addressing emerging issues in technical communications.

United States Distance Learning Association (USDLA)
140 Gould Street, Suite 200B
Needham, MA 02494–2397
www.usdla.org

The association's purpose is to promote the development and application of distance learning for education and training. The constituencies served include K through 12 education, higher education, continuing education, corporate training, and military and government training.

Appendix C

Resource Sites
and Conferences

Resource Sites

There are a number of excellent sites that offer practical advice on every aspect of e-learning. The following list is limited to twenty-five sites I find most helpful. Many of these sites offer newsletters or discussion groups; these are free and they provide a great way to keep tabs on what's happening and alert you to new content at the site.

Instructional Design

ASTD Learning Circuits
www.learningcircuits.org

Big Dog's HR Link Page—Training and Development Subjects
www.nwlink.com/~donclark/hrd/hrdlink.html

Distance-Educator
www.distance-educator.com

TeleEducation New Brunswick
http://teleeducation.nb.ca/

The Node
www.thenode.org/

E-Learning Meta Sites

Electronic Training Village
www.trainingvillage.gr/etv/

Learnativity
www.learnativity.com/

TCM.com
www.tcm.com/trdev/t2.html

The eLearning Jump Page
www.internettime.com/e.htm

The Learning Post
www.elearningpost.com/

The Training Professional's Gateway
http://homepage.tinet.ie/~mjcollins/

Knowledge Management

Brint WWW Virtual Library on Knowledge Management
www.brint.com/km/

Sveiby's What Is Knowledge Management
www.sveiby.com.au/BookContents.html

Electronic Performance Support Systems

EPSS.COM!
www.epss.com/index.htm

EPSS Info Site
www.epssinfosite.com

General Business and Technology

FastCompany
www.fastcompany.com/homepage/

Harvard Business School Publishing
www.hbsp.harvard.edu/home.html

How Stuff Works
www.howstuffworks.com/

LineZine
www.linezine.com

MeansBusiness.com
www.meansbusiness.com/

Web Design

Jakob Nielsen's Website
www.useit.com

MIT Disabilities Resources: Universal Design and Web Accessibility
http://web.mit.edu/ada/waccess.html#principles

Web Monkey
http://hotwired.lycos.com/webmonkey/index.html

Web Pages That Suck
www.webpagesthatsuck.com/

Web Style Guide
http://info.med.yale.edu/caim/manual/contents.html

Conferences and Expositions

Advances in technology make e-learning an evolving field. Conferences for every skill level are held to review changes and to highlight challenges facing e-learning leaders. Here is a list of annually held conventions, conferences, and exhibitions. The dates and frequency of conferences vary, and the names of the conferences are frequently changed for marketing reasons. The links here are a starting point.

American Society for Training and Development Conference & Exposition
www.astd.org/virtual~community/conferences/

Conference designed for individuals who are new to training and wish to learn practical training methods and the technologies for learning how to utilize technology to deliver training.

Association for Educational Communications and Technology International Conference

www.aect.org/events/

The conference provides an in-depth review of new developments in educational communications and practical usage of technological advances for online learning.

Chief Learning Officer Conference

www.linkageinc.com/

Linkage provides conferences that focus on timely issues related to HR, leadership, technology, and learning (i.e., a CLO conference). Conference topics vary with calendar and industry trends.

Computer Education Management Association Europe Conference

www.cedma-europe.org/conferences/

CEdMAE's conferences look at industry issues such as instructor resourcing, education administration, measuring education value, and selling and marketing education.

Computer Education Management Association National Conference

www.cedma.org/guestevents-national/html

CEdMA's national conference is for online educational training professionals. Topics reviewed include distance learning as a solution to the skills gap, current trends in the education marketplace, and learning media.

Computer Training World Conference & Exposition

www.influent.com/ctw2000/body.html

Conference for IT training professionals to learn the latest technology from multiple seminars and demonstrations as well as learn techniques for industry gurus regarding cutting-edge issues in managing, creating, and delivering online training.

Corporate University Symposiums & Exposition

www.corpu.com/conferences/

Presentation and demonstrations of leading-edge technologies, seminars on e-learning strategies, employers' expectations for a chief learning officer, vendor selections, and developing an e-learning curriculum.

E-Learning Conference & Exposition

www.eventshome.com/clients/advanstar/elearning/200

Conference for individuals interested in online training, distance learning, and enterprise collaboration. Reviews of new e-learning methods and solutions.

Education Technology Conference & Exposition

www.salt.org/ed-conf/conference/

Seminars in technology application in schools and colleges, technology systems, and e-learning and knowledge management systems.

E-Media World Conference in Educational Multimedia, Hypermedia, & Telecommunications

www.aace.org/conf/emedia

Conference on the advancements in the knowledge, theory, and quality of learning technology at all levels of information technology.

Information Technology Training Conference

www.ittconference.org

Conference focuses on the issues important to the IT training industry. Conference includes technology training sessions and presentations by industry experts.

International Conference on Advanced Learning Technologies

www.lttf.ieee.org

Conference brings together researchers, academics, and industry practitioners involved in the design and development of emerging learning technologies to review development trends and challenges in the field of online learning.

International Performance Improvement Conference

www.ispi.org/conference

Conference identifies performance expectations, gaps, and requirements of individuals and organizations. Review of performance management tools and how to integrate performance-driven "best practices" into an organization.

KM World Conference

www.infotoday.com/

The KM World conference and exhibition focuses on strategies, tools, content management, collaboration and knowledge sharing, e-learning, and organizational effectiveness.

Mait's Multimedia & Networks Aided Training Exhibitions & Conference
www.maitsexpo.com/efodl.htm

The European Federation for Open & Distance Learning (EFODL) holds an annual conference on technological developments driving the growth of e-learning.

OnLine Learning Asia
www.vnuonlinelearning.com.sg

Conference that reviews products and services for online learning; analysis of current state of the Asian and U.S. online learning markets. Panel discussion by industry experts and product demonstrations showcase session.

OnLine Learning Europe
www.vnuonlinelearning.com.uk/

Product demonstrations and panel discussions similar to OnLine Learning USA Conference, but from a European perspective. Hands-on learning labs and workshops.

OnLine Learning USA Conference
www.onlinelearningconference.com

Conference on e-learning design and development, future trends, building successful and sustainable e-learning strategy, and key trends and e-learning implementations. Conference also offers hands-on learning labs.

Techlearn Conference
www.techlearn2001.conference/

Conference explores the intersection of learning and technology and the future of e-learning.

TeleCon
www.teleconexpos.com/

TeleCon addresses diverse industry segments such as education, finance, and the government/military. The conference focuses on using technology to collaborate, communicate, and connect with employees, partners, and customers.

Training Conference & Exposition

www.trainingconference.com

Conference for IT managers and developers offering seminars and workshops on designing effective training programs, how to evaluate e-learning, and building digital learning strategies.

Training Directors' Forum

www.trainingdirectorsforum.com

TDF focuses on the specific needs of senior training executives. Conference addresses topics such as ROI, performance improvement, and advances in technology-supported learning.

WBT Producer Conference & Exposition

www.influent.com/wbt2001/index.hmtl

Learning event for managers, designers, and developers of online instructional information.

WebNET

www.aace.org/

This annual conference serves as a multidisciplinary forum for the exchange of information on research, development, and applications of all topics related to the Web. This encompasses the use, applications, and societal and legal aspects of the Internet in its broadest sense.

World Conference on Open Learning & Distance Education

www.fernuni~hagen.de

Conference that examines development trends in open learning, virtual training, and e-learning for individuals and organizations.

Appendix D

Selected Bibliography

Adult Education

Brookfield, S.D. (1986). *Understanding and facilitating adult learning.* San Francisco: Jossey-Bass.

Brookfield, S.D. (1987). *Developing critical thinkers: Challenging adults to explore alternative ways of thinking and acting.* San Francisco: Jossey-Bass.

Brookfield, S. (2000). *The skillful teacher: On technique, trust, and responsiveness in the classroom.* New York: John Wiley & Sons.

Caudron, S. (2000). Learners speak out: What actual learners actually think of actual training. *Training & Development, 54*(4), 52–57.

Cranton, P. (1996). *Professional development as transformative learning: New perspectives for teachers of adults.* San Francisco: Jossey-Bass.

Culling, A. (1999). Practising theory. *Adults Learning, 10*(7), 18–21.

Doherty, P.B. (1999). Learning in the next millennium. *Journal of Instruction Delivery Systems, 13*(3), 713.

Jakupec, V., & Garrick, J. (Eds.). (2000). *Flexible learning, human resource and organizational development: Putting theory to work.* London: Routledge.

Jordan, S., & Jackson, N. (2001). Is skills training good for you? *Adults Learning, 12*(5), 14–16.

Knowles, M.S. (1975). *Self-directed learning: A guide for learners and teachers.* New York: Association Press.

Knowles, M. (1980). *The modern practice of adult education: From pedagogy to andragogy* (rev. ed.). New York: Cambridge.

Kolb, D.A. (1984). *Experiential learning: Experience as the source of learning and development.* Englewood Cliffs, NJ: Prentice Hall.

Mezirow, J. (Ed.). (2000). *Learning as transformation: Critical perspectives on a theory in progress.* San Francisco: Jossey-Bass.

Saba, F. (2000). Adult education and training. *Distance Education Report, 4*(3), 1.

Taylor, K., Marienau, C., & Fiddler, M. (2000). *Developing adult learners: Strategies for teachers and trainers.* San Francisco: Jossey-Bass.

Tennant, M. (1997). *Psychology and adult learning.* London. Routledge.

Vella, J. (2000). *Taking learning to task: Creative strategies for teaching adults.* San Francisco: Jossey-Bass.

Wlodkowski, R.J. (1998). *Enhancing adult motivation to learn: A comprehensive guide for teaching all adults.* San Francisco: Jossey-Bass.

Distance Education

Belanger, F., Jordan, D.H., & Jordan, D. (2000). *Evaluation and implementation of distance learning: Technologies, tools and techniques.* Hershey, PA: Idea Group Press.

Brown, B.L. (Ed.). (2000). *Web-based training.* ERIC Digest No. 218. (ERIC Document Reproduction Service No. ED 445 234) [Online] www.ericacve.org/fulltext.asp.

Driscoll, M. (1999). Web-based training in the workplace. *Adult Learning, 10*(4), 21–25.

Keegan, D. (1993). *Theoretical principles of distance education.* London: Routledge.

Lee, W.W., & Owens, D.L. (2000). *Multimedia-based instructional design: Computer-based training, web-based training, and distance learning.* San Francisco: Jossey-Bass.

Schreiber, D.A., & Berge, Z.L. (1998). *Distance training: How innovative organizations are using technology to maximize learning and meet business objectives.* San Francisco: Jossey-Bass.

Simonson, M., Smaldino, S., Albright, M., & Zvacke, S. (2000). *Teaching and learning at a distance: Foundations of distance education.* Upper Saddle River, NJ: Merrill/Prentice Hall.

Simpson, O. (2000). *Supporting students in open and distance learning.* London: Kogan Page.

Williams, M.L., Covington, B., & Paprock, K. (1999). *Distance learning: The essential guide.* Thousand Oaks, CA: Sage

E-Learning

Alessi, S.M., & Trollip, S.R. (2000). *Multimedia for learning: Methods and development.* Boston, MA: Allyn & Bacon.

ASTD Learning Circuits. (2001, April). *E-learning evaluation method gains support in Canada* [Online] www.learningcircuits.org/jul2000/jul2000_newsbytes.html#july4

Beer, V. (2000). *The web learning fieldbook: Using the world wide web to build workplace learning environments.* San Francisco. Jossey-Bass.

Clark, R.C. (1999). *Developing technical training* (2nd ed.). Washington, DC: International Society for Performance Improvement.

Colbrunn, R.R., & Fan Tiem, D.M. (2000). From binders to browsers: Converting classroom training to the web. *Performance Improvement, 39*(2), 35–40.

Huang, H. (2000). Instructional technologies: Facilitating online courses. *Educational Technology, 40*(4), 41–46.

Hartley, D.E. (2000). *On-demand learning: Training in the new millennium.* Boston, MA: HRD Press.

Hoffman, J. (2001). *The synchronous trainer's survival guide.* [Online]. www.insynctraining.com/

Horton, W.K. (2000). *Designing web-based training: How to teach anyone anything anywhere anytime.* New York: John Wiley & Sons.

Kruse, K. (1999). *Technology-based training.* San Francisco: Jossey-Bass.

Lee, W.E., & Owens, D.L. (2000). *Multimedia-based instructional design: Computer-based training, web-based training, and distance learning.* San Francisco: Jossey-Bass.

Lewis, N., & Orton, P. (2000, June). The five attributes of innovative e-learning. *Training & Development, 54*(6), 47–51.

Oliver, R. (1999). Exploring strategies for online teaching and learning. *Distance Education, 20*(2), 240–54.

Palloff, R.M., & Pratt, K. (1999). *Building learning communities in cyberspace: Effective strategies for the online classroom.* San Francisco: Jossey-Bass.

Rosenberg, M.J. (2000). *E-learning: Strategies for delivering knowledge in the digital age.* New York: McGraw-Hill.

Whalen, T., & Wright, D. (2000). *The business case for web-based training.* Boston, MA: Artech House.

Zielinski, D. (2000). Can you keep learners online? *Training, 37*(3), 64–66, 68, 70, 72, 74–75.

Instructional Design

Bloom, B.S., Hastings, J.T., & Madams, G.F. (1971). *Handbook on formative and summative evaluation of student learning.* New York: McGraw-Hill.

Dick, W., Carey, L., & Carey, J.O. (2000). *The systematic design of instruction.* Reading, MA: Addison-Wesley.

Gagne, R.M. (1985). *Conditions for learning* (4th ed.). New York: Holt, Rinehart & Winston.

Gagne, R.M., Briggs, L.J., & Wagner, W.W. (1992). *Principles of instructional design.* Fort Worth, TX: Harcourt Brace.

Gustafson, K.L. (2000). Designing technology-based performance support. *Educational Technology, 40,* 38–44.

Hara, N., & Schwen, T.M. (1999). An instructional development model for global organizations: The GOAL model. *Performance Improvement Quarterly, 12*(4), 99–116.

Heinich, R., Molenda, M., & Russell, J. (1989). *Instructional media and the new technologies of instruction* (3rd ed.). New York: Macmillan.

Jonassen, D.H., Tessmer, M., & Hannum, W.H. (1999). *Task analysis methods for instructional design.* Mahwah, NJ: Lawrence Erlbaum.

Merrill, M.S. (1994). *Instructional design theory.* Englewood Cliffs, NJ: Educational Technology Publications.

Mager, R. (1997). *Preparing instructional objectives: A critical tool in the development of effective instruction.* Los Angeles: Center for Effective Performance.

Morrison, G.R., Ross, S.M., & Kemp, J.E. (2000). *Designing effective instruction* (3rd ed.). New York: John Wiley & Sons.

Park, I., & Hannafin, M.J. (1993). Empirically based guidelines for the design of interactive multimedia. *Educational Technology, Research and Development, 41*(3), 63–85.

Reigeluth, C. (1999). *Instructional-design theories and models: A new paradigm of instructional theory.* Mahwah, NJ: Lawrence Erlbaum.

Richey, R.C. (Ed.). (2000). *The legacy of Robert M. Gagne.* Washington, DC: Office of Educational Research and Improvement (ERIC Document Reproduction Service No. ED 445 674).

Rossett, A. (1987). *Training needs assessment.* Englewood Cliffs, NJ: Educational Technology Publications.

Rossett, A. (1998). *First things fast: A handbook for performance analysis.* San Francisco. Jossey-Bass/Pfeiffer.

Rothwell, W.J., & Kazans, H.C. (1996). *Mastering the instructional design process: A systematic approach.* San Francisco: Jossey-Bass.

Shotsberger, P.G., & Vetter, R. (2000). The handheld web: How mobile wireless technologies will change web-based instruction and training. *Educational Technology, 40*(5), 49–52.

Smith, P., & Ragan, T. (1999). *Instructional design* (2nd ed.) New York: John Wiley & Sons.

Zemke, R. (1999, July). Toward a science of training. *Training, 36*(7), 32–36.

Zemke, R., & Kramlinger, T. (1982). *Figuring things out: A trainer's guide to task, needs, and organizational analysis.* New York: Perseus Press.

Knowledge Management and Knowledge Economy

Allee, V. (2000, Fall). eLearning is not knowledge management. *LineZine.* [Online] www.linezine.com/indexfall00.htm

Brown, J.S., & Duguid, P. (1991). *Organizational learning and communities of practice: Toward a unified view of working, learning, and innovation.* [Online] www.parc.xerox.com/ops/members/brown/papers/orglearning.html

Cohen, E., & Prusak, L. (2001). *In good company: How social capital makes organizations work.* Cambridge, MA: Harvard Business School Press.

Davenport, T.H., & Prusak, L. (1999). *Working knowledge: How organizations manage what they know.* Cambridge, MA: Harvard Business School Press.

Heijke, J.A.M., Muyksen, J., & Heijke, H. (Eds.). (2001). *Education and training in a knowledge-based economy.* New York: St. Martin's Press.

Kelly, K. (1997). *New rules for the new economy.* [Online] www.wired.com/wired/archive/5.09/newrules.html

Liebowitz, J. (2000). *Building organizational intelligence: A knowledge management primer.* New York: CRC Press.

Millison, D. (2001). Learning by the rules. *Knowledge Management, 4*(7), 62–64.

Morey, D., Maybury, M., & Thuraisingham, B. (Eds.). (2000). *Knowledge management: Classic and contemporary works.* Cambridge, MA: MIT Press.

Neef, D. (Ed.). (1997). *The knowledge economy.* London: Butterworth-Heinemann.

Nonaka, I., & Takeuchi, H. (1995). *The knowledge-creating company.* London: Oxford University Press.

Stuller, J. (1998, April). Chief of corporate smarts. *Training,* 34–37.

Wenger, E. (1999). *Communities of practice: Learning, meaning, and identity.* Cambridge, MA: Harvard University Press.

Wenger, E. (2001). *Supporting communities of practice: A survey of community-oriented technologies.* [Online] www.ewenger.com/tech/index.htm

Web Design

Campbell, K. (1999). *The web: Design for active learning.* [Online] www.atl.ualberta.ca/articles/idesign/activel.cfm

Crawford, C. (2000). *Understanding interactivity.* [Online] www.erasmatazz.com/book.html

Kristof, R., & Satran, A. (1995). *Interactivity by design: Creating & communicating with new media.* San Francisco: Hayden Books.

Mok, C. (1996). *Designing business: Multiple media, multiple disciplines.* New York: Macmillan.

Nielsen, J. (1999). *Designing web usability: The practice of simplicity.* New York: New Riders Publishing.

Satran, A., & Kristof, R. (1995). *Interactivity by design: Creating & communicating with new media.* San Francisco: Adobe Press.

Williams. R., & Tollett, J. (1997). *The non-designer's web book: An easy guide to creating, designing, and posting your own web site.* Minneapolis, MN: Peachpit Press.

Krug, S., & Black, R. (2000). *Don't make me think! A common sense approach to web usability.* New York: Que Press.

Workplace Learning

Aldrich, C. (2000). Customer-focused e-learning: The drivers. *Training & Development, 54*(8), 34–36, 38.

Cofer, D.A. (2000). *Informal workplace learning.* Practice Application Brief No. 10. ERIC/ACVE [Online] www.ericacve.org/searchinput.asp.

Cross, J. (2001). A fresh look at ROI. *Learning Circuits.* [Online] www.learningcircuits.org/2001/jan2001/cross.html

Dobbs, K. (2000). Simple moments of learning. *Training, 35*(1), 52–58.

Fotz-end, J. (2000). *The ROI of human capital: Measuring the economic value of employee performance.* New York: AMACOM.

Garrick, J. (1998). *Informal learning in the workplace: Unmasking human resource development.* London: Routledge.

Marsick, V.J., & Volpe, M. (Eds.). (2000). *Advances in developing human resources: Informal learning on the job.* San Francisco: Berrett-Koehler.

Matthews, P. (1999). Workplace learning: Developing a holistic model. *Learning Organization, 6*(1), 18–29.

Yeung, A.K., Ulrich, D.O., Nason, S.W., & VonGlinow, M.A. (1999). *Organizational learning capability: Generating and generalizing ideas with impact.* New York: Oxford Press.

Appendix E

Matrix of Web-Based Training Types*

	Web-Based Training			
	Web/CBT	**Web/EPS Systems**	**Web/VAC**	**Web/VSC**
Purpose	To provide performance-based training with measurable goals and objectives	To provide practical knowledge and problem-solving skills in a just-in-time format	To provide group learning in a non-contiguous time environment	To provide group learning in a real-time environment
Types of Learning	Well-structured problems that require transferring knowledge, building comprehension, and practicing application of skills	Ill-structured problems that require analysis and synthesis of elements, relationships, and organizational principles to produce solutions	Less structured problems that require application, analysis, synthesis and evaluation to produce new ideas, plans, or products	Ill-structured problems that require the synthesis and evaluation of information and shared experience to produce new ideas, plans, or products

*There are many variations of these approaches, and different approaches are often used in combination.

Web-Based Training

	Web/CBT	Web/EPS Systems	Web/VAC	Web/VSC
Roles of Facilitator or WBT Designer	*Manager of instruction:* controls, predicts, directs, and assesses the learning outcomes; communicates with learner	*Organizer of content:* locates, analyzes, abstracts, indexes, and classifies information into learning modules	*Facilitator of group learning:* guides instruction, provides resources, evaluates outcomes, and communicates with learners	*Coordinator of learning experience:* participates as a co-learner, recommends learning direction, but does not determine direction or evaluate outcomes
Roles of Learner	Takes active role practicing new behaviors; receiving feedback; and communicating with instructor	Takes initiative to direct own learning; determines the level of detail; and assesses the success of instruction	Guided by facilitator as an individual or as a member of a group; participates in instructional activities; and receives feedback	Active participant in a collaborative learning process with facilitator and peers, participates in dialogue and reflects on experience
Methods	Drill and practice, simulations, reading, questioning, and answering	Problem solving, scientific method, experiential method, project method	Experiential tasks, group discussions, team projects, self-directed learning, discovery method	Dialogue and discussions, problem solving, and maximum interaction
Interactions	Multimedia, hypertext, hypermedia, simulations, application exercises, e-mail, listserv, and bulletin boards, communication with instructor	Multimedia, hypertext, hypermedia, bulletin boards, notes conferences, modules of Web/CBT, and e-mail access to facilitator and peers	Multimedia, hypertext, hypermedia, bulletin boards, notes conferences, modules of Web/CBT, and e-mail access to facilitator and peers	Synchronous audio- and video conferencing, shared whiteboards, shared applications

Netiquette

Netiquette refers to a set of guidelines for online behavior. The guidelines presented here are general and can be used to help shape the guidelines for your own Web-based training program.

Checklist for Participating in Mailing Lists*

Questions to ask oneself before posting a message to a mailing list or listserv:

1. Is the message being sent to the appropriate destination—the whole list versus one or more selected individual(s)? If your reply is no longer related to the subject of the list, you should send it privately to the person who wrote the original message. Also, if the original sender volunteered to summarize responses, you should generally send your message privately to him or her.

2. Is the subject line descriptive of my message? A descriptive subject line will include specific, concise information about the content of a message.

3. Have I included only enough of any past messages that my message refers to so that other list members know what I am referring to? Delete as much of the original as you can, such as headings, signature files, and any part of the message you are not replying to.

4. Is my message as brief as possible, and have I referred interested parties to a website or other method of getting additional information (or offered to send more information via e-mail for those who want it)? The longer the message, the less chance people will read it.

5. Have I attempted to express appreciation to list members who have made a useful contribution to the list? Send a private thank you message to people who go out of their way to help you.

6. If I have disagreed with someone else's ideas, have I attempted to avoid a personal attack against him or her?

7. Have I attempted to ignore or defuse anything that I consider a personal attack against me?

8. Does my message say something more than "me too"? If all you say is "I agree," do not send your message to the entire list. If you give another example of the point being made, or in some other way add new content, then you can send your message to the list.

9. Have I offered to summarize the replies to any question I asked? Certain questions will elicit many responses, and if you think your question will be of this type, it is easier for readers to use the information if it is provided in one message.

10. Have I signed the message and included my e-mail address in the body? You need to include your e-mail address in the body, because some lists do not include the header with your address.

11. Did I proofread the message? Messages with spelling and grammatical errors can reflect poorly on the writer.

Appendix G

Glossary

360-Degree Review	A performance review in which individuals evaluate themselves and receive feedback from other employees and organization members.
Active-X	A programming language used to develop interactive applications that are downloaded and executed from within a Web browser.
ADA	See Americans with Disabilities Act.
Adaptive Testing	An application that statistically determines one's ability to correctly respond to a series of questions.
Adaptive Tests	Tests in which a test taker's performance on each question helps the computer pick subsequent questions. The test gets harder or easier as it proceeds, depending on how well the student does.
Affinity Groups	A group of people who are formally or informally connected by a similarity or shared

	set of characteristics such as job titles, experience, or interests.
Alpha Class	A formative evaluation of a Web-based training program that determines the program's effectiveness once development has been completed.
Americans with Disabilities Act (ADA)	A law that prohibits discrimination on the basis of disability in employment and services provided by state and local governments, private companies, and commercial facilities. Although this law was originally applied to the physical world, it also applies to the cyberspace world.
Applets	A small Java program that can be embedded in an HTML page.
Application	A program such as a word processing or a spreadsheet package that bundles a set of instructions or computer codes to accomplish a task such as writing a letter or creating a balance sheet.
Application Service Providers	Companies that host, manage, and/or maintain packaged business applications on their own servers in their own data center(s) and deliver them to customers over the Internet for a fee.
Application Sharing	The ability for two or more learners to work on a shared piece of software. For example, a group of learners can work together to create a spreadsheet to be turned in for an assignment.
Asynchronous Learning	Educational events that take place independently in time (i.e., a learning exchange between students and facilitator(s) that is delayed by minutes, hours, or days).
Attitudinal Skills	Abilities related to teaching learners to behave in a particular manner, such as teaching people

to choose to recycle or to reduce the amount of salt they consume.

Audio Board
An electronic component that is required for a computer to have sound.

Authoring Tool
Software that allows for the creation of tutorials, CBT courseware, websites, CD-ROMs, and other interactive programs.

Awareness
The ability to see an indicator informing one that colleagues are online.

Bandwidth
The amount of network capacity available to carry files, e-mail, and other materials from one place on the network to another.

BBS
See Bulletin Board Systems.

Blended Solutions
Educational interventions involving multiple delivery modes such as traditional classroom and Web-based training or multiple kinds of learning such as self-paced e-learning and live virtual classroom programs.

Browser
An application that enables users to access various kinds of Internet and intranet resources such as HTML files, video, audio, and images.

Bulletin Board Systems (BBS)
A computerized meeting and announcement system that allows people to carry on discussions, upload and download files, and make announcements without the people being connected to the computer at the same time. This is also referred to as a threaded discussion.

Certification Programs
Testing and assessment programs that verify a learner's ability to perform at a defined level of competence.

Chat
A real-time conferencing capability between two or more users on a local network (LAN), on the

	Internet, or via a BBS. The chat is accomplished by typing on the keyboard, not by speaking.
Cognitive Skills	Abilities in the intellectual domain such as balancing a checkbook or completing a tax form.
Collaboration	A process by which people work together.
Common Gateway Interface (CGI)	A small program that takes data from a Web server and does something with it, such as putting the content of a form into an e-mail message or turning the data into a database query.
Curriculum	A series of courses organized in a prescribed path.
Critical Reflection	The ability of the learner to draw on experience and question underlying assumptions.
Design Document	A detailed blueprint that provides the development team with the specifications needed to produce the final product.
Distance Learning	Instructional interactions in which the teacher and learners are separated by time, space, or distance.
Dumbing Down	The process of revising training material by removing sophisticated interactions and complex multimedia segments.
E-Learning	Any kind of learning that is mediated by an electronic medium.
E-Learning Portal	A website providing access to training services such as courses, collaboration tools, and testing.
Electronic Performance Support System (EPPS)	A computer system that provides quick assistance and information without requiring prior training to use it.
EPPS	See Electronic Performance Support System.
Extensible Markup Language (XML)	An open standard for describing data from the W3C. It is used for defining data elements

	on a Web page and business-to-business documents.
Firewall	A method for keeping a network secure.
Flowchart	A detailed version of the navigation map that guides the work of the development team.
Forum	See Threaded Discussion.
Helpdesk	An organization that end users can call for assistance with their hardware or software problems.
Hosted Solutions	A combination of hardware, software, connectivity, and support services managed by a vendor rather than by the organization consuming the services.
HTML	See Hypertext Markup Language.
Hypermedia	Any media (text, sound, graphics, video, and animation) that can be chosen by a learner, connected, and displayed in a non-linear manner.
Hypertext	Any text that can be chosen by a learner and which causes another document to be retrieved and displayed.
Hypertext Markup Language (HTML)	A coding language used to make hypertext documents for use on the Web. Using HTML text on a Web page can be linked to resources (images, sound, video, and text) on another page on the Internet.
Instant Messaging	Software that informs users when any individuals in their list of "buddies" (colleagues, workgroup members, friends, etc.) log onto the network so they can chat and/or share an application.
Instructional Strategy	An overview of how the information will be presented and how students and facilitator(s) will interact in a training program.

Interactivity	The ability to provide control, direct attention, and coordinate the communication among the students, instructor, and content.
Internet	A subset of the World Wide Web that is accessed via graphic browser.
Internet Relay Chat (IRC)	A multi-user, live, real-time text-based conference via the Internet or intranet.
Intranet	An internal network that can stand alone or be connected to the Internet.
IRC	See Internet Relay Chat.
JAVA	A network-oriented programming language invented by Sun Microsystems that is specifically designed for writing programs that can be downloaded to a computer through the Internet and immediately run on that computer.
Learning Content Management Systems	Software applications that label, track, and manage learning objects (PowerPoint slides, quiz questions, video clips, illustration, course modules) and then organize them for delivery in infinite combinations.
Learning Management Systems (LMS)	Any use of Web technology to plan, organize, implement, and control aspects of the learning process.
Learning Objects	Modular building blocks that can be interchangeably used to create new courses from a common set of blocks.
Listserve	A software product that manages distribution lists for e-mail.
LMS	See Learning Management Systems.
M-Learning	The use of mobile devices such as laptops, personal digital assistants, cell phones, and other devices to deliver training, instruction, or information that contribute to knowledge transfer.

MOO	See Multi-User Object-Oriented Environment.
MUD	See Multi-User Dungeon or Dimension.
Multimedia	The use of two or more of the following elements in a computer-based training program: text, images, video, sound, and animation.
Multi-User Object-Oriented Environment (MOO)	One of several kinds of multi-user role-playing environments.
Multi-User Dungeon or Dimension (MUD)	A text-based multi-user simulation environment. In this environment learners can create things that stay after they leave, which other users can interact with in their absence, thus allowing a world to be built gradually and collectively.
Navigation Map	A graphical depiction of how the program is organized at a high level.
Netiquette	The etiquette or rules of behavior for the Internet.
Newsgroups	A discussion group on USENET devoted to talking about a specific topic. See also Threaded Discussions.
Notes Conferences	See Threaded Discussion.
Off-the-Shelf Programs	Web-based training programs that provide instruction for non-proprietary topics and are offered for sale to the general public.
Operating System	The master control program that runs the computer.
Opportunity Statement	An explanation of how the training program will improve productivity, reduce cost, and increase profitability for an organization.
Participatory Evaluation	The process of involving the learners in the review of the training program.
Plug-In	A small piece of software that adds features to a larger piece of software. Common examples are

	plug-ins for the Netscape® browser and Web server.
Praxis	The process of learners exploring a topic, taking action, and reflecting on the outcome of their action.
Production Value	The perceived or relative quality and sophistication of the media in a program.
Program Script	A detailed blueprint of the audio, the visuals, and the interactions planned for a Web/virtual synchronous class.
Psychomotor Skills	Abilities that involve physical movement ("motor") as well as a mental ("psycho") component.
Rapid Prototype	A Web-based training program with just enough functionality to assess the effectiveness of the program.
Records Management	The creation, retention, and scheduled destruction of an organization's documents, reports, and files.
Repurposing	The process of revising training material for use in an alternative format.
Screen Real Estate	That amount of space available on the video display terminal or screen.
Search Engine	A software application that locates words, phrases, and files on a website.
Server	A computer processing unit that is shared by a number of users and dedicated to performing a specific task such as processing mail or managing print requests.
Servers Side Authoring	A phrase used to describe authoring tools that are used via a browser and do not require the person creating or authoring courseware to have the application on his or her computer.

The authoring application resides on a server shared by a number of people.

Simulation
A simplified representation of an actual event, concept, or process with which the learner can interact.

SME
See Subject-Matter Experts.

Spamming
The act of sending unwanted e-mail to a large number of people.

SQL
A specialized programming language for sending queries to databases.

Storyboarding
A technique used to pictorially display how a program will unfold.

Streaming Media
Refers to the continuous transmission of data, typically audio or video.

Subject-Matter Experts (SME)
People who are highly skilled and knowledgeable in a given topic area.

Synchronous Events
Those taking place in real time.

Systematic Design of Instruction
The process of developing training and instruction using a structured and repeatable technique.

Templates
Pre-designed documents or files formatted for learning activities such as quizzes, pages in lessons, and exercises.

Thin Client
A small application in a client/server environment that performs very little data processing. The client processes only keyboard input and screen output, and all application processing is done in the server.

Third Party Content
See Off-the-Shelf Programs.

Threaded Discussion
A running log of remarks and opinions about a subject. Users e-mail their comments, and the computer maintains them in order of originating message and replies to that message.

Training Management Systems	Refers to a software application or manual process for tracking traditional instructor-led training activities such as scheduling and registration.
Treatment	A description of the program's style and overall approach.
Try-Out Learners	A group of learners who are similar to the intended audience and who will test the Web-based training program.
Uniform Resource Locator (URL)	The standard way to give the address of any resource on the Internet or an intranet.
URL	See Uniform Resource Locator.
Virtual Classroom	A group of students working together in a Web-based environment to learn. This refers to both synchronous and asynchronous applications.
Virtual Lab	A software application that enables terminal emulation and allows learners to access simulations of laboratory environments for practice.
W/CBT	See Web/Computer-Based Training.
Web/Computer-Based Training (W/CBT)	A Web-based multimedia methodology that features drill and practice, simulations, reading, questioning, and answering.
Web/Electronic Performance Support System (W/EPSS)	A Web-based job aid for just-in-time training that focuses on problem solving, the scientific method, and experiential methods of instruction. **W/EPSS** See Web/Electronic Performance Support Systems.
Web/Virtual Asynchronous Class (W/VAC)	A Web-based collaborative learning methodology that features discussions, problem solving, and reflection as instructional strategies.

Web/Virtual Synchronous Class (W/VSC)	A Web-based group learning methodology that employs experiential tasks, discussions, and team projects as instructional strategies.
Webmaster	A person who designs, manages, and maintains an organization's website.
What You See Is What You Get (WYSIWYG)	This refers to displaying text and graphics on screen the same as they will look in print.
Whiteboard	The electronic equivalent of chalk and blackboard, but between remote users. Whiteboard systems allow network participants to simultaneously view one or more users drawing on an on-screen blackboard or running an application.
World Wide Web (WWW)	The global network of networks.
W/VAC	See Web/Virtual Asynchronous Class.
W/VSC	See Web/Virtual Synchronous Class.
WWW	See World Wide Web.
WYSIWYG	See What You See Is What You Get.
XML	See Extensible Markup Language.

Index

A

ABCDs, objectives using, 41
Abstract prototypes, 238–239
Accountability, WBT and, 12
Active participation, community spaces and, 140
ADDIE model: blueprint development and, 199–200; cautions with latter phases, 233–234; design document worksheet for, 218; e-learning and, 4; instructional systems design and, 82–83; phases overview, 83–91; SMEs and, 235; WBT and, 23
Administrators, LMS functions for, 72–73
Adult education: principles of, 39–58; tenets of, 4
Adult learners: characteristics of, 45–47; designing tests for, 144–145; resistance to videoconferencing, 191
AICC (Aviation Industry CBT Committee), 31
Alessi, S. M., 41, 82
Alpha-class evaluation, 236, 243–245
Americans with Disabilities Act, 94
Analysis: as kind of cognitive skill, 108; pilot implementation and, 254; as videoconferencing strategy, 193
Analysis phase (ADDIE): components of, 86–91; features, 83; SMEs and, 235
Animation: as asynchronous tool, 167; as multimedia development tool, 67
Annual Industry Report (Training), 5
Answers: creating plausible, 149; responding with alternative tools, 152. See also Questions
AOL, as community space, 139
API (application program interface), 36
Appendices, in strategic plans, 283
Application/job task question format, 145, 153–154
Application sharing, 167, 169, 182–187
Aptitude, for computer-based learning, 90
Architecture: hosting *versus* owning, 78; scalability of, 36
ASP (application service provider), 76–77
Assessment: guidelines for, 39–43; needs assessment phase, 28; performance-content matrix and, 50; rapid

prototyping and, 237; via quizzes/tests, 142; web-based training options, 145–162
Assessment applications (software application vendors), 300–301
Assumptions, documenting in design document, 201
Asynchronous interactions: compared with synchronous, 132; defined, 129; options available, 133–162
Asynchronous programs, 29
Asynchronous tools, 167, 169–172
Attention, directing, 131
Attitude, for computer-based learning, 90
Attitudinal skills: resources needed, 14–15; teaching, 106; type of learning, 104–105
Audience: analysis of, 83; defining, 88–90; as design document introduction, 201; draw on experiences of, 179; identifying learners representative of, 240; influence on prototype, 239; with Internet access, 268; pilot implementation and, 247–249; targeting/profiling, 157
Audio software applications, 67
Audioconferencing: JIT development and, 167; scripting template, 197; as synchronous tool, 169; with visuals, 172–182
Authoring, 273
Authoring tools: e-learning platform and, 68–70; software application vendors, 302–303; technology trends, 278–280; websites, 70
Authority (champion responsibilities), 30

B

Background (design document), 201
Backup plans, 255
Benchmarking: the competition, 36; strategic plans and, 281
BlackBoard.com (discussion group software), 137
Bloom, B. S., 107, 108
Bloom's taxonomy of educational objectives, 108
Blueprint development: editor responsibilities, 29; instructional

designer responsibilities, 28; overview, 199–231
Broadcast messaging, community spaces and, 140
Brookfield, S. D., 47
Budgets: champion responsibilities, 30; defined in design document, 211–215; as design document section, 202; design document worksheet for, 220; influence on prototype, 239; in strategic plans, 282; for WBT, 21–23
Business issues, WBT-based, 5–21
Business managers, 28, 30
Business (resource sites), 310

C

Caffarella, R. S., 47
Calendars, community spaces and, 140
Campbell, K., 130
Carey, J. O., 82
Carey, L., 82
Champions: compared with project managers, 31; finding, 30–32; pilot implementation and, 253–254; training team and, 25–30
Chapman, Bryan, 63–64, 276, 277
Chat. See Instant messaging; Internet Relay Chat (IRC)
Chief information officer (CIO), 284
Chief learning officer (CLO), 284–285
Children learners, 57
Chin, Yegin, 10
Chronological structure, 48
Clark, Ruth, 43
Class discussion, as real-time audio strategy, 181
Class size. See Participation
Classroom teaching: blending with WBT, 107; W/VSC programs and, 167
Clip art, storyboards and, 229
Closing section: ending on time, 194; in program scripts, 224; for programs, 180–182
Cognitive skills: defined, 13; kinds of, 107–109; problems with poor, 54; teaching, 106; type of learning, 104–105

About the Author

Dr. Margaret Driscoll is a member of the IBM Mindspan Solutions team. She is a featured speaker at national and international training events. Her work has appeared in the *Journal of Performance Improvement; Training & Development;* the *Multimedia and Internet Newsletter; Technical Training;* and *Communications Week.* She is active in the American Society for Training and Development and the Association for the Advancement of Computing in Education.

Dr. Driscoll has rich experience consulting to Fortune 1000 companies involved in selecting, evaluating, and implementing e-learning. Her work includes experience in industry sectors such as high tech, financial services, pharmaceutical, medical, and academic environments. Her recent activities include researching trends on corporate learning, exploring the role of collaborative tools in informal learning, and participation in the design of next generation e-learning technologies. She conducts short courses and presentations world-wide on e-learning, adult education, return on investment for instructional technology, and collaborative learning. She is an adjunct professor at the University of Massachusetts and Suffolk University in Boston. Dr. Driscoll holds an MEd in instructional technology from Boston College, an MBA from the University of Massachusetts Boston, and an MA and EdD from Teachers College, Columbia University in New York City.

How to Use the CD-ROM

System Requirements

Windows PC

* 486 or Pentium processor-based personal computer
* Microsoft Windows 95 or Windows NT 3.51 or later
* Minimum RAM: 8 MB for Windows 95 and NT
* Available space on hard disk: 8 MB Windows 95 and NT
* 2X speed CD-ROM drive or faster

Macintosh

* Macintosh with a 68020 or higher processor or Power Macintosh
* Apple OS version 7.0 or later
* Minimum RAM: 12 MB for Macintosh
* Available space on hard disk: 6MB Macintosh
* 2X speed CD-ROM drive or faster

NOTE: This CD requires Netscape 3.0 or MS Internet Explorer 3.0 or higher. You can download these products using the links on the CD-ROM Help Page.

Getting Started

Insert the CD-ROM into your drive. The CD-ROM will usually launch automatically. If it does not, click on the CD-ROM drive on your computer to launch. You will see an opening page. You can click on this page or wait for it to fade to the Copyright Page. After you click to agree to the terms of the Copyright Page, the Home Page will appear.

Moving Around

Use the buttons at the left of each screen or the underlined text at the bottom of each screen to move among the menu pages. To view a document listed on one of the menu pages, simply click on the name of the document. Many of this CD's Word®

documents contain links to websites, if you use Word 98 and you connect to a site, you must click on the BACK button in your browser to return to the Word document. In addition, websites offered for further information may have changed or been discontinued after press time. To quit a document at any time, click the box at the upper right-hand corner of the screen.

Use the scrollbar at the right of the screen to scroll up and down each page.

To quit the CD-ROM, you can click the Quit option at the bottom of each menu page, hit Control-Q, or click the box at the upper right-hand corner of the screen.

To Download Documents

Open the document you wish to download. Under the File pulldown menu, choose Save As. Save the document onto your hard drive with a different name. It is important to use a different name, otherwise the document may remain a read-only file.

You can also click on your CD drive in Windows Explorer and select a document to copy it to your hard drive and rename it.

In Case of Trouble

If you experience difficulty using the *Web-Based Training, Second Edition* CD-ROM, please follow these steps:

1. Make sure your hardware and systems configurations conform to the systems requirements noted under "Systems Requirements" above.

2. Review the installation procedure for your type of hardware and operating system. It is possible to reinstall the software if necessary.

3. You may call Jossey-Bass/Pfeiffer Customer Service at (800) 956-7739 between the hours of 8 A.M. and 5 P.M. Pacific Time, and ask for Technical Support. It is also possible to contact Technical Support by e-mail at *techsupport@JosseyBass.com*.

Please have the following information available:

* Type of computer and operating system

* Version of Windows or Mac OS being used

* Any error messages displayed

* Complete description of the problem

(It is best if you are sitting at your computer when making the call.)